Go M·A·D!

GO MAKE A DIFFERENCE: 2

OVER
500
DAILY WAYS TO
SAVE THE PLANET!

THINK
BOOKS

A Think Book

First published in 2003 by Think Publishing

Think Publishing
The Pall Mall Deposit
124-128 Barlby Road
London W10 6BL

Tel: 020 8962 3020
Fax: 020 8962 8689

Email: watchdog@thinkpublishing.co.uk

Editors: Jo Bourne, Emma Jones
Tips Editor: Vicky Bamforth
Sub Editor: Malcolm Tait
Design: Lou Tait
Illustration: Thomas Boivin

Research and compilation: Annabel Short with: Melissa Andrews, David Balch,
Laure Baudon, Emily Ruth Brooker, Simon Calder, Philippa Crighton, Simon
Crawshaw, Emmanuelle Delabarre, Manisha Ferdinand, Liz Fox, Yvonne Gavan,
Kathryn Harter, Matt Havercroft, Katrine Kjoeller, Niki Lewis, Robin
Mannering, Susannah McMicking, Simon McWhirter, Kate Milner-Gullard,
David Mitchell, Les Pickford, Christiane Risch, Faye Smith, Rebecca White,
Sebastian Mackenzie Wilson.

www.thinkpublishing.co.uk

© Think Publishing 2003

Researched and compiled by Think Publishing
Printed and bound by William Clowes Ltd
Distributed by Airlift Book Company

Papers supplied by William Clowes are natural, renewable and recyclable
products. They are made from wood grown in sustainable forests. The logging
and manufacturing processes conform to the environmental regulations of the
country of origin.

ISBN 0-9541363-2-2

THANKS TO

This book has only been made possible
with the help and enthusiastic support
of many organisations and individuals and our
thanks go to:

BTCV, Butterfly Conservation, Campaign to
Protect Rural England, Forum for the Future,
Friends of the Earth, Friends Provident,
Geographical magazine, Natural Collection,
Solartwin, The Body Shop, The Ecologist
magazine, The Ramblers' Association, The Soil
Association, The Wildlife Trusts, Unit[e],
John Humphrys, Tony Juniper, Jonathon Porritt,
Harry Ram, Anita Roddick, John Vidal.

We would also like to thank all our advertisers
who have supported this book.

CONTENTS

At Organico we are proud to work with dedicated organic growers and manufacturers who are passionate about the foods they produce.

We sell foods under our own brand as well as under many different supplier names. The common thread is food quality. No artificials, no nasties, no cheap tricks. Just delicious tasting foods from organic ingredients.

Award-winning pasta,
sauces and condiments

The only range of sustainably-fished
tinned fish in UK

Pure pressed organic juices
straight from the fruit

High-fruit jams, fruit purées
and compotes

A pioneering range of
Organic baby foods

Soups and condiments from
the sierra of Andalucia

A full range of cold pressed
vegetable oils

Available in quality independent stores UK-wide
For local stockists or more information,
call 0118 9510 518 or email info@organico.co.uk
or check us out on www.organico.co.uk

WHY GO MAD?

There is only one world, and we all have a role in looking after it. But what can we as individuals really do to make a difference? Well, the answers are here in this little book. In the pages that follow are the details that can enable every one of us to tread more lightly on the planet that sustains us.

Whether the challenge is protecting local green spaces or fighting global climate change, the fact is that the most important force for change is you and me. If we don't do anything, then probably nothing much will happen. Small actions, by contrast, can have a vast impact. Simple deeds like writing letters, recycling waste, saving energy and being thoughtful about what we buy can have quite awesome influence on the world we live in.

What's better still is that we can all choose how much to do and how to make our individual actions fit with our busy lives. That is why Go MAD! 2 is so powerful. The hundreds of actions set out here provide everyone with the means to make a difference.

The greatest threat to our planet is people believing that the decline of our common environment is inevitable. Nothing could be further from the truth. If we all play a small part, big change is possible. Go on, Go Make a Difference.

Tony Juniper
Executive Director
Friends of the Earth

THE FUTURE STARTS HERE

It's often said that the failure of people to adopt a green lifestyle is a reflection of inherent selfishness. The assumption is that a shift towards the kind of society that stands a chance of lasting beyond the next generation is one that only a monk could tolerate.

But that couldn't be further from the truth. The most damaging aspects of modern industrial society are not things that we would miss were they to be replaced. Who would mourn the end of pesticides or a reduction in packaging in supermarkets? Who would feel oppressed if instead of promoting low grade industrial food production our taxes were spent on support for local organic produce?

There are any number of ways in which we can make a difference. For some people it is easier than others. It's hard for many to buy local organic produce when local shops have been bankrupted by politically advantaged out-of-town supermarkets. It's hard to unhook oneself from cars when the transport infrastructure so favours them. Without systemic or political change, our own individual actions are somewhat crippled.

But we are also part of an economy that responds to consumer stimulation. When enough people choose to power their homes with renewable energy we will see a snowball effect and before long, Britain will be carbon neutral. After all, the consumer persuaded supermarkets to abandon GM foods, and it is working mothers in New Zealand who are responsible for the initiation of a 'zero-waste' strategy.

Go MAD! 2 is primarily a guide to ecological living. But it is also a guide to ecological renewal, with vital information on how we can all get involved in pushing for change at the policy level. Combined, this process is irresistible.

Zac Goldsmith
Editor, The Ecologist

HOW TO USE THIS BOOK

The tips in this book have been compiled and updated using information from over 300 leading environmental sources and organisations, from global charities to individual suppliers of environmentally friendly products.

The 14 chapters cover all aspects of life – from birth to death via shopping, holidays, DIY and petcare – for there is nothing we do as human beings that doesn't touch the wider world.

Each tip highlights a small, practical, positive way that can help you make a difference to the world around you. They fall into three types: things you can do in order to make a difference, things you shouldn't do in order to make a difference and ways for you to make a difference by joining or helping an organisation and getting more involved. Websites and telephone numbers are given wherever possible so you can find out more; full contact details are in the directory on page 241.

Help us with the next edition
We have taken every care to make sure the information in Go MAD! 2 is correct at the time of going to press, but things do change. If the contact details given don't work, or you'd simply like to comment on a particular tip, email us at watchdog@thinkpublishing.co.uk or write to

Go MAD! 2,
Think Publishing Ltd,
The Pall Mall Deposit,
124-128 Barlby Road,
London W10 6BL.

To find out how you can contribute to the next edition, please turn to page 239.

And help yourself
You can also use this book to raise funds for your organisation. Call Tilly at Think Publishing on 020 8962 3020 to find out more.

I live in an Ecover home

Ecover cleaning products
help eliminate unnecessary
chemicals from your
home and from the
environment.

✔ *Brilliant cleaning*

✔ *Based on plant &
mineral ingredients*

✔ *No unnecessary
chemicals*

✔ *Protects your home
and the environment*

For an information
pack call *01635 574553*
or visit our website at
www.*ecover.com*.

ECOLOGICAL
WASHING-UP LIQUID
WITH LEMON AND ALOE VERA

ECOVER

NATURALLY MILD ON YOUR HANDS

for people who care

HOME SWEET HOME

Ecology begins at home. Whether you're decorating, buying furniture, gardening or simply cleaning, you can now Go MAD with tools, materials and products that have less impact on the environment than ever before.

And we've never been better informed – visit the Greenpeace chemical kitchen at **www.greenpeace.org.uk** for some shocking truths about the products that make our environment 'cleaner'. If you're building, or even making simple repairs, CAT, the Centre for Alternative technology **www.cat.org.uk** supplies a whole range of fact sheets on everything from heating your greenhouse to sheep's wool insulation.

Think, though, before you go 'changing rooms' or landscaping the garden – do you really need to do it in the first place? The kindest solution for the environment is generally that which has the lowest impact. Sometimes it's nicer to do nothing, sit back and let the grass grow.

NEXT TO GODLINESS

There's nothing clean about chemicals

When you're cleaning your house you're often doing the opposite to the environment, and also to your health. Our lifestyles have never been so full of chemicals – by the 1980s the world chemical output was 500 times greater than in 1940. There are now 60,000-70,000 synthetic chemicals in regular daily use. Increasingly the link is being made between the chemicals we use and the rise in certain diseases – the incidence of cancers, for example, increased 77% between 1981-2 and 1991-2. More than 400 toxic chemicals (some of which are used in the home) have been discovered in human blood. For more information on the effects of chemicals in the blood visit The Ecologist website www.theecologist.org

How many chemicals are there in your body?

When Elizabeth Salter-Green, director of WWF UK's toxic programme volunteered for a fat-cell test to establish the presence of chemicals in her body, she found that levels of contamination were far above normal. More worryingly were the traces of DDT and PCBs that were found – chemicals that have already been banned in the UK. The results spurred her into making some lifestyle changes – she now eats only organic non-processed food, avoids bleach and pesticides in her home, never dry-cleans her clothes and avoids parks and farms where spraying takes place. Her contamination levels have significantly reduced as a result. Visit **www.wwf.org.uk/chemicals/feature.asp** to find out more.

Use oxygen enhancing products to clean your clothes

Phosphates are used as water-softeners, and when they're discharged into the water supply they stimulate excessive algal growth. These 'algal blooms' starve water of oxygen, killing plant and fish life, and disrupt the sewage treatment process. For every litre of washing powder you use, 20,000 litres of water are required to treat it until it can re-enter our water system safely. And it's not the detergent that cleans the clothes anyway – it's the water. All detergents do is separate the oxygen molecules to a 'wetter' water to penetrate the fabric deeper and thus remove most dirt.

Alternatives to detergents do exist – Safewash's T-wave laundry discs (**www.safewash.com**) and Ecoball (**www.ecozone.co.uk**) offer clean, inexpensive, chemical free cleaning. Visit **www.naturalcollection.co.uk** or call Ecozone on **0870 600 6969.**

Avoid products containing chlorine

Chlorine is highly corrosive, capable of damaging the skin, eyes and other membranes. It can irritate the skin, eyes and lungs and research has linked exposure to chlorine with birth defects and cancer. If mixed with other cleaning solutions it can produce deadly gases.

Detergents transfer their chlorine into the air through a process called volatilisation – when you open the dishwasher the steamy mist that comes out is full of chlorine. Chlorine concentrations in the upper atmosphere have quadrupled over the past 25 years. Each chlorine atom released is capable of destroying tens of thousands of ozone molecules. Other chlorine-containing products to avoid are chlorine bleach, chlorinated disnfectant cleaners, mildew removers and toilet bowl cleaners. Find ecological alternatives at
www.greenbrands.co.uk

Beware of carpet cleaners

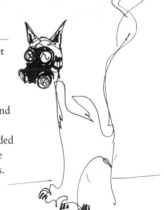

Perchorethylene is used in many carpet and upholstery cleaners. It's a known carcinogen, which may be responsible for anaemia, damage to the liver, kidneys and nervous system. Carpet and upholstery cleaners that contain ammonium hydroxide should be avoided too – they're corrosive and can irritate the eyes, skin and respiratory passages.

Use fragrance-free cleaners

Avoid cleaners that use synthetic musk fragrances. They are potential hormone disrupters and have been found in fish, mussels, human body fat and breast milk. Use products with citronella instead or open the windows and create a homely fragrance by boiling some cinnamon.

Use baking soda to clear your drains

Many commercial drain cleaners contain corrosive and toxic products such as sodium or potassium hydroxide, hydrochloric acid and petroleum distillates that kill aquatic life and make water even more expensive to treat – there's no need for them! Flushing drains with a solution of boiling water, baking soda and vinegar, then using a plunger will work just as well. And never flush cleaning products down the drain, they can corrode water pipes and kill sewage-eating bacteria.

Avoid commercial furniture polishes

Furniture polishes are petroleum distillates, which are flammable and have been linked with skin and lung cancer. They also contain nitrobenzene, a chemical that is highly toxic and easily absorbed through the skin. Ecozone has alternatives, visit **www.ecozone.co.uk**, 0870 600 6969.

Use Borax as a cleaner instead

Borax is a naturally occurring mineral made of sodium, boron, oxygen and water that has been used as a cleaner for decades. It is effective as a natural anti-bacterial, cleaning, fungicidal, and bleaching agent. You can use it to clean your fridge, wash your laundry and to remove stains from your rugs. Local hardware stores and chemists sell borax – if you can't see it, ask for it.

Avoid products containing triclosan

Triclosan is an antibacterial chemical based on an antibiotic that is used widely in the home to make germ-free utensils such as chopping boards. The ever-increasing use of antibiotics has been linked to the appearance of super bugs – resistant bugs for which there is no treatment. Triclosan has been found in human breast milk and it may lower the body's immune system and ability to fight off other bugs.

Make your own cleaning products

It doesn't take much effort to make cleaning products yourself. For washing powder mix 1 cup of finely grated soap, 1 cup of washing soda, and 2 tsp of lavender oil. To remove oil on clothing, rub white chalk into the stain before laundering. Use bicarbonate of soda to clean sinks and baths, vinegar to clean windows, washing soda crystals in water to clean floors, a paste of baking soda and water to clean ovens and microwaves, three parts olive oil to one part vinegar to polish furniture and soda paste to polish silver.

READER TIP – MELANIE CLARE
Use essential oils and alcohol for cleaning too!

Essential oils have such a wide range of practical uses around the home. Use pine oil as a bathroom cleaner – a tiny drop freshens the loo and plug hole. A refreshing antibacterial room spray can be made out of vodka, water and two drops each of lemongrass, lavender and tea tree oil. And to ward off insects in summer and generally freshen the air, use lemon oil or citronella.

Avoid washing clothes at 50°C

No textiles need to be washed at 50°C. By changing all 50°C labels on clothing to 40°C a clothing company can cut energy used during the lifecycle of its clothes by 10%. Marks and Spencer did this and saved the equivalent amount of energy needed to run all its 300 UK stores for four months. If you have clothes with 50°C on the label, why not write to the manufacturer or shop asking them to change all labels to 40°C.

Don't use commercial mothballs

Common mothball crystals contain nitrophenols, dichlorobenzene (para-DCB) and napthalene vapour, giving them their smell. However, these are all toxic chemicals which hang around a long time in the environment. Para-DCB is a known human carcinogen and repeated exposure at high levels can damage the nervous system and lungs. High levels of napthalene can lead to headaches, fatigue, confusion, nausea and vomiting. Make sure you store your woollens in air-tight storage containers or use natural alternatives: cedar wood or a mixed herb bag including dried rosemary, lavender, cinnamon, cardamom seed, cloves, tansy, wormwood, southern wood and pyrethrum flowers.

Just because it's on the floor...

Don't automatically toss anything that has been worn once or ended up on the floor into the laundry bin. Is it truly dirty? You could cut the number of loads you wash by half by airing it and putting it back in the cupboard if it isn't!

READER TIP – AGNES BODDINGTON
Cleaner cleaning cloths

Invest in Microtex cloths to clean every area of your house. Microtex fabric is made up of thousands of tiny micro-fibres that attract dirt using only a little plain warm water. No cleaners, detergents or sprays are needed, so your cleaning will help the environment, too. Look out for the cloths in your local hardware shops.

Become a toxic expert – learn about your brands!

Brands of cleaning products you've used for years may be highly toxic or polluting your home – but their manufacturers will keep on making them as long as people buy them. So find out which brands are bad and why, and boycott them.

Greenpeace's campaign against toxins is a mine of information on how chemicals affect our lives. Their 'toxic kitchen' has details of the pros

and cons of different products used in all parts of the home: visit
www.greenpeace.org.uk/Products/Toxin or call 01179 268 893.

Alternatively find out all about chemicals in cleaning products at
www.arcania.co.uk/greentree/features/clean.htm

READER TIP – NICK SMITH
Don't let wire coat hangers breed

Take wire coat hangers back to the dry-cleaners' rather than
allowing them accumulate in your wardrobe. You'll save space, and
the shop will be grateful too.

HOME IMPROVEMENTS

What are you really doing when you do it yourself?

*The back-to-back home improvement programmes that appear on TV
may inspire you to give your house a makeover. But often the products
and methods they promote are designed to look good, without
considering the harm they can do to your health and the environment.
In terms of energy and toxicity, buildings and construction are among
the most wasteful and polluting areas of modern life. But there are
ecological alternatives.*

*Visit the Association of Environment Conscious Building **www.aecb.net**
or call 01559 370 958. The Green Building Store will help you choose
which products to buy and which to avoid. Contact them at
www.greenbuildingstore.co.uk or call 01484 854 898. In the end
though, if you really want to be happy with the place you live, it's a
state of mind, not a coat of paint that will make the difference. And as
you anguish over which shade of buttermilk to paint the hall,
remember those without homes – buy the Big Issue.*

Estimate the cost of your DIY to the environment

All buildings affect the environment. How disruptive or harmonious
they will be as time progresses depends on how you build and

maintain them. Is your house well insulated and energy-efficient so that it emits low levels of CO_2? Have you harnessed the energy of the sun, water or wind power? Are your building materials recycled or do they come from sustainable sources? Do they have a minimal effect on the environment, and will they need to be maintained often?

Do you choose materials that don't damage the ozone layer or your health? Do you conserve as much water as possible when you build? And have you taken into account the wildlife living around your home? The choices you make – either in building, repairing or redecorating – all count.

Sharpen your tools

Buy a sharpening stone from a hardware store. It'll cost £2.50 or thereabouts, and save you pounds on the cost of new tools. Chisels, screwdrivers, garden shears, edge-cutting lawn tools and even saw blades can be restored to pristine condition with very little effort. Tools cost money to make, and use resources in their manufacture, so sharpen them regularly and make them last for years.

READER TIP – IAN CARE
Influence design for the better

When you buy a new house or build an extension, you can influence the design. Make the best use of natural light and heat – it has a far greater effect than replacing bulbs with 'energy savers' – if you plan your windows carefully you may not need that extra light at all. Have you planned the angle of the roofline so that it can accommodate a solar heating device?

This requires more thought than just accepting the standard or choosing between options presented but the positive effects make it worth it.

Only use boron-based wood preservatives

Wood preservatives don't just kill the pests they're designed to. They're also killing the environment. The pesticides they contain are nerve poisons and their fungicides are toxins, which harm the environment during their production and after they've been applied. When buying a wood preservative, check the tin to ensure it's made from boron. Boron is a naturally-occurring mineral, preservatives made from it are less harmful. They're the only kind approved by the Association for Environment Conscious Building, **www.aecb.net** or 01559 370 908. Visit Auro Organic Paint Supplies at **www.auroorganic.co.uk**

Check the labels and avoid solvent-based paint

Modern gloss paints can contain up to 50% solvents and volatile organic compounds (VOCs) which enter the surrounding air throughout the paint's lifetime. If inhaled or absorbed through the skin VOCs may irritate the eyes, nose and throat, affect the nervous system and damage internal organs. The World Health Organisation says that decorators are faced with a 40% increased chance of lung cancer as a result of continued exposure.

Solvent paints also have a high product-to-waste ratio – every tonne of paint produced results in 30 tonnes of waste, so use natural paints made from plant and mineral bases. Visit **www.ecosolutions.co.uk**, 01934 844 484; **www.auroorganic.co.uk**, 01799 543 077; and **www.greenshop.co.uk**, 01452 770 629.

Donate your left-over paint

Did you know that of the 350 million litres of paint sold in the UK each year, 45 million litres remain unused? The Community Re-Paint scheme run by Save Waste and Prosper runs paint collection schemes – sorting out paint and redistributing it to community projects, housing associations and schools. Visit **www.communityrepaint.org.uk** for more information or call 0113 243 8777.

Install a solar water heater

A solar water heater in an average sized house can save up to a tonne of CO_2 emissions a year. They do not need bright sunlight to work effectively – diffuse light is just as efficient. They needn't be expensive to install either. The Low Impact Living Initiative will show you how. They run courses on building a solar hot water tank, building compost toilets, and green DIY. Visit **www.lowimpact.org**

Avoid ozone depleting chemicals in insulation

Insulation uses HCFCs – which are used as a replacement for the CFCs responsible for depleting the ozone layer. HCFCs are also harmful to the ozone, yet insulations that have low HCFCs may also contribute to global warming. Use cellulose, cork and foamed glass as alternatives. For more information visit the Green Building Store at **www.greenbuildingstore.co.uk**

Buy wood from a sustainable source

There's a strong demand for sustainable wood, or wood from managed plantations, which has led some manufacturers to make claims about their wood that are dubious. The best way of making sure wood is from a sustainable source is by becoming an online member of TRADA (the Timber Research Development Association) **www.trada.co.uk**, who have a comprehensive information service. The Forest Stewardship Council also provide information. Visit **wwwfscoax.org**

Avoid chipboard and MDF

Chipboard and MDF (medium density fibreboard) have a high formaldehyde content. Formaldehyde is a recognised carcinogen, which also irritates the lungs, throats and eyes. It can take 2 to 3 years before a product has finished releasing formaldehyde fumes. Instead, use softwood or European plywood, and for kitchen worktops choose conifer.

Use recycled materials

Look for reclaimed, vintage or antique building materials such as
baths, radiators and wood floors. They are unusual, stylish, often less
expensive and come with a history too. Visit **www.salvo.co.uk** or
www.buildrecycle.net for suppliers and products.

Rent power tools or share them with neighbours

That small cheap electric drill was probably made in a sweatshop on
the other side of the world, its production and transportation
consuming unnecessary amounts of energy and causing pollution.
Why not hire tools, or invest in more durable ones that can be pooled
with neighbours? Letslink, the community sharing scheme, will help:
www.letslinkuk.org, 020 7607 7852.

Campaign for the re-use of empty homes

For every homeless person in England, there are 7 empty homes.
Across the UK there are over 700,000 empty homes – and 10%
of these belong to local authorities. Unused housing puts unnecessary
pressure for development on greenfield sites, wastes resources
and creates ghost areas and crime hotspots in towns and cities.
The Empty Houses Agency campaigns to raise awareness of the
problem of empty properties and promote solutions to bring
empty homes into use. In 2002 23,000 empty houses were filled.
Join the Community Action on Empty Houses Campaign around
your area, visit **www.emptyhomes.com** or call 020 7828 6288.
Londoners can report any empty house they know of on a special
hotline: 0870 901 6303.

Donate unused tools to charities

Unused and unwanted tools can be given to Tools for Self-Reliance,
a charity that refurbishes tools and sewing machines into kits to
go to tradesmen from Africa. They ship goods worth more than
£500,000 each year to people building their communities in
Tanzania, Zimbabwe, Uganda, Mozambique, Sierra Leone and
Ghana. To find out how you can help visit their website at
www.tfsr.org.uk

This land is our land

More than 50% of the energy we use goes on constructing and maintaining buildings. The Land is Ours is a group that campaigns for access to the land, its resources and the decision-making processes affecting them. The group occupy derelict land, build environmentally friendly houses and gardens and highlight the misuse of urban land and the lack of affordable housing. For more information contact **www.tlio.org.uk**

Find an environmentally conscious builder

For a list of environmentally friendly architects, earth builders, thatchers, wildlife consultants, insurance companies, housing associations and manufacturers contact the Association for Environment Conscious Building, which promotes environmentally sensitive building – visit **www.aecb.net**. If you're doing it yourself, visit the association's message board to get answers to your questions.

READER TIP – NEIL ALLDRED
Home Audit

Visit **www.homecheck.co.uk** to get a detailed survey of your postcode and find out what's been happening in your area. The results include information on pollution, landslides, flooding and other hazards.

 TOP TIP – BENFIELD ATT
Build your own home!

Brick-and-mortar homes have turned our planet into a huge concrete village... break the mould! 9 out of 10 new self-build homes in the UK are now built from state-of-the-art timber technology. A timber home uses one-tenth of the non-renewable energy used to construct a brick-and-mortar home, and saves you money because it is both energy-efficient and is built within weeks, rather than months. You can go further by adding eco-products such as slate-effect roof tiles made from recycled car tyres, or rock foundations instead of cement. For more information on environmentally friendly homes and building products contact Benfield ATT, 01291 437 050, **www.adtimtec.com**

TABLE TALK

Cut down on clutter

It's easy to think another piece of furniture will help make the house more cosy, but sometimes the more clutter we fill the house with, the less space is left for ourselves! The furnishing business is a massive industry that doesn't always take into account that our home environment should be in harmony with our wider environment. When you're buying furniture, think about where it has come from and what process it has gone through to get to your home.

Recycle curtains

Curtains are resource-intensive in the amount of material they require – so don't leave them to fester in the garage or dump them in the rubbish. Find your nearest textile recycler at **www.wastepoint.co.uk/ wasteconnect**, 01686 640 600. Or get in touch with the Curtain Exchange at **www.curtainexchange.net**. And why don't you buy a pair of vintage recycled curtains from them rather than a new pair?

Recycle your furniture and wood

Every year over £13 million worth of furniture is recycled and distributed to people who can't afford to buy new furniture. But demand for cheap recycled furniture still outstrips supply by up to 50%. Don't throw away your unwanted furniture – recycle it and help someone else build up a home. For details of a recycling point near you contact The Furniture Recycling Network on **www.reuze.co.uk**. Some local authorities also recycle wood. Find out if your local authority does – visit **www.reuze.co.uk** or contact your local authority directly.

Buy recycled furniture

Whether it's a gorgeous antique, a G-plan sideboard, a reclaimed rocking chair, or an armchair made from plastic bottles, recycled furniture is stylish, individual and kind to trees. For information on fairs and where to buy antiques visit **www.antiquesworld.co.uk**. A good place to sell and buy second hand furniture is **www.ebay.co.uk**. For furniture made from cable reels visit **www.reelfurniture.co.uk**. Their furniture is fully seasoned and finished with eco-friendly lacquers. Visit **www.re-formfurniture.co.uk** for furniture made from polythene bottles. For information on recycled wood visit **www.smartwood.co.uk**. Smart wood was set up by the Rainforest Alliance, to certify reused, reclaimed, recycled and salvaged wood products.

Don't buy furniture treated with brominated flame retardants

Brominated flame retardants are a group of chemicals used in fabrics, computers and plastics to counteract the spread of fires. They contribute to indoor air pollution and build up in the environment because they don't biodegrade. Several of them are also proven to be hormone disrupters, interfering with the daily functioning of the body, and they can also disrupt the thyroid hormone and contaminate human breast milk. Some countries have banned them and some major furniture suppliers such as IKEA have stopped using them, but always check the company's policy when you buy new furniture. For more information contact Friends of the Earth or visit **www.foe.co.uk/resource/press_releases/19990718090047.html**

Synthetic carpets vs natural flooring

Carpets hide a number of evils. The carpet, as well as its underlying pads and glues, can release formaldehyde – a known carcinogen – into the air for months or even years. Carpets are also a haven for house-dust mites that aggravate asthma. Most cleaning products for carpeting contain solvents and glycol ethers – chemicals that may cause irritation and coughing when inhaled. There's a range of alternatives – including carpets made from paper and plastic bottles! Visit **www.naturalcarpets4u.com** or opt for a reclaimed wood floor.

Avoid furniture made with formaldehyde

Formaldehyde is a bonding agent used to glue wood and make insulating foam. It is also used in latex paints, fabrics, and cheap furniture and MDF. It can take up to 3 years for all the fumes to be released – and inhalation can cause flu-like symptoms, rashes, cancer and neurological illnesses. Avoid buying furniture with formaldehyde, and if you're using MDF, make sure it's formaldehyde-free.

Never buy wooden furniture from old growth forests

Over 78% of the world's original old-growth forests have already been logged or degraded. If you do buy new furniture, ask the retailer where the wood comes from and whether it comes from a sustainable source. Consumer pressure DOES work. In 1991, Friends of the Earth launched a campaign against the stocking of 'unsustainably-sourced' tropical timber by the 'big six' DIY chains. The campaign became a consumer boycott and by June 1994, all six had agreed to stop selling mahogany. Mahogany imports fell 68% by 1996. Contact the Rainforest Action Network to find specific campaigns against companies, which are destroying our rainforests at **www.ran.org**. They also have information on how to buy alternatives to old-growth wood.

PEST CONTROL

The pesticide problem

Most people associate pesticides with farming, yet 80% of our exposure to them comes from our homes and gardens. In 2001 4,893 tonnes of pesticides were bought in the UK and that figure is rising by 38% per year. If you do use pesticides, keep yourself informed about their ingredients. Approximately 1 teaspoon of pesticide concentrate could affect 200,000 people a day. Many people are completely unaware of the harmful content of the products they use, as the packets don't always explain their contents.

Pesticides are designed to kill – before you buy them, think about how your use of them will affect other people (particularly children), domestic pets and wildlife. Make a difference in your own pest control at home or in the garden. Contact Pesticide Action Network

UK – *an excellent source of information at* **www.pan-uk.org** *or call 020 7274 8895. There are invariably alternative environmentally friendly methods of pest prevention and control.*

Dispose of chemicals properly

Of the 4,893 tonnes of chemicals that we bought in 2001 only 5–10% will be disposed of in special facilities, 20-30% will end up down the drain where they will pollute the water table and endanger wildlife, and the rest will sit on the shelf – where they may pose a threat to humans. Water companies use millions of litres of water to purify our drinking water and the cost of the energy used is added to YOUR water bill. Make sure you dispose of chemicals and pesticides properly by taking them to a special facility. Support the Pesticide Action Network's campaign to organise proper disposal of harmful chemicals. To find out more visit **www.pan-uk.org**

Don't spray fly sprays!

One squirt of a chemical fly spray, and the toxic gases emitted will stay in the air for 72 hours. Chemicals such as dichlorvos and pyrethrines that are found in fly sprays also kill bees and aquatic life when their residues enter water systems. Perversely, they can also cause fly populations to increase, by strengthening their resistance to pesticides and killing species that are natural predators. 'Integrated pest management' is the term given to controlling pests without resorting to chemicals, and involves altering the local environment to make it less attractive to pests. In the case of flies, this would involve cleaning out rubbish bins, disinfecting them and making sure there's no decaying food lying around. Natural fly deterrents include lemon, cloves, pine and cedar oils.

Strike a balance

Pests play a vital role in the life cycle of nature, and for some pests, no matter how hard you try to get rid of them, they will always come crawling back into your garden to fulfil this role. So instead of trying to kill off the pest, try adapting the environment to minimise their impact. If a weed is taking over a shady area of your garden, prune back a tree to allow light through or plant something that flourishes in shady conditions to drive it out. With insects and other pests, try eradicating their food supply and the pest – over time – will move on.

If you get nits, avoid chemical head lice treatments

Chemicals used in head lice treatments can disrupt the immune system, cause burning sensations, skin irritation, hyperactivity and dizziness. Instead of using chemical treatments, thoroughly wash the hair with normal shampoo and conditioner, then wide comb the hair to straighten it, then systematically fine-comb the hair from the roots to the tips to remove hatched lice.

Get rid of any products that contain Lindane

Lindane is an organochlorine pesticide that was banned from use in the UK in June 2002. It has been linked with breast cancer, and may disrupt the endochrine system. In June 2002 an 8-year-old girl died after swallowing a tiny amount of ant powder that contained lindane. Because of its known dangers, it was banned for use throughout the EU. Check that you do not have any remaining in your cupboard and dispose of it properly if you do. Visit **www.pan-uk.org/banlindane** to find out more.

★ TOP TIP – THE NATURAL COLLECTION
Ladybird ladybird...

Ladybirds eat greenfly. Encourage them to breed in your garden with a silver birch ladybird house, which provides a safe environment for 100 ladybirds to live and breed. Larvae are supplied with the house – simply place them on the plants with the greenfly infestation – they'll consume up to 8,000 greenfly a day. Hang the house up nearby – the ladybirds will take up residence as they grow! Visit the Natural Collection **www.naturalcollection.org** or call 0870 331 3333 for more information.

Use non-toxic methods of snail and slug control

Chemical slug treatments do not degrade, so their toxins remain in the environment indefinitely. And as slugs are the hedgehog's favourite food, you will be indirectly poisoning hedgehogs too. There are several simple ways of deterring slugs from eating your beans or hostas. Inter-plant vulnerable species with lavender or rosemary – slugs don't like spiky aromatic plants – or spread ash, beer or eggshells on the earth. For patio pots put a strip of copper round the base of the pot – they won't go near it. Slugs' natural predators are frogs, so encourage frogs into your garden by providing a rock pile shelter for them to make a home.

Use a fly swat

Houseflies are a nuisance and a health hazard. But resorting to chemical sprays doesn't solve the problem in the long run. Flies often come down the chimney in summer – so block your chimneys with cardboard, cover food and secure domestic waste. If you can't get rid of one annoying critter – use a fly swat.

Install a bat box

Unlike many other insects mosquitoes are very short-sighted and have to rely on their sense of smell. If you get bitten, you may not notice it straight away as the mosquito injects an anaesthetic into the skin. Only when the anaesthetic has worn off will you start itching. If your garden is providing a home to mosquitoes, there are plenty of things you can do without reaching for chemicals. Make sure any stagnant water is covered and if you have a pond stock it with mosquito predators – frogs, dragonflies, and fish. Alternatively install a bat box. A bat will eat around 3,000 mosquitoes and gnats every night. For information visit **www.naturalcollection.com** or call 0870 331 3333.

Support the victims of the world's worst chemical poisoning on the Day of no Pesticides

One night in 1984 in the Indian city of Bhopal, there was a leak of almost 40 tonnes of deadly gases into the atmosphere from Union Carbide – a American factory that produced pesticides. Parts of the city were surrounded by a chemical fog so thick that people could hardly see.

It was the world's worst industrial pollution – to date over 20,000 people have died and more than 150,000 are now chronically ill. But the story is not over yet. There are still about 25 deaths every month, the contaminated factory site has never been cleaned, victims have not been properly compensated and Union Carbide and its new owner Dow Chemical continue to deny liability and refuse to pay for a clean-up. The anniversary of the Bhopal poisoning – 3rd December – is marked as Day of No Pesticides. Support the Bhopal victims' campaign for justice and make a donation to help them with their medical costs. Visit **www.bhopal.org** for more information and **www.pan-uk.org** for information about Day of no Pesticides.

CLEAR WATER

Elixir of life

Water is one of the most important resources on our planet – and with 60% of our body made of water it's vital for human survival. It transports blood and food around the body and helps remove waste. It also lubricates the joints, keeps our eyes in shape, is essential to the maintenance of our body temperature and to the development of foetuses. Yet we do not have an abundance of water. Of the total water supply on the earth – 326 million cubic miles – only 0.3 per cent can be consumed by humans. Use water thoughtfully – the average person in the UK now washes away a staggering 1,050 litres of water a week – and be conscious, even in rainy places, what it takes to get that clean water piped to your home.

Filter out the chemicals

Much of the water we use has undergone quite a transformation since it first fell from the sky. Water is treated with chemicals, which find their way back into the environment when we use it a second time. Even ultra-violet light is now part of the used water treatment process.

Some of these chemicals may be harmful – chlorine for example, which is used to kill bacteria is a bleaching agent that destroys proteins in the hair and skin, it can dry hair out and make sensitive skin itchy. To filter out the chlorines in your household water visit the Fresh Water Filter company at **www.freshwaterfilter.org.uk**

It takes 6 litres of water to make a pint of beer...

...10 litres to make a newspaper, 27 litres to make a plate of French fries, 150 litres to make a cotton shirt and 20,000 litres to make the body of a steel car. There is a culture of wastefulness in some industries, despite the fact that companies can make great savings by auditing their water use. The UK government, for example, fitted controllers to urinals in their cabinet offices to stop them flushing continuously and saved 3,500 cubic metres of water and £2,600 a year. Think about the things you use – the more processed they are the more water is likely to have been used in production. For more information contact Friends of the Earth or visit **www.foe.co.uk/campaigns/**

KIDS – Help your school to save water

On average schools in the UK spend £2,500 a year on water (although a large secondary school could spend as much as £20,000). Schools that carefully manage their water consumption could, together with an effective education programme, reduce their water use by two-thirds. A secondary school with 600 pupils could save as much as £5,000 a year – enough to buy eight new computers. To find out how you can make sure your school is saving water visit **www.eco-schools.org.uk**

Use short bursts of water from the tap when you brush your teeth

You can waste up to 4.5 litres of water by just leaving the tap on while brushing your teeth. Just using short bursts of water to rinse your toothbrush can save 80% of the water that you normally use.

Only use a washing machine with a full load

A single washing machine cycle uses up to 100 litres of water, and the average family uses their washing machine five times a week. That's 26,000 litres a year.

Why use drinking water for flushing the toilet, washing your clothes and watering your plants?

Use rainwater instead! Flushing the loo accounts for over a third of our water use, laundry for 12% and irrigation for 7%. To really make a difference, invest in a rainwater collection system that will enable you to use rainwater for all these activities. You can also arrange to have your bath water recycled through your cistern – it's a small matter of plumbing. But if that's a bit daunting, install a large water butt for your gardening and some washing needs. Contact the Centre of Alternative Technology for advice, **www.cat.org.uk** 01654 702 400.

Take showers instead of baths

The average bath uses about 80 litres of water while the average shower uses something between 30-49 litres. Having a shower saves a significant amount of water, and time too!

Save water in the garden

Sprinklers use 300-650 litres of water an hour. If you leave them on for 8 hours a night, that's a minimum of 2,400 litres! Avoid sprinklers and try to use a watering can instead. Also only water plants during the evening or early in the morning. Not only does this save water, it prevents leaves from getting burnt in strong sunshine. Other water-saving garden tips include: installing a water butt to catch rainwater, building a soak-away, leaving grass cuttings on the lawn, mulching around plants with organic compost and using drought tolerant plants, such as lavender and thyme instead of bedding plants that are very heat sensitive and require more water.

Use appliances carefully

Use front loading washing machines rather than top loaders. Energy efficient washing machines now use less than 50 litres of water per wash (on average older machines use 100). Energy efficient dish-washers also use as little as 16 litres of water per cycle. When you buy new appliances check their water consumption on the energy-rating label to find out how much water they use. Visit The Green Building Store for more information on products **www.greenbuildingstore.co.uk** and **www.environment.agency.co.uk/savewater** for information on the energy rating scheme.

Check your system for leaks

The average family in the UK now uses around 5,000 litres of water a week, but out of this over 16% is lost due to leaks. That's a staggering 800 litres of lost water a week! Check your water meter just before you go to bed and then re-check in the morning. If it shows an increase have your water system checked – it could save you money in the long run. For more information check **www.h2ouse.org**.

And while you're checking for your own leaks, make sure your local water company isn't wasting water either. In some areas of the UK more than one third of water is lost through leaking pipes. Find out about your local water company's record – if it's bad write to them to protest that consumers should not have to pay rising costs if the company won't invest more of its profits in water consumption.

Kit out your house with water-saving devices

Spray taps let out a smaller volume of water but achieve the same results as normal taps. Low-flow showerheads can be fitted to maximise water coverage and minimise the water used. And a dual flush toilet saves thousands of litres a year by discharging a small amount of water for liquid waste and a larger amount for solid waste. Contact the Centre for Alternative Energy for more details at **www.cat.org** or call 01654 702 400.

Help bring clean water to the billion people who need it

We take water for granted. But over a billion people in the world don't have safe water to drink. That's one in six of the world's population. And 2.4 billion don't have access to adequate sanitation. That means that one child dies from diseases caused by lack of safe water every 15 seconds. Water Aid is a charity that helps over 500,000 people from the poorest communities provide themselves with a better quality of life through water, sanitation and education. It also lobbies for more sustainable water policies on a global level. To become a supporter visit **www.wateraid.co.uk**.

GREEN FINGERS

The Eco-garden

Your garden is an ecosystem teeming with life; and just as it contains its own micro-ecosystems, it is also part of the ecosystem of the surrounding area. Encourage biodiversity, by thinking about what species you plant and about the materials you use in your garden. Where do they come from, how were they made and what knock-on effects do they have? For more information contact The Wildlife Trusts for a leaflet on wildlife gardening 01636 677 711 or **www.mylinkspage.com/wildlife.html**. *HDRA – the Henry Doubleday Research Association is a mine of information on gardening methods. Visit* **www.hdra.org.uk** *or call 0247 630 3517.*

Turn your windowsill into a garden

You don't need a garden to grow things… think chillies in window boxes, tomatoes in grow bags and herbs on the kitchen windowsill. Read *The Window Box Allotment* by Penelope Bennett for ideas including wormeries and compost heaps in confined spaces, or *The Edible Container Garden: Fresh Food from Tiny Spaces* by Carol Klein, Michael Guerra and Patrick Whitefield.

Don't use a fuel-powered lawnmower

One fuel mower produces as much pollution in one hour as 40 cars. Use an electric mower – or better, a manual mower – instead. And bear in mind that grass is not always greener anyway. Grass needs a lot more water and treatment against weeds than other hardier ground covers, and the more ground area covered by grass the less area available for other species. Devote a larger area of your garden to other types of habitat such as rockery, flowerbeds, a wild area or a vegetable patch.

Don't poison your garden

Private gardens make up a significant proportion of green space – in cities, and provide a refuge for urban wildlife. What you do with your garden can make a vital difference to the survival of species in your area. Don't resort to chemical warfare – learn more about the pests in your garden and search out other ways of dealing with them. Visit **www.essexwt.org.uk/Leaflets/poisons.htm** for information.

Don't treat fencing with creosote

Breathing in creosote fumes irritates the windpipe, and if it gets into food or drinking water it can cause burning in the mouth, stomach pains, convulsions and kidney problems. Creosote dissolves in water and can then get through the soil to groundwater, where it takes years to break down. Why not create a hedge or tree border instead, or build a wall from old bricks with crevices that can become a home to plants, insects and beetles? Old brick walls are a haven for wildlife and can also support a variety of species or creeper.

Avoid using water-worn limestone in your garden

The British Isles hold the world's most significant areas of limestone pavement, of which only 3% has escaped damage by man. It has been sculpted by glaciers and weathered for over 10,000 years resulting in a unique splintered appearance, with fissures that are home to rare plants, snails and butterflies. Water-worn limestone, used in rockeries, is also known as Irish limestone, Cumbrian stone or weathered limestone. There are several alternatives – sandstone, granite deep-quarried limestone or York stone, as well as re-constituted and artificial substitutes made from fibreglass or cement.

Save our allotments!

Allotments are a vital breathing space in city areas and give people who have no access to gardens a chance to develop green fingers. Over the past two decades there has been a 43% drop in the number of allotments in the UK. The National Society of Allotment and Leisure Gardens campaigns to protect allotments. Find out about their work and get involved at **www.nsalg.co.uk** or call 01536 266 576. The Wavendon Allotment and Garden Society has a database of allotment sites around the UK - **www.btinternet.com/~cbownes/wags** has details.

Don't use peat compost

Over 90% of Britain's peatbogs have been damaged or destroyed – mostly in the last 50 years. Some are thousands of years old, and in their trapped remains researchers and archaeologists have found seeds, plant remains, artefacts and even bodies – such as the 2,300 year-old man 'Pete Marsh'. These have helped us to understand our climate, environmental history and early civilizations.

Gardeners use up 70% of all the peat used today in the UK. The area of lowland raised bog in the UK has diminished from an original 95,000 hectares to approximately 6,000 hectares today. Buy peat-free compost and make sure that the plants you buy are also in peat-free compost. To find out more visit The Royal Botanical Gardens website **www.rbgkew.org.uk** or call Friends of the Earth for information about gardening without peat, 020 7490 1555, **www.foe.org.uk.** Find out more about our disappearing peat bogs and what you can do to help from Plant Life, an organisation that works to conserve Britain's wild plants. Visit **www.plantlife.org.uk** or call 020 7808 0100. The Scottish Wildlife Trust also has a peat bog campaign at **www.swt.org.uk**

Urban foxes aren't pests

Foxes survive in a range of different environments – they can adapt easily to urban areas and eat many different types of food and it is now quite common to see them in cities. The Wildlife Trusts believes they have become an important part of the city's ecology and should be tolerated rather than persecuted. If a fox becomes a nuisance in your garden don't remove it by killing, trapping or transporting it – another fox will quickly take its place. Visit **www.wildlondon.org.uk** for humane and effective ways of controlling foxes in your garden.

Furniture in the garden

You don't have to make your garden hi-tech to enjoy it! Avoid energy wasting gadgets such as patio heaters – put on a warm jumper! If you must install lights in the garden – go for solar powered. When you buy wooden garden furniture avoid tropical hardwoods such as teak – which is fast disappearing. If you have to buy teak, make sure it's either reclaimed or from sustainable forests. To learn more, contact Global Witness who have researched the garden furniture industry. Visit **www.globalwitness.org/campaigns/forests/garden_furniture/** and become a supporter.

★ **TOP TIP** – MALCOLM TAIT, WILDLIFE EDITOR
Be hedgehog aware

If you're planning a late autumn bonfire, carefully turn the contents over first. A hedgehog may have begun its hibernation inside.

Wildlife Walks is a guide to over 500 of the UK's top nature reserves. Call 0870 101 9700 or visit **www.wildlifetrusts.org** for information.

COOL COMPOST

Back to the soil

Almost a third of our domestic waste could go straight onto the compost heap. Instead, 27 million tonnes of organic waste – food scraps and tea bags – go to landfill each year where deprived of oxygen they do not biodegrade. There is no reason why it should not be turned into compost, returning the nutrients and energy from your leftover food back to the soil where they can be re-used. Composting reflects the world's cyclic patterns – recycling waste and reaping the benefits as you watch your garden grow, rather than the destructive resource-waste conveyor belt.

Your plants love compost because...

• it slowly releases nutrients that benefit plants when they need them – unlike chemical fertilisers, which are released in a 'rush'

• it helps sandy soils to retain water (so you save on water too!)

• it helps to suppress plant diseases and weeds without introducing chemicals into the ground

• it insulates soil and retains warmth in cold weather – plants are better protected from frosts.

Spread the word

Compost Awareness Week is held every year around the world to encourage homes, businesses and schools to start composting. Show your support for composting by joining one of the planned activities such as competitions to grow sunflowers, educational drives and roadshows. For more information visit **www.compost.org.uk**

Not just for the green fingered...

Composting is easy. You throw your leftovers – uncooked food waste such as fruit and vegetables, tea bags, egg shells and coffee grinds together with your garden waste – such as mowings, old plants, flowers, weeds and leaves into a pile in the garden. With the help of worms and other creepy-crawlies, they'll decompose into 5-star plant food. You'll save on plastic rubbish bags, buying nutrients for the soil and water. The earth will be saved from yet more contaminating landfills and your plants will thrive. For information on how to create a compost heap visit The Composting Association **www.compost.co.uk**, The Henry Doubleday Research Association at **www.hdra.org.uk** and Waste Watch at **www.wastewatch.org.uk**

Get started!

Compost bins are easy to get hold of at garden centres, but even better, make your own from old tyres, scrap timber, bricks or wire mesh. By building your own bin you can recycle materials, which might otherwise find their way to the scrap heap.

Local authorities also run discount home composting schemes...

By 1999 some local authorities had supplied almost a million compost bins to home composters. In other areas, there are municipal composting bins and garden rubbish collection schemes. Find out what your local authority is doing at **www.compost.org.uk/**

KIDS – Go MAD with worms

Set up a worm-composting bin, either inside your house or out. Worms eat your kitchen waste and convert it into rich dark compost by passing it through their bodies. Each worm can recycle half its own bodyweight of waste every day – if you have a bin-full of worms, that's a lot of composting. You can buy worm-composting bins, but why not make your own? The best types of worms to use are tiger worms and red worms. Contact Wiggly Wigglers for more details. Visit **www.wigglywigglers.co.uk**, or call 0800 216 990.

Feed your compost heap with fibre

All your paper and card which cannot be recycled can be composted. That includes tissues, kitchen towels, the tubes from toilet rolls, cereal boxes and egg boxes. Like people, compost heaps need fibre to keep healthy (otherwise they go soggy!) Fibre keeps air spaces in the compost, so your heap will be bursting with beneficial creepy-crawlies.

Give your flowers coffee and watch them grow

Did you know that coffee-grounds are perfect compost material? Next time you're about to empty the coffee pot, tip it onto the flowerbeds instead of the bin. And if you use a paper filter – well that can go on the compost heap too! If you've got a serious compost heap 'brewing' in the back garden, ask local coffee shops to donate their coffee-grounds – or take them to the nearest municipal compost heap.

Other good things to compost are old prunings, straw and hay, hamster and rabbit bedding, eggshells and autumn leaves. Avoid cooked food and meat.

No garden? No excuse!

Find out where your nearest community composting project is. And if there isn't one in your area, set one up. The Community Composting Network provides composting sites around the UK that each serve about 100 households. The compost made from their organic waste is distributed around the community either for free or at a cheap price, and it's also used in local parks. Contact the Community Composting Network at **www.othas.org.uk**, or call 0114 258 0483.

Give your composting a turbo boost

Serous composters who want to cut down on landfill should look out for an Eco Food Waste digester. Unlike conventional composting bins, it can digest cooked food too. For more information visit Green Cone at **www.greencone.com**

Aaah, how I love my daily breath of fresh air...

COMPOST

HAPPY FAMILIES

There are so many ways – at all stages and in all areas of their lives – in which family members can collectively do their bit. Economies of scale are the key. Families consume more, waste more and spend more than individuals, so changing habits makes more of a difference. They also benefit from the ripple effect – if one family member starts recycling, volunteering or eating organic, others are likely to follow.

Doing your bit doesn't have to cost more in terms of time and money, either. Sometimes it's just a matter of thinking before you act, or consciously deciding *not* to do something. Make the world one of your family's priorities, and there'll still be a world for your family's families to grow up in.

LOVE CONQUERS ALL

Green recipes for love and romance

Try to care about the world as you care about each other. After all, it's love that makes the world go round.

Candlelit romance

Turn off the lights and eat by candlelight. It's more romantic and you'll save energy, too! Take care in your choice of candles, though – paraffin candles are made from petroleum residues so do neither your health nor the environment any good. Use natural beeswax or vegetable-based candles that biodegrade and are smoke-free. They last twice as long and burn brighter! Try **www.101candles.com** for ideas.

Choose a green mate

Find a partner you can make a difference with by joining a 'green' dating agency – try Natural Friends at **www.natural-friends.com**, 01284 728 315, or Evergreen, **www.evergreenagency.co.uk**, 01992 632 250.

For a more subtle approach, Friends of the Earth have groups across the country which meet to discuss and campaign together. Visit **www.foe.org.uk** or call 020 7490 1555.

Give your loved one a locally-grown plant on Valentine's day

The blossoming bouquets in florists' windows have usually been cultivated in mass plantations on the other side of the world, doused in pesticides and fed vast quantitites of water in locations where water is scarce. They're then transported thousands of miles to reach their point of sale. Choose a locally-grown bouquet or plant for your Valentine, instead.

Good for the planet, good for your Valentine!

Don't give commercially made food or chocolates as presents. They're likely to be full of sugar and additives and wrapped in unnecessary packaging. Instead, make it personal and give them an edible gift. Home-baked biscuits are fun to try, while organic truffles or even home-made chocolates are delicious indulgences.

Condom etiquette

We're pretty responsible when it comes to using condoms, but not so good at disposing of them. Every year in the UK almost 150 million are flushed down the toilet, clogging water treatment filters and causing sewage overflows on rivers and beaches: and let's face it, wrinkly rubbers are unwelcome guests when you're wading through rock pools! Latex condoms are biodegradable in landfill so stick to latex and put them in the bin. For more information visit **www.bagandbin.org**. And if you're indulging in a bit of alfresco loving, don't leave the evidence behind!

Stay closer to home

Heathcliff and Cathy's stormy love affair took place in the wild moors of the Pennines, Henry VIII romanced Anne Boleyn at Hever Castle in Kent and Tintern Abbey near the Forest of Dean inspired one of Wordsworth's greatest poems. Some of the world's most up-lifting places are found in parts of Britain's remote and beautiful countryside, so you don't need to travel to far-flung places for romance. Turn to literature for inspiration, or visit **www.sawdays.co.uk**

KIDS – Make a friend out of cress

Take a small tray. Plant cress seeds in the shape of a friend's name, and give the tray to that friend. Tell them to water it regularly and wait. They'll be surprised when shoots start to spring up and spell their name – a perfect present to show you care about someone.

Get together and cool it!

All over the world, people have achieved change through linking their voices together, whether it's halting plans for the construction of an incinerator, or saving a species from extinction. One of the biggest threats to the future of our planet is global warming. CO_2, the main heat-trapping gas, is at the highest levels the planet has seen for 20 million years. Link up with people planet-wide to turn the heat down before it's too late. ClimateArk is a great campaigning tool against global warming – visit **www.climateark.org**

WELL MATCHED!

Weddings that don't cost the earth

The symbolism in traditional weddings implies that there are parallels between the union of two people and the union of those people with the earth. But now a wedding is far more likely to cost the earth, than bring us closer to it.

Couples spend an average of £11,200 on a wedding. But you don't have to follow the crowd and run up the same bill. A green wedding saves not only your pocket but also the environment, and it is no more difficult to arrange.

Send invitations on recycled or handmade paper

This is so much more original than bleached white heavily embossed traditional cards. Some paper comes ready-sprinkled with flower petals, or you can use plain paper and decorate each card individually with feathers, petals and leaves. Visit **www.recycled-paper.co.uk** for

inspiration and paper supplies or call them on 01676 533 832. For all types of wedding stationery from invitations to place names, as well as photo albums and frames, contact Dakini, an Irish company committed to fair wages and environmental concerns. Visit **www.dakini.ie** or call 00 353 9177 6747.

Have an ethical wedding list

This is a great opportunity to introduce some of your friends to the benefits of green life. Ask for a wind-up radio or solar powered garden lights. You can set up a wedding list at **www.ethicalmatters.co.uk** or **www.greenfibres.com**

Tree of life

Rather than collecting more household goods, ask your guests to donate a tree to the MarryMe wood. This scheme, run by Future Forests, will help protect the climate by absorbing greenhouse gas carbon dioxide. The trees are native species planted in natural woodlands protected from development for at least 40 years. Visit **www.futureforests.com** for more information. Alternatively you could celebrate by planting an apple or pear tree in your garden!

Ask your guests to make a donation to your favourite charity

For advice on easy ways to set this up, without spending time collecting donations while busy organising your wedding, visit **www.justgiving.com/events** and click on *Weddings*.

Cut down on cars

Save the environment from the pollution of all those cars carrying just one or two people to your wedding. Include clear directions in the invitation for how people can reach the wedding by public transport and details of places for them to stay nearby. Try to persuade friends to join up in cars together, and when you arrive at the church, do it in the ultimate style – by horse, or horse-drawn carriage.

All that glisters is not gold...

Don't swap rings that have been made from materials excavated using cheap labour in exploitative conditions. Diamonds mined by insurgent groups in Sierra Leone and Angola cause misery to millions, while gold is mined with cyanide, which is highly toxic to both humans and the environment. The Kimberley Process, launched in January 2003, requires governments and the industry to implement import/export control to prevent conflict diamonds from fuelling war and human rights abuse. Visit **www.kimberleyprocess.com** for more information.

BUT, there is currently no way of knowing whether a cut diamond is a conflict diamond or one that has been legally harvested. If you must have a ring, buy antique, or melt down and recast an old one.

For an alternative to diamonds, **www.silverchilli.com** offers a range of silver jewellery bought at fair trade prices from Mexican craftsmen. Visit the website for more inspiration and to shop online.

Make your own wedding cake

This way you can ensure that all the ingredients are organic, locally produced and the eggs are from free-range chickens.

The Campaign for Real Food is a group of caterers providing freshly prepared food from natural ingredients and local produce wherever possible – call 020 7771 0099 for more information. For vegetarian or vegan caterers, call More Food for Thought on 020 7836 9072 and for organic champagne visit **www.ethicalmatters.co.uk**

Don't celebrate with toxic flowers

Flowers are laced with pesticides – so much so
that when you sniff a commercially grown
rose you breathe in a small amount of toxic
fumes. Buy local, farm or garden-grown
flowers instead.

Make sure your confetti doesn't hang around

If you throw plastic confetti at the
happy couple on their wedding day it will
still be around in a landfill site when they celebrate their silver
wedding anniversary. Choose a biodegradable alternative – recycled
paper, rosebuds or dried bougainvillea petals. Visit **www.wedding-
favours.com** or **www.scentsations.uk.com** for biodegradable
confetti. Better still, collect flower blossoms or petals yourself.

A flash send-off

No need for a plush Rolls Royce or a flashy open top car to drive
off into the sunset. Bring romance and originality to your wedding
by leaving your guests on a tandem, a rickshaw or a hot air
balloon. For good ideas visit **www.tourismconcern.org.uk**

Make your honeymoon matter

Explore the possibility of becoming eco-tourists on your
honeymoon. Visit **www.exodus.co.uk**,
www.exploreworldwide.com or **www.responsibletravel.com** for
eco-friendly holidays which include wilderness trails, hideaway hot
springs in the forest and scuba diving in some of the world's most
romantic destinations. In 20 years' time you'll be able to go back,
and find it's still there!

BIRTH RIGHT

Green tips for eco-babies

Excited parents-to-be and their families, encouraged by advertising, can spend huge sums with little consideration for the impact they are having on the environment, not to mention the money they waste on products they probably don't need or won't use for longer than a few months. It's easy to spend £2,000 on baby paraphernalia before and during the first year of a child's life... make those first 21 months calmer and easier by cutting down on clutter and making sure everything you buy is simple and natural. Think in terms of the essentials: clothing and nappies, a pram, a cot and feeding equipment.

Buy second-hand baby clothes

Second-hand baby clothes are cheaper, as well as being well-worn and more comfy. And if you aren't keeping baby clothes for future children of your own, pass them on again to friends or take them into your local charity shop.

You can also buy and sell unwanted baby items on the internet. Visit **www.baby-things.com** and **www.preloved.co.uk/go/gaga** or get information on local nearly-new sales from The National Childbirth Trust **www.nctpregnancyandbabycare.com**, 0870 770 3236.

Breast over bottle?

Breast-feeding helps protect your baby against infection because antibodies are passed from mother to baby through the breast milk. On average breast-fed babies have fewer infections in early life than babies who are bottle-fed, and it's thought that babies who are breast-fed are also less likely to develop obesity, diabetes and heart disease. Breast-feeding is also good for mums – it reduces their chances of developing breast cancer and helps weight-loss after giving birth. It's also free!

Formula milk is made with artificial additives and a huge amount of energy is needed to turn cow's milk into formula. If you do need to buy formula milk, there are organic varieties available – try **www.hipp.co.uk**

For breast-feeding advice contact La Leche League **www.laleche.org.uk** (020 7242 1278) and for general feeding information, visit the National Childbirth Trust at **www.nctpregnancyandbabycare.com** or call the breast feeding line on 0870 444 708.

Don't let your baby be a victim of hand-me-down poisons

Mothers may unwittingly pass on chemicals or contaminants to their baby through being unknowingly polluted themselves. A WWF survey found that more than 350 man-made contaminants have been found in mothers' milk. These pollutants are thought to be linked to reduced intelligence and subtle behavioural effects in children. For more information visit **www.wwf.org.uk** or America's Natural Resources Defense Unit **www.nrdc.org/breastmilk/envpoll.asp**

Untreated cotton bedding

Synthetic bedding can expose a baby to formaldehyde, solvents and other chemicals. Babies' bedding should be made from cotton, wool, hemp or silk – these natural fabrics breathe and feel more comfortable. Don't forget that non-organic cotton is treated with pesticides and chemical fertilisers that remain in the material after it has been treated. Contact **www.borndirect.com** or **www.gossypium.co.uk**, 0800 085 6549 for organic bedding and baby clothes.

Take action against infant deaths

The World Health Organisation (WHO) estimates that 1.5 million infants die around the world every year because they are not breast-fed. Instead they are given aggressively marketed milk substitutes mixed with unsafe water. Where water is unsafe a bottle-fed child is up to 25 times more likely to die as a result of diarrhoea than a breast-fed child. In 1981, an international marketing code was set up to regulate the industry, but some companies continue to violate that code.

Baby Milk Action is part of the International Baby Food Action Network and campaigns to expose these violations and make milk substitute companies take responsibility for their actions. Find out how you can help at **www.babymilkaction.org** or call 01223 464 420.

Choose organic food for your babies

Organic baby-food is already bought by 60% of mothers, and is available in most supermarkets and small retailers. Friends of the Earth have found high levels of pesticides in non-organic baby food. Pesticide residues have more impact on babies than adults as the amount they eat in proportion to their body weight is higher. Visit Hipp at **www.hipp.co.uk**, 0845 050 1351 and find out about Babynat at **www.organico.co.uk**, 020 8340 0401. Both specialise in producing organic baby-food.

If you want to make your own organic baby food get information from other mothers and exchange recipes at **www.babyorganix.co.uk** or **www.child.com** or **www.mumsnet.com**

THE BOTTOM LINE

Nappy facts

Nappies are one of Britain's major waste problems. The average baby will get through a total of 5,480 – which is the equivalent of two trees – during its early years. Each day eight million disposable nappies are thrown away accounting for 4% of landfill waste, where they can take 500 years to decompose – and there is also the risk that viruses from human faeces can seep into groundwater supplies. As many as 100 viruses can survive in soiled nappies for up to two weeks, including the live polio virus excreted by recently vaccinated babies.

It's not only babies' disposables that are harmful to the environment – older children and adult incontinence pads are, too. For information on eco-friendly incontinence pads and incontinence laundries, contact the Extra Large Real Nappy Network on 01386 701 428.

READER TIP – TRACEY FARWELL
Is it worth the sacrifice?

It takes a cup of crude oil to produce the plastic for one disposable nappy. Use environmentally friendly nappies presoaked in an environmentally friendly nappy soak (**www.thebabycatalogue.com**) and then throw them in the washing machine using Eco-balls (**www.ecozone.co.uk**), not washing powder.

Disposables cost the environment – and us – more

With cotton nappies, you'll bear more of the environmental cost in terms of water and energy (if you wash them at home) but this is very little compared to nappy production costs and will make a substantial saving to the environment.

The financial cost of disposable nappies per child per year has been estimated to be £1,200. But the cost of keeping one child in shaped cloth nappies has been estimated to be £300, and that includes washing. Think what you could do with an extra £900 a year!

But it's not just the money. A paediatrics professor has recently discovered that nappies lined in plastic can increase the temperature of a baby boy's scrotum by up to 1% – interfering with the baby's cooling patterns and possibly decreasing fertility levels as an adult.

And some nappies contain a super-absorber crystalline made of sodium polyacrylate which turns into a gel on contact with urine. This chemical was linked to toxic shock syndrome in tampons, and was removed from them in 1985.

Which would you prefer to wear?

Cloth nappies have come a long way since the squares with safety pins. They can come in different shapes and sizes, colours and prints, with elastic or Velcro fastenings, breathable fleece or silk covers and biodegradable liners. The Real Nappy Association estimates that 15% of parents use them. If you were to wear them on your bottom, which would you choose – a sweaty plastic disposable or a breathable cotton fleece lined one? Contact **www.realnappy.com**, 01983 401959.

Buy eco-disposables

If you're going on a long journey where changing and washing nappies is difficult, make sure you use eco-disposable nappies instead. Their manufacturing process does far less harm to the environment than normal disposables, not least because they don't contain bleaching agents. They are also free from perfumes and other chemicals which may harm your baby's skin. Visit **www.spiritofnature.co.uk** for more details.

Go velcro

Pins too much hassle? Buy Velcro fastening cotton nappies. Visit **www.earthwisebaby.com**, 01908 587 275 and **www.ecobabes.co.uk**, 01353 664 941 for ranges of easy-to-use cotton nappies.

Keep it dry

Keep your baby's bottom as dry as possible – and don't use moist tissue wipes. This reduces your baby's likelihood of contracting nappy rash, a reaction to chemicals in the urine and faeces. And if you thought that cotton nappies meant a higher chance of nappy rash – WRONG! Research by the American Medical Association found that nappy rash occurs in 54% of babies using disposable nappies and only 18% of babies using cloth nappies. Moist baby wipes are full of chemicals such as alcohol, preservatives, fragrances and moisturisers – babies' skin is even more sensitive to these artificial chemicals than yours.

Never flush a disposable nappy down the toilet

The bleaching agent in nappies can pollute waterways, and damage wildlife, fisheries and ultimately humans. The super-absorbent gel in disposable nappies absorbs water and the nappies swell so much they block pipes. Any nappies that do get through the sewerage system will eventually end up on our beaches. Lovely.

Use a nappy washing service

Nappy services use 32% less energy than home washing, and 41% less water. They also make life much easier for you. Contact the National Association of Nappy Washing services to find out about services in your area. Visit **www.changenappy.co.uk** or call 0121 693 4949.

Maternity wards should use cotton nappies too

Most women put their first nappy on their baby at hospital, so it makes sense for hospitals to encourage them to use cotton nappies to start with. Join the campaign for the NHS to use cotton nappies and lobby your local hospital to do so. Contact the Womens' Environmental Network for more information at **www.wen.org.uk**.

READER TIP – GRACE EDWARDS
Wear a nappy!

Support Real Nappy Week by wearing a nappy – a clean one of course! Last year mums whose babies wear real cloth nappies supported Real Nappy Week by wearing scraps of terry nappy on their lapels – a great conversation point and a good way of spreading the news.

Help make the change

Real Nappy Week is a nationwide campaign to get people to switch from disposable to cotton. Get involved at **www.realnappy.com**. The Real Nappy Association will also tell you all you need to know about cotton nappies, where to buy them and what to consider when buying. Also visit The Nappy Lady **www.nappylady.co.uk**, and the Women's Environmental Network **www.wen.org.uk** which organises nappy activists' workshops.

KIDS' STUFF

Early learners

Kids learn best by doing. One of the best things parents can do to make kids more aware of the environment is to lead by example. Show kids how to save water by turning taps off when they brush their teeth, and how to separate rubbish and recycling cans and plastic bottles at the bottle bank. Walk or cycle with them to school and local shops to save fuel, and point out interesting plants, animals and birds on the way. If you are aware of environmental issues, your children will become aware of them too!

The right to a healthy environment

International law gives children the right to education, but not – as yet – to live in a healthy and sustainable environment. Find out what other parents in Europe are doing to create safe and sustainable lives for their children.

Examples include car-free days, safe public transport initiatives and alternatives to the gas-guzzling school run. For more information visit **www.europa.eu.int/comm/environment/youth/air/kids_on_the_move_en.html**

Turn city kids green

If your kids are growing up in a city centre, take them to a green space – a park or a city farm – to learn more about how the countryside supports cities. There are over 60 city farms throughout the UK which breed livestock and grow crops – **www.farmgarden.org.uk** has all the details. If there aren't any green spaces near you, find out how you can create one. Visit the British Trust for Conservation Volunteers website **www.btcv.org/ppawards/ppawardsintro.html** for information on the green spaces and community initiatives, a project that helps communities to develop or improve accessible 'green spaces' in urban and rural areas across England.

Horse-riding

Seeing the countryside on the back of a horse is a great way of getting back to nature. There are stables all over the country that offer riding lessons, and there are several organisations that organise riding holidays. Details of these can be found at **www.horse-directory.co.uk**

Children's environmental holidays

If you send your kids on adventure holidays, choose a holiday that combines the excitement of activity with discovery of the natural world. The Field Studies Council runs eco-adventure holidays in the Lake District for children from eight years upwards; details are available at **www.field-studies-council.org**. Meanwhile, the Young People's Trust for the Environment runs Environmental Discovery Holidays for people aged 8-16 during the summer in Dorset. Visit **www.yptenc.org.uk/docs/residential_hols.html** for more information.

Start volunteering early

Young people are the decision-makers of the future, so encourage them to get involved and volunteer when they're young. The Young Person's Trust for the Environment is packed with courses, facts and ideas for kids aged 5-16 years and their teachers/parents. Search **www.yptenc.org.uk** for more information.

Visit environment museums or open spaces

The best way to get children to care about the creatures and plants around us, is to help them learn about them first. **www.uk-tourist-attractions.co.uk/attractions/wildlife/index.cfm** lists safari parks, bird sanctuaries, sealife centres and zoos. (Visiting a zoo may be controversial, but it may be the only way some kids will ever experience wildlife and understand the conflict between humans and animals). Other museums well worth visiting are The Natural History Museum **www.nhm.ac.uk**, the Earth Centre near Doncaster, (**www.earthcentre.org.uk**) and the Eden Project (**www.edenproject.co.uk**) in Cornwall. The IMAX cinema has informative films on the natural world **www.bfi.org.uk**

Kids – Go fly a kite

Have you ever tried flying a kite off the side of a hill on a windy day?
Kite surfing is an international sport and kites come in all shapes and
sizes. For new and second hand kites try **www.kiteshack.co.uk**.
Alternatively make your own kite out of a bin liner, some sticks and a
bit of sticky tape! It's cheap and easy – **www.reeddesign.co.uk** will
show you how.

Kids – Make recycled paper

Only 25% of the world's paper is recycled. If this were increased to
50%, up to 8,000,000 hectares of forest worldwide could be saved
from destruction! Help recycle by making sure all the paper –
particularly newspaper – in your house is recycled. You can also make
recycled paper – visit the Young People's Trust for the Environment
www.yptenc.org.uk/docs/actionsheets/recycling_paper.html to find
out how.

Kids – Help birds nest in your area

Build them nest boxes! Some birds return to the same box each year,
and as long as you don't disturb them, you can watch them as they
establish a home for their offspring, feed them and teach them to fly.
To find out more visit the Young People's Trust for the Environment
www.yptenc.org.uk/docs/actionsheets/nestboxes.html

Kids – Make a frieze of endangered species

Thousands of animal species are threatened with extinction – from
elephants which are killed for their ivory tusks to tiny insects in the
Amazon who die out when their habitat is destroyed. Your
own children may never be able to see them. Find out
which animals are endangered and draw pictures
of them – then stick them around your bedroom
wall. Find out how to protect an animal from
extinction – ask your parents and look on the
internet.

Kids – Form your own environmental club

Find out about the wildlife in your area, how the creatures live, where they live, what they eat and how they survive. Visit **www.beetroot.org.uk/environment_resources.htm** for information, advice and support. Learn more about biodiversity in your backyard from **www.biodiversityday.org**

Kids – Persuade your parents to get you a bicycle

50% of car journeys in Britain are shorter than 5 miles. Don't let your family's car choke Britain with smoky car fumes that contribute to climate change, polluted air and health problems. Persuade your parents to put away the car keys and walk on local journeys, or better still get bikes for everyone, including you!

Kids – Learn more about the environment and make new friends

A new website aimed at 12-16 year olds has lots of information about air pollution, dealing with waste, conserving water, and protecting endangered animals. There are also competitions, games and suggestions for group activities. Young people can join the Green Buddies Network through the site.
www.europa.eu.int/comm/environment/youth/index_en.html

PLAY SCHOOL

Toys and games that make a difference

Toys can do so much damage. Often made on the other side of the world by children who receive next to nothing for their labour, they are transported from country to country, burning up fuel, and wrapped in packaging that contributes to global waste. And how often have you given a brand new toy to a young child only to find them playing with the cardboard box it came in? Why not Go MAD with the toys you give – it'll be fun for you as well as the children.

Play safe

Are your children playing with toys that are safe? Look for the lion mark – a triangle with a lion inside it. This shows it has been made by a member of the British Toy and Hobby Association and meets government safety requirements. About 95% of toys sold in the UK are made by members of the association so it's not difficult to avoid the few that aren't. For more information visit **www.btha.co.uk** or call 020 7701 7271. Never buy a child a toy if it is aimed at an older kid – they can be especially dangerous for children under three. Check toys with loose or small parts that a young child could choke on, toys with sharp edges or finger traps, loose ribbons and small toys sold with food.

Join a toy library

In 2000, £1.76 million was spent on toys in the UK – that's an average of over £150 a year spent on every child. But you don't have to spend a fortune to keep up with the latest toy craze: join a toy library where (for a small fee) you can borrow toys, join play sessions and meet other families. There are over 1,000 toy libraries in the UK, run by the National Association of Toy & Leisure Libraries. Call them on 020 7387 9592 to find out your nearest library or visit **www.natll.org.uk**

Avoid plastic toys

Plastic toys, especially PVC toys, can contain phthalates, harmful chemicals thought responsible for altering testes development as well as liver and kidney damage. Some toys made in Asia contain up to 55% phthalates by weight. Workers who produce these products have been found to suffer from a high level of liver and other cancers. Some researchers put the risk of liver cancer in vinyl plastics workers as high as 200 times greater than average.

Don't let your child's toys be someone else's killer. Wooden toys are much kinder to the environment and last longer too. Small World Toys make wooden toys and traditional games with non-toxic paint that conforms to European safety standards, for details visit **www.smallworldtoys.co.uk**. Contact the toy maker's guild **www.toymakersguild.co.uk** to find out where you can buy handmade wooden toys.

Children should play with toys, not make them

Michael Eisner, CEO of Disney, pays himself US$133 million a year, or about US$63,000 an hour. It would take a worker in Bangladesh sewing Disney garments for 12 cents an hour 210 years to earn what Eisner does in an hour. When Bangladeshi workers came to America to highlight their situation, they said they had to work over 15 hours a day, seven days a week, were denied maternity benefits, beaten and paid just 15 cents for every US$17.99 Disney shirts they sewed. Disney responded by cancelling their order, causing all the women to lose their jobs. Join the campaign to stop Disney's exploitation on **www.nlcnet.org/campaigns/shahmakhdum**

Bring fairness to the toy industry! Buy fair trade toys

In 1996 children working on assembly lines in Haiti were paid 1p an hour to make Pocohontas pyjamas for Disney. The International Labour Organisation estimates that over 100 million children are working throughout the world. Over 95% of these children are found in the developing countries. Fair trade shops sell toys made to strict ethical rules, and manufacturers get a fair price for making them. Find out more from traidcraft at **www.traidcraft.co.uk** or the British Association of Fair Trade Shops on 01189 569361. The Natural Collection sells wooden animal jigsaws using non-toxic paints which are made by a craft enterprise in Sri Lanka. For details visit **www.naturalcollection.com**

Save community playing fields

Recreational space is a vital part of every community. Yet despite its importance, an average of one playing field every day comes under threat from building development, such as new houses and car parks. Once this land is built on, it's lost forever. The National Playing Fields Association is responsible for acquiring, protecting and improving our fast disappearing playing fields and playgrounds. Visit its website – **www.npfa.co.uk** – to find out if any playing fields near you are under threat and support its campaigns.

Don't let killing become fun

In the 21st century virtual killing has become child's play. But children under the age of 8 are not able to separate fact from fiction. The Lion and Lamb Project, **www.lionlamb.org**, a US organisation set up to change attitudes, shows parents how violent games affect children and suggests more constructive alternatives. Another US organisation, the National Institute on Media and the Family runs Kidscore, a rating system that evaluates films, TV shows, videos and games from a family friendly perspective; visit **www.mediafamily.org**

Play a green game

Too many games encourage children to become rampant property speculators, or global investors. The Green Board Game Company makes games that encourage knowledge of the natural world and are made of recycled products and wood from sustainable forests. The game *Into the Forest* is designed for children to discover the world of natural food chains with players 'eating' and 'being eaten' just as they would in the wild. Visit **www.greenboardgames.com** for details.

Toys to understand the environment

An Australian study recently found that 6 out of 10 children who use computers at school and children as young as 9 were being treated for chronic RSI pain. Don't expose your children to 'Nintendo thumb' by buying them more computer games. To find out more contact the Body Action Campaign, **www.just.dial.pipex.com**.

Encourage children to learn more about the outdoors. The Natural Collection sells three games – a transparent wormery, a giant plant kit and a solar energy kit designed to get children out of doors to learn more about the environment. Visit **www.naturalcollection.com**

Recycle them

If your child has grown out of a toy, it's not useless – another child will still get hours of fun from it. If you're a toy hoarder, do you really think your grandchildren will want to play with toys that are 50 years old? Better for someone else to get use out of them now.

Make your own

Transform colourful old clothes into stuffed toys, beanbag toys or rag dolls. Some clothes will have a whole new lease of life in a fancy dress box . Look on the Blue Peter website for tips and ideas
www.bbc.co.uk/cbbc/bluepeter/makes

Choose batteries carefully

Most batteries contain toxic metals such as cadmium, mercury and nickel that leak into the environment when they are thrown away. When you do buy batteries choose alkaline manganese batteries which are free from toxic heavy metals. And how about buying a solar-powered battery charger? You can find them at **www.getethical.com**

Global toys

With more and more toys being imported from outside the UK, children can learn all about other cultures by simply playing with toys from overseas. Try **www.fairtradeonline.com**, which sells children's gifts from all over the world, or the Parrot Fish company, which sells shadow puppets from Indonesia, masks of Gods and wedding saris from India – all designed to educate kids about other cultures. Visit **www.parrotfish.co.uk**

GRASS ROOTS

Back to basics with eco-education

Habits die hard. If you're brought up thinking green, it's easier to stay thinking green. Schools are the perfect place for environmental initiatives. They are crowded and busy places that consume a lot of resources. Environmental projects can help create a sense of community and participation while providing excellent teaching resources. And who knows – children may start bringing their good habits into the home and influencing their parents.

Meanwhile we need to put the brakes on the increasing corporate takeover of our schools. In a school in America, for example, PepsiCo donated US$2 million to build a football stadium in exchange for exclusive rights to sell its soft drinks in all 140 of the district's schools and to advertise in school gymnasiums and on athletics fields. That deal is estimated to earn the company US$7.3 million over 7 years. Education or exploitation?

Travel to school on foot or by public transport

At 8.50am one in five cars on urban roads is taking children to school. One in four children travel to school by car – twice as many as 20 years ago. Contrary to popular belief, in slow-moving traffic pollution levels are actually higher inside the car than out. Children who walk or cycle to school are usually fitter than those dropped at the gate, and arrive for lessons more alert. In the UK 1% of kids cycle to school, while in Denmark, which has pioneered a cycle to school campaign, over 60% of kids do. Sustrans is a sustainable transport charity. They facilitate School Action Plans in partnership with pupils, parents, teachers, the police and the local authority to provide safe routes to schools for children. Visit **www.sustrans.org.uk** or call 01179 268 893.

Education is a basic human right...

It's as fundamental as food and shelter. An education is the key to every child's development, bringing out their potential and helping them deal with the challenges of a changing world. It is also one of the most effective ways of breaking the poverty cycle. Around the world 120 million primary school age children are not in school. In Nepal, only 44% of children complete primary school, and in Angola only 4% do. To find out more, and see what you can do to help, visit **www.unicef.org**, or **www.savethechildren.org.uk**

Get planting!

Growing food at school is a fun way of learning about the lifecycle of a plant and becoming more aware of where food comes from. And you don't even need a garden! Herbs can be grown on windowsills, and carrots, tomatoes and potatoes can be grown in buckets on a balcony. You can take this even further and encourage your school to make a conservation area, where you can all work together to make an exciting, growing garden. For ideas on how to start a garden in your school, visit the Kids section of the Aggie Horticulture website **http://aggie-horticulture.tamu.edu**

Rubbish in the classroom

Kids – ask your school to put recycling bins in the classrooms for white and coloured paper, and cans. See **www.wastewatch.org.uk** for information, arrange for a 'robot cycler' to come to your school to teach everyone about recycling, and join the Schools Waste Action Club.

Bring the outdoors in

The countryside is a fantastic learning resource and studies have shown that children who spend time learning outdoors and in close contact with nature often develop better interaction and initiative skills, while children living in urban areas often miss out on its benefits. The Countryside Foundation is a charity that runs a scheme to bring the countryside into the classroom using excellent learning materials. Alternatively the class can be taken to the countryside on an educational field trip, or simply for a ramble. Find out more at **www.countrysidefoundation.org.uk** or call 01422 885 566. Find out about your nearest 'wild places' at Friends of the Earth website **www.foe.co.uk/wildplaces**

Save energy at school

UK Schools account for 25% of public sector energy costs, spending around £350 million on energy and releasing 8 million tonnes of CO_2 each year. One secondary school managed to save £10,000 of its annual fuel costs after an energy saving project. Imagine what you could buy with that! Two-thirds of a teacher, nearly 2,000 textbooks or 25,000 bars of (fair trade) chocolate! Find out what your school can do contact; the Four Seasons Project on **www.4seasons.org.uk**

An AK47 is small, light and simple enough to be used by a child of 10

In some countries it can be bought for as little as US$20. More than 300,000 children are being used as child soldiers around the world and since 1990 two million children have been killed and six million children have been seriously injured in wars. Support the campaign for an end to the use of children in warfare – visit the Coalition to Stop the Use of Child Soldiers at **www.child-soldiers.org** and support Amnesty International's child solder letter writing campaign at **http://web.amnesty.org**

Don't let education become a commodity; say NO to GATS

Students, teachers, campuses… normally we don't think of these as profit-making resources, or the institution of education as a market. But with the General Agreement on Trade in Services (GATS), all this may be up for grabs. GATS could start to replace the principles of learning with those of profit-making. Find out more about Education International at **www.ei-ie.org** who want to have education removed from the scope of GATS. If you are a student, campaign to turn your university into a no-GATS zone. Visit the students' campaigning group People and Planet at **www.peopleandplanet.org**, or call 01865 245 678 for more information.

FETCH!

Turn your pets green

Pets in the UK get it pretty easy compared to most. Hundreds of millions of pounds are spent annually on pet products by animal-loving Britain, which is not difficult considering pets are present in over half the UK's households. Worldwide, the petcare industry is worth US$27.5 billion, and is predicted to rise to US$40 by 2010. An industry of such proportions won't leave the environment unscathed.

Then there are the pets themselves. Could your treatment of them be greener? It's not just about being kind to them, it's about being kind to the environment, too.

Rescue your pet

Keeping a family pet will help kids understand animals better. By taking responsibility for a pet they will learn about animal welfare first hand. If you're thinking about a cat or dog, get one from an animal shelter – there are thousands of mistreated or abandoned animals which need safe homes and caring owners. Contact Battersea Dogs home (for dogs as well as cats) at **www.dogshome.org**, Cats Protection, which has branches all round the country at **www.cats.org.uk** or Rescuepet at **www.rescuepet.net**.

If you can't have a pet at home, encourage your kids to volunteer for the RSPCA – they welcome young volunteers. See their website: **www.rspca.org.uk** for details.

Put a bell around your cat's neck

Domestic cats can plague local wildlife, killing birds, frogs, mice, and voles, which can also litter people's lawns. A survey in 1997 estimated that the UK's 7.5 million pet cats could be killing at least 300 million animals and birds every year. Putting a bell round their neck could help to reduce that number significantly – a trial conducted by the RSPB found that a bell reduced predation by 35%, a sonic collar by 44%. Try keeping them indoors at night during the birds' breeding season, too.

Don't feed your pets plastic

Your pets are just as happy chewing and scratching on home-made toys as they are on resource-depleting, environment-damaging plastic. With a little care and attention, your pet can be your best friend – and the environment's, too. Screwing up a used sheet of paper into a cat's football can provide hours of fun, time and again. Visit Bluepet **www.bluepet.co.uk** or call 024 7639 6961, for some healthy, chewy alternatives.

Homeopathy for pets

Applying arnica to bruises or giving aconite for a fever works just as well for pets that are poorly. And as there's no difference between human and animal remedies – you don't have to buy them specially. Get advice from the British Association of Homeopathic Veterinary Surgeons before you start, on 01367 710 475.

Scoop that poop

The 6.8 million members of the British canine population produce 900 tonnes of excrement a day. That's the equivalent of 15 million sausages! Dog excrement can contain the minute eggs of roundworm, which can live for up to two years in the soil. Once inside the human body they can burrow through the gut, damaging the liver, lungs, eyes and can lead to blindness. Children playing in parks are most at risk, so take a scoop with you, bag it and then bin it!

Dry not canned

The UK spends £600 billion a year on canned pet food. Tins can be recycled by their production and transportation requires energy and effort that's greatly reduced when you buy dry food in bulk. Find out about organic and vegetarian options from Bluepet at **www.bluepet.co.uk**, or call 024 7639 6961.

Don't use commercial sprays

A female flea can lay around 25 eggs a day. If they all survive there could be 750 new fleas after just one month and 22,500 after two, wriggling about your pet and anything they come into contact with. But many of the commercial sprays, which act by attacking the fleas' nervous systems are associated with reproductive problems in pets. Use a non-toxic flea collar, try adding garlic pills or brewer's yeast, which can be bought in pet shops, to your pets' food or make a herbal flea collar. Visit the Pesticide Action Network at **www.pan-uk.org** for more information and alternatives.

Biodegradable kitty litter

Instead of filling up the landfill with plastic bags of dirty cat litter, try using biodegradable cat litter, made from recycled paper. Bio-Catolet Cat litter is made from 100% paper, biodegradable, dust and odour free and available in many pet shops. The cat litter can be composted, but cat faeces should be removed as they could attract pests.

Look after the animal you love

Pets can be treated for a wide range of illnesses now – ranging from a slipped disc to suspect lumps. But the treatment can be very expensive. You can insure your animals for as little as £6 a month for a cat and £9 a month for a dog. If you insure with the RSPCA you can receive a range of benefits, including the cost of up to £4,000 per illness. And 10% of your premium will be donated to the RSPCA to help animals less fortunate. Visit **www.rspca.org.uk**, 0870 333 5999.

Have your cat neutered

One female un-neutered cat can be responsible for 50 million offspring and descendants if it has two litters each of six kittens. The surging cat population means that thousands are abandoned each year – in 2002 the RSPCA re-homed 82,936 cats, and had many more on waiting lists.

Exotic Pets? Just say NO

Exotic animals don't make pets. They grow faster, live longer, are unpredictable and dangerous if they escape. In 2001 an RSPCA inspector found a two-metre boa constrictor in an abandoned flat in Wales. Hungry and aggressive, it had escaped from a tank in a nearby flat. The same year, terrapins the size of dinner plates started killing ducks in a London lake, thought to have been dumped after the Teenage Mutant Ninja Turtle craze. Visit the RSPCA **www.rspca.org.uk** for more information – in 2000 3,700 exotic animals were dumped, found neglected or handed in to them.

Stamp out pet cruelty

Did you know that puppies bred intensively throughout the world to be sold in UK pet shops are often kept in dark, cold and cramped conditions and are looked after by people more concerned with making money than the welfare of animals? Indiscriminate breeding increases the risk of genetic and behavioural problems and puppies are often separated from their mother at a very young age. Help the National Canine Defence League campaign against puppy farming; **www.ncdl.org.uk** or call 020 7837 0006.

Support the campaign against trafficked animals

A single shipload of green iguana can contain 2,000-5,000 creatures, carrying them thousands of miles, often illegally, from their native habitat to an unnatural one in captivity and allowing their natural population to decline. Iguanas are the most commonly traded animals in the UK, but Britain imports a total of over one million live reptiles and amphibians a year, including boas, pythons, chameleons and geckos. It's not only reptiles, but also birds, fish and mammals who are swept up in this trade. Find out how you can help stop it at **www.traffic.org**, or call Traffic International on 01223 277 427.

CHRISTMAS CRACKERS

Top tips for a green Christmas

At Christmas we go into an all-consuming, all-disposing frenzy. On the weekend before Christmas in 2002, British consumers spent a total of £630 million – up to £823,000 per minute. Our concerns for the environment get thrown out of the window along with the wrapping paper, the dead Christmas tree and the left-over roast potatoes… but it doesn't have to be that way. Before you buy something, ask yourself – Do I really need it? How long would I use it for? Can I borrow it? Can I do without it? If the answer is still yes, then ask yourself: Is it recyclable? How will it be disposed of?

READER TIP – DAVID NILAND
Give a Christmas tree

For just £10 you can dedicate a tree from a choice of woods as a present. In return you'll receive a certificate stating the dedication and naming the tree's location. Trees are a lifelong gift and make an excellent present for weddings, anniversaries and christenings, too. Contact the Woodland Trust, **www.woodlandtrust.org.uk** for details.

Recycle your cards

We have become so wound up in giving and receiving presents that the traditional spirit of Christmas is under threat. An estimated 1.7 billion Christmas cards are sent each year in Britain – the equivalent of 200,000 trees. In Lapland the reindeer's habitat and the lifestyle of the indigenous Saami people is under threat because 95% of old forests have been lost in Finland and Sweden – where 40% of the UK's paper comes from. If more old forests aren't preserved, Rudolph may become a thing of the past. Make sure your Christmas cards don't go to waste – take them to a Woodland Trust recycling point at WHSmith.

Buy charity Christmas cards

Buy Christmas cards from charities and donate up to 20% to less fortunate people at the same time. Check on **www.christmas-cards.org** or **www.charitycards.co.uk** for details. Some charities, such as the Blue Cross and the Royal National Lifeboat Institution make recycled cards. Or send an ecard instead.

Support Buy Nothing Day

Instead of rushing to the shops to buy something – why don't you *not* buy something instead? Buy nothing day is organised to challenge the consumer culture and switch off from shopping for a day. It normally takes place at the end of November. For information and tips on what to do instead of shopping on that day visit **www.buynothingday.co.uk**

Closing the loop

There's no point recycling rubbish if you don't buy recycled products – after all the recycled products have to go somewhere! In 2002 we used 83 square kilometres of wrapping paper (which could cover an area larger than Guernsey) at Christmas. This year make sure your paper is recycled; you can buy recycled gift wrap and matching envelopes at recycled paper supplies **www.rps.gn.apc.org**, and wrap your presents with string, ribbon and wool rather than sticky tape.

Recycle your Christmas tree

Five-and-a-half-million Christmas trees are bought each year, most of which are thrown out after Christmas, creating enough tree waste to fill the Albert Hall 3 times over. Either buy a proper Christmas tree with roots and plant it in the garden afterwards or contact your local authority to see if they have a scheme which chips Christmas trees into garden mulch.

If you're buying a turkey, make it organic

Of the 10 million turkeys eaten at Christmas, most have been reared intensively in huge, windowless sheds holding up to 2,500 birds each. The birds have been genetically selected to grow as fast as possible, are

fed antibiotics and are so overweight they cannot mate naturally.
Appetising? Visit compassion in World Farming **www.ciwf.org.uk** for
more information.

KIDS – make your own Christmas cards and decorations

Britain produced about 2.25 million tonnes of festive rubbish in 2000.
Hardly any of this was recycled. But house decorations can be made
from recycled and scrap paper – old newspapers and magazines make
great paper chains and scrap materials can be used to make Christmas
tree ornaments. This makes more sense than spending £20 on a
sparkly angel which has been made by children in a far-eastern sweatshop, then flown half the way round the world to be thrown away
after a few days perched on a Christmas tree.

How will someone dispose of your present?

Avoid presents that rely on disposable parts, such as the paper filter
on a coffee machine – look for a model with a permanent filter and
choose solar powered chargers rather than batteries. The best presents
are ones that will help their owners be kinder to the environment – a
recycling paper kit, a worm bin compost kit, a sponsor an animal
scheme, a subscription to *The Ecologist* or a copy of this book!

Give someone else a happy Christmas

Christmas can be the worst time of year for people who have no one
to share it with. Think about donating some money, or time to a
charity that works with the homeless, elderly people or those suffering
from domestic violence. Think small! The mainstream charities, which
everyone knows about, will be inundated with Christmas donations –
choose a small, specific charity that really needs your help. And how
about remaining loyal to it over the years with a direct debit?

For a register of all UK charities and their contact details go to
www.charity-commission.gov.uk, or call 0870 3330123. And you
can be linked to a local volunteering project by Timebank. Visit
www.timebank.org.uk or call 020 7401 5420.

KIDS – Recycle your toys by giving them as gifts at Christmas

Millions of kids around the world will receive nothing for Christmas because their parents can't afford presents. But you can recycle your unwanted toys and make a Christmas present for someone less fortunate – last year over 1 million other British children did. Throughout the year collect unwanted toys in a shoebox and in November pop in some sweets, paper and crayons, a photo of yourself and a £2 donation to cover transport costs. Wrap the box in (recycled) Christmas wrap and stick a label on saying whether it should be for boys or girls and roughly what age you think the box would suit. Take it to your nearest Kwikfit or other designated collection point. From there it will be taken abroad and given to a child in need. Contact Samaritan's Purse International on 020 8559 2044, or visit **www.samaritanspurse.org**

PRESENT AND CORRECT

Make a difference when you give

Sometimes it seems as if the year is one long gift-buying spree – with Christmas, Easter, Mother's Day, Father's Day, Valentines, leaving parties, something to bring back for the folks from holiday, not to mention birthdays!

And what might the present be? Something made in China, transported to the US, then distributed to a UK warehouse before making its way to a local shop, burning up thousands of miles of transport fuel in the process. Then there's the wrapping paper, the gift tags and the ribbon bows which end up in the dustbin the following day. We spend so much money on the many presents we give, and use up so much of the world's resources in the process.

With a little planning, we can find a way of giving presents, which are thoughtful, original, and a real pleasure to receive. And which make a positive difference to the environment as well.

Give a recycled present

Wastewatch is full of good ideas and details of where you can find original recycled gifts. Go to **www.wastewatch.org.uk** or phone the Waste Watch Wasteline on 0870 243 0136. Charities also run year-round mail order services and are a good source of recycled present ideas.

Give a gift of time

Your time is valuable, so give it as a gift! It will mean more than a hurriedly bought present. Why not arrange for yourself and your friend to go on a trip to the theatre, a concert, the cinema or a sporting event? No wrapping involved, and the memory will last longer than chemical bath products or socks.

Don't give mass produced flowers

The beautiful bunch of roses you buy in a florists or supermarket has probably been grown in a greenhouse the other side of the world at a huge environmental and social cost. In Colombia, with a flower industry worth 600 million, two-thirds of flower workers suffer from illnesses caused by pesticide exposure. One-fifth of the chemicals used there are carcinogens or toxins, the use of which is restricted in the US! It is still difficult to source organic flowers in the UK – try farmers' markets for locally grown cut flowers, or choose an organically grown plant instead –visit **www.redhens.co.uk**. Alternatively, grow your own – visit **www.hdra.org.uk** and take a look under 'muck and magic'.

Give a squirrel!

Well, not exactly. But through wildlife charities you can organise for a rare squirrel, seal, puffin or owl to be adopted as a present. The money you spend on the present (often as little as £15) goes towards the organisation's work to protect that endangered species. Two organisations that do this are The Wildlife Trusts – visit **www.wildlifetrusts.org.uk**, 01636 677 711 – and the Barn Owl Trust, visit **www.barnowltrust.org.uk**, 01364 653 026.

Give to Make a Difference

Make a present of a year's membership of an environmental organisation. Most rely on their membership to be able to do the work they do. Hunt around for a small organisation that has a specific relevance for the person receiving the present. There are thousands, ranging from the British Beekeepers Association or the British Hedgehog Preservation Society to the British Cave Research Association. For an extensive list and website links go to **www.ethicaljunction.org** or call 0161 236 3637 for information.

Give presents that make us more aware

For little thank yous and stocking fillers buy fair trade presents – organic chocolate, handmade smellies, beeswax candles, recycled paper notebooks and pencils. And for someone who has everything, get them a wind-up phone charger. 3 minutes of wind-up will provide 8 minutes of conversation – there's no better way of learning about the cost of energy. Visit **www.greenshop.co.uk** for more ideas.

READER TIP – JUDI BRILL
Give to make a difference

Mercy Corps offer a series of kits which they describe as a unique way to honour your friends, loved ones or business associates with a gift that means the world for families and children in pain. Examples of these kits are an Afghan Education Kit, a Food Kit and a Child Health Kit. You can use Mercy kits to mark birthdays, weddings and anniversaries, and are the perfect gifts for people who have everything. Find out more at **www.mercycorps.com**.

Choose fair trade over flowers

Instead of buying flowers, choose a fair trade basket from **www.greenshop.co.uk** and fill it with fairtrade goodies – luxury organic truffles, drinking chocolate, chutneys, preserves and biscuits from **www.beantreeorganics.com**

CELEBRATIONS – GREEN STYLE

Throw a party – save the world!

Parties are big business these days – especially for kids, and there's a whole industry devoted to making your celebrations go with a bang. Party poppers, paper hats, instant fancy dress kits – it all adds up to a whole pile of rubbish at the end of the evening. If you don't want to spend hours filling those binliners with junk, plan a green party.

Avoid helium balloons

Helium is the second most abundant element in the known universe. Here on earth it is mined in conjunction with natural gas – mostly from around Amarillo in Texas. It's used for cooling MRI machines, deep scuba diving, cryogenic and superfluid research, the manufacture of optical fibres – and party balloons.

Helium is formed from the radioactive decay of uranium and is a very slowly renewable resource – most of earth's stocks eventually drift out into space. By 2012, it's estimated that there will be a severe shortage of helium (apart from the huge stockpile in the US dating from WWII) and prices will rocket.

Helium balloons are fun, but all things considered, staggeringly irresponsible. They use a valuable resource to drift around the world, depositing foil or treated latex that litter and can be swallowed by wildlife – dead turtles have been found beached with balloons hanging from their mouths.

If you want balloons at your party, use environmentally friendly natural latex balloons instead – they biodegrade at the same rate as an oak leaf. For more information visit **www.talking-balloons.co.uk**

Don't clog up landfill with cards

We spend millions giving cards – for birthdays, anniversaries, valentines, weddings, Mother's Day, Father's Day, Easter, congratulations… this list goes on. But it's commiserations for the environment – at Christmas alone an estimated 1 billion cards (17 for every man woman and child in the UK) end up in our bins. Send recycled cards – visit **www.ethicalwares.co.uk** or send ecards instead check **www.bbc.co.uk** for animated cards for all occasions and recycle the cards that are sent to you.

Slave to chocolate

Britons eat more chocolate per capita than any other country – over £1.20 per person per week. It's hard to believe that the type of chocolate we choose will determine whether a family can put food on the table, or a child goes to school. But the prices that most cocoa growers get for their crops make it difficult for them to survive at all. Buy Green and Black's Maya Gold, Traidcraft organic fairtrade chocolate and Divine chocolate which is fairtrade. For more information visit **www.ethicalmatters.co.uk**

Party in the countryside with care

Don't use disposable barbecues in the countryside. In dry weather the heat can penetrate the ground, causing parched soil to burn below the surface. This is a real danger to plant, animal and human life. If you want to have an outdoor barbecue party, have it on the beach, or in your garden. And don't add to the mountain of litter – take a bag and clear up any rubbish after you.

Make Halloween more green

Traditionally Halloween celebrated the change of seasons from Autumn to Winter, and was at one time considered to be the beginning of the year. Return this festival to its environmental beginnings. Avoid the glow-in-the-dark green plastic and make your own Halloween figures and games – jack-o-lanterns out of pumpkins, creepy string spiders, floating beeswax candles. Visit **www.ethicalmatters.co.uk** and **www.pumpkin-carving.com**

DOWN TO EARTH

Make a difference in death as well as life

*Death is part of the cycle of life – and just because we stop, it doesn't mean everything else does. While we may not be around to appreciate it ourselves, we don't stop making a difference when we're dead. And arranging a green funeral, in a woodland burial site can be more personal than a conventional one, with poems, songs and readings. Visit **www.alternativeceremonies.co.uk** for details on arranging an alternative woodland and environmental ceremony.*

Go for burial instead of cremation

In the UK, 440,000 people – 74% – are cremated, the largest proportion in Europe. Cremation releases toxins into the atmosphere, such as hydrogen chloride and formaldehyde. And crematoria discharge 1,300kg of mercury emissions in the UK every year. The mercury comes from amalgam fillings in teeth and its emissions will pollute the air, contaminate rivers and endanger the health of those you leave behind – it can attack the nervous system and cause brain damage.

How about a cardboard coffin – or even making your own?

Each year 437,000 wooden coffins are burned in the UK. Do you really want to see those trees going up in smoke? Cardboard coffins are biodegradable and much cheaper than wooden coffins, costing as little as £53. Funeral directors J.E. Gillman & Sons, 0208 672 1557, sells chipboard-based veneered coffin using wood from managed sustained-yield forests for £45. For a truly personal coffin you could even make your own! The Natural Death Centre has details, visit **www.naturaldeath.co.uk**, or call 020 8208 2853.

Have a tree planted in your memory or Go MAD and be buried in a wood

There are now over 160 woodland burial sites in the UK, and more are seeking planning permission. Woodland burial returns your body to nature – carbon is locked underground and land is saved from development. Many woodland burial sites are run by farmers and wildlife trusts. And what better headstone could you have than a living tree. Visit **www.naturaldeath.co.uk** or call 020 8208 2853 or try the Funeral Company at **www.thefuneralcompanyltd.com** 01908 225 222.

Taking your organs with you? Donate them instead!

Over 5,500 people are currently waiting for a transplant and by the end of the year 400 of them will have died because they won't receive organs in time. Pick up a donor card from your local doctor's surgery, get one online at **www.uktransplant.org.uk**, or call 0845 606 0400.

Keep campaigning after you've gone – write an eco-will

In 2002, £991 million was bequeathed to the top 500 charities in legacies. Why don't you write an ethical will? Visit **www.ethicalwill.com** and preserve your legacy of values and hopes for future generations. Leave something or a charity or environmental organisation which means a lot to you. And on the subject of wills, if relatives are not going to need your old furniture, how about leaving it to a local community centre, school or old people's home?

POWER DRILLS

In the next 20 years, global energy consumption is projected to rise nearly 60% due to population growth, urbanisation, and economic and industrial expansion, according to the Worldwatch Institute Report *State of the World 2003*. Estimates of electricity consumption are even more dramatic, running at a staggering 70%. Much of this rise is in the developing world, and the improvements this will bring to quality of life are immeasurable – but it's what it takes to generate the electricity that's worrying.

Renewable energy targets have been set by the British Government – by 2010 they intend for 10% of electricity to be generated by renewables such as wind, with the hope of reaching 20% by 2020. Whether this will happen depends on a tangle of funding, technology and ultimately profit. And that's still only 20%. Power isn't just lighting, heating and cooking – everything you buy has a power history behind it – clothes, household items and even fresh fruit and vegetables. To make a difference, we need to use less energy. Get started now.

ENERGY SAVIOURS

Cleaner ways to power your home

We're all responsible for global warming – it's not just a problem for someone else to sort out. It's now one of the greatest threats to the global environment, so we need to take action now. 25% of the UK's total CO_2 emissions come from our homes, so our actions can have important implications. An average house produces 6 tonnes of CO_2 every year – that's more than the average car. By reducing our household energy consumption, we can take responsibility for global warming. Find out more about how to save energy from the Energy Savings Trust at **www.saveenergy.co.uk***, 0845 727 7200 or from Action Energy at* **www.actionenergy.org.uk***, 0800 585 794.*

Save energy when you boil water

When you make a cup of tea, coffee or a hot drink, only boil the amount of water you need. If everybody did this for just one day, we could save enough energy to light every street lamp in the UK the following night.

Turn the iron off when you only have one thing left to iron

Irons stay hot after they've been switched off, and so it will still be hot enough to iron the last item very well. Although this might seem a very small thing, it gets us into the habit of making small energy-saving actions that, collectively, can make a much bigger difference.

Don't leave your TV on standby

When you go to bed, switch off your TV, rather than leaving it on stand-by. If everyone in the UK did this over £50 million could be saved each year. That's the equivalent to 200 million cups of tea! And if you decide to upgrade your TV set, don't throw it away – take it to a second hand shop so someone else can use it.

Don't use the dryer – hang up your clothes

Tumble-dryers are the most energy-consuming appliances we use in the home. If you do buy one, remember that gas appliances cost half as much to run as electric ones and produce 33% less greenhouse gas.

Share appliances with your neighbours

How often do you really use that steam carpet cleaner? Or that garden shredder? Or that high-pressure washer? By sharing appliances, you can save energy and also form links within the local community. Local Exchange Trading Schemes (LETS) are a good way of organising tool-pools. Find out more at **www.letslinkuk.org**, 020 7607 7852.

Go MAD with alternative energy sources

You can install small-scale renewable energy systems in your home, and they needn't cost the earth. Solar water heaters, solar panels and wind generators all help provide alternative sources of energy. For information about buying your own domestic wind turbine, contact the British Wind Energy Association at **www.bwea.com**, 020 7689 1960. For more general information on renewable energy, contact the Centre for Alternative Energy **www.cat.org.uk** or 01654 705 950 and the National Energy Foundation **www.greenenergy.org.uk**, 01908 665 555.

Buy green electricity

Shop around to get the greenest electricity you can – and not always for a higher price. Get hold of the free leaflet 'Guide to Buying Green Energy' from Friends of the Earth **www.foe.co.uk**, 020 7490 1555. The green credentials of mainstream suppliers are graded in the leaflet, so by choosing one higher up the table you can help shift the entire industry towards greener energy. Or try **www.greenprices.com** and **www.uswitch.com**, 0845 601 2856, which have lots of information on green energy options. Simplest of all, switch to Unit[e], which provides energy from renewable sources across all of Europe. Visit **www.unit-e.co.uk** or call 0845 601 1410 for details.

★ **TOP TIP** – UNIT[E]
Get home generation

Unit[e] currently operates in England and Wales, sourcing its energy from small-scale hydropower and wind farms across the UK.
If you install a small wind turbine in your garden, a solar PV panel on your roof (find out about government grants, below) or a small hydro plant in a river, you can power your home and sell surplus units to Unit[e]. To find out more email generation@unit-e.co.uk or visit **www.unit-e.co.uk**

Voice your support

Write to your local MP supporting the Sustainable Energy Bill/your local wind farm/your local community renewable project.
www.unit-e.co.uk

★ **TOP TIP** – FRIENDS OF THE EARTH
Switch to Green Energy

Want to help stop climate change? Changing your electricity supplier to one that uses green energy – from renewable sources like wind and biomass – is a great start. And since 1998, when the energy market was opened up to competition, it's been possible.

Now there's a new law that says all suppliers have to buy some green energy (currently 3%). A large number of suppliers offer a confusingly wide range of green electricity tariffs.

So how do you choose the best? Friends of the Earth has already worked it out for you, and ranked the different tariffs in a league table. Check it out at **www.foe.co.uk/campaigns/climate/press_for_change/choose_green_energy/index.html**, or call Friends of the Earth Information Service on Freephone 0808 800 1111.

Change to the leading green electricity product today[1]

5 reasons to switch to unit[e]

1 **Rated No. 1 by Friends of the Earth** as the cleanest greenest choice of electricity.

2 **It's easy** You can sign up in less than 10 minutes - call us on 0845 456 1640 or visit www.unit-e.co.uk.

3 **Only 100%** unit[e] is the only UK supplier that supplies _only_ 100% renewable products.

4 **Committed to renewable** unit[e] supports the renewable energy industry by buying electricity from small scale UK generators including renewable electricity generated by individuals and businesses, as well as investing in its own generation.

5 **Know you are making a difference** unit[e] customers can keep up to date with developments at unit[e] and aspects of the renewable electricity industry through the unit[e] newsletter, email newsletter and our website.

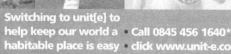

Switching to unit[e] to help keep our world a habitable place is easy

• **Call 0845 456 1640***
• **click www.unit-e.co.uk**

*lines are open 8.30am to 6.30pm Monday to Friday

unit[e]

unit[e], Monkton Park Offices, Monkton Park Chippenham SN15 1ER

Grants for solar energy

The UK government is offering grants towards the installation of solar electricity equipment for householders, business or social housing groups. Call the helpline on 0800 298 3978 or visit **www.est.org.uk**. You could save between 40% and 60% on total installation costs.

HOT TIPS FOR HEATING

Give your house a heating makeover

Every house is different, so tailor energy-saving devices to your home's requirements. There are currently over 50 Energy Efficiency Advice centres across the UK offering free independent advice on how to make your home more efficient, especially through regulating your heating. To find your nearest one, visit the National Energy Foundation at **www.natenergy.co.uk***, or call 01908 665 555. To get expert advice from heating, glazing and insulation experts trained to help you choose the best energy efficiency options to suit your needs, contact the Energy Saving Trust on 020 7222 0101,* **www.est.co.uk**

Calculate your home's energy rating

Saving energy will reduce your household bills as well as improve the environment. There are lots of simple, cheap improvements you can make to save energy – such as insulating your front door! Check how energy-friendly your house is and get some tips for improvement! **www.eere.energy.gov/energysmartschools/quiz/quiz.html**

Exclude draughts

Check for draughts and stop heat escaping from your house. Test your windows by holding a ribbon up to the window frame – if it flutters, air is coming in, and heat will be going out! Draughtproofing can make a big difference to heat leakage, so take steps to cure the problem. Also, close doors when the heating is on to reduce draughts and keep the house snug and warm.

One degree of separation

In the summer, turn your thermostat down a few degrees and in the winter set your thermostat a few degrees higher. For each one-degree change, your family can save up to 10% on your home's heating bill and cut down on greenhouse gas emissions. And don't underestimate the power of warm clothing – pop on an extra layer if you feel chilly!

READER TIP – DAVID READ
Install or upgrade heating controls

You can save a lot of energy by only heating the rooms you need to use. Thermostatic radiator valves enable you to control every temperature separately. Installing these together with heating time-switches and thermostats could save you up to £60 a year. Time-switches automatically turn your heating and hot water on and off at pre-programmed times. Visit **www.future-heating.co.uk** or call 020 8351 9360.

READER TIP – SIMON FORT
Go solar

You can obtain 70% of your household's hot water needs from solar thermal panels installed on your roof. Alternatively, covering your roof with PV (photo voltaic) panels can provide up to 50% of your electricity needs and save around 34 tonnes of greenhouse gases over their lifetime. Contact the National Energy Foundations renewable energy website **www.greenenenergy.org.uk** or the centre for Alternative Energy at **www.cat.org.uk**, 01654 702 400, for details. You can also visit **www.future-heating.co.uk**, 020 8351 9360.

Condensing boilers

Condensing boilers are the most efficient type of boiler, converting 88% of fuel into heat compared to only 72% for standard boilers. They also save an extra 12% on heating costs. When your current central heating system breaks down, make sure you replace it with a condensing boiler. They work by containing an extra heat exchanger, so when the boiler works at peak efficiency the water vapour produced in the combustion process condenses back into liquid, releasing extra heat. Find out more from the National Energy Foundation **www.natenergy.org.uk** or call 01908 665 555.

KEEP COOL

Fridge tips

Fridges and freezers are probably the single most expensive electrical appliances to run in the house, costing an average £55-65 each per year. We can't get enough of them, however, throwing away 2.5 million per year as we seek replacements.

Keep temperature between 3°C and 5°C

Fridges don't need to be kept cooler than 3°C. Below this temperature they are wasting energy, and your money! Put a thermometer in your fridge so you can keep an eye on the temperature.

Keep coils free from dust

Get that feather duster out! When dust gathers on the condenser coils at the back of your fridge, energy consumption can increase by 30%.

Buy a fridge-saver plug

You can save 20% of your fridge's running costs by buying a saver plug to replace your existing fridge or freezer plug. When the motor is first switched on in the appliance, full system power is needed. But once it's running, full power is no longer necessary. The plug senses this, and cuts power to the motor in short bursts without changing the operation of the fridge. Every time the red light shows, savings are being made. Buy your plug from SavaWatt (**www.savawatt.com** or 01789 490 340).

Free-stand your fridge

Your fridge works most efficiently if it's free-standing and in a cool environment. If possible, move your fridge to maximise its efficiency.

Don't site your fridge next to the cooker or boiler...

...or leave a good gap between them. Don't leave the fridge door open for longer than necessary, as cold air will escape. Avoid putting hot or warm food straight into the fridge; allow it to cool down first. Defrost your fridge regularly to keep it running efficiently and cheaply.

Never dump, recycle!

The UK disposes of about 2.5 million consumer fridges and half a million larger commercial fridges each year. These contain an estimated 2,000 tonnes of CFCs and HCFCs, which are ozone-damaging chemicals. Since 1st January 2002, all fridges must have their insulation removed before they are recycled or scrapped, in order to prevent the release of CFCs into the atmosphere. So make sure you take your old fridge to a recycling plant that can deal with it safely. Find your nearest one at **www.wastepoint.co.uk** or call 01743 343 403.

Now cool it!

Not only can you recycle your old fridge safely, you can now buy 100% ozone-friendly fridges. 'Greenfreeze' fridges are widely available and work on a mixture of propane and butane. This means they don't contain any of the polluting CFCs, HFCs or HCFCs.

The Electricity Association in the UK has shown that two German 'Greenfreeze' models were 39% and 55% more energy-efficient than the equivalent British Hotpoint models. Also, make sure your new fridge is energy-efficient, which means it can use up to 70% less energy. They cost an average £50 extra, but within 18 months you'll have made this back through cheaper running costs. Look for the energy consumption ratings that are required to be displayed on all models. Grade A means the appliance is the most efficient, and grade G means it is least efficient.

Contact the Energy+ project at **www.energy-plus.org** or call 01865 281 211. They give details of 438 Energy+ energy efficient fridges and freezers from 13 participating manufacturers.

BRIGHT IDEAS

Greener lighting

The Energy Savings Trust wants the Government to reduce VAT on energy-saving light bulbs to 5%. A step in the right direction, but in the meantime, what can you do to cut down on the energy-guzzling light you use?

Be a glow-worm

Use your muscles to generate electric light with a clockwork torch. BayGen clockwork torches – created by British inventor Trevor Bayliss – use a winding handle to energise a constant force spring, and turning the crank provides enough energy to provide light for half an hour. The concept is catching on, and will help light the way for many people in developing countries, without resorting to expensive batteries. You can also buy other clockwork items, such as radios, along with torches in large travel shops.

Other products are being considered for the Personal Power Generation treatment, too. So, stand by for wind-up cell phones, laptops and global positioning systems! Visit **www.iwantoneofthose.com** or call 0870 241 1066.

If every household in the UK used one energy efficient light bulb, we could close a power station

When your light bulb runs out replace it with an energy efficient one – they last 12 times as long! Over their lifetime an 11-Watt bulb saves

£35 and a 20-Watt bulb saves £57. If you have strip lights, don't send the fluorescent tubes to landfill – each tube contains enough mercury to pollute 30,000 litres of water beyond a safe level for drinking. Contact **www.reuze.co.uk/fluro_tubes.shtml** for recycling schemes.

Fill your house with sunlight

Tube skylights transform dark houses and mean you can keep the electric light off longer. These flexible tubes distribute light around the home by means of a reflector and prisms in a roof dome. Find out more from Solalighting Ltd at **www.solalighting.com**, 0845 458 0101.

Don't use halogen security lights

Almost half of lighting complaints to local authorities are related to domestic security lights. These often use 150-Watt halogen lights that are over-sensitive and are set off by roaming cats or blowing litter. Not only does this waste large amounts of electricity, it also means they're not an effective warning system, because neighbours become accustomed to the constant glare. Halogen lights are not that effective either, because the glare is so bright it darkens the shadows, providing more places for burglars to hide. Replace your wasteful halogen light with a low-power compact fluorescent light that's cheaper, more effective, and kinder to your neighbours and the environment.

Help put the stars back in the sky

Everyone should be able to see the stars. But over the past 40 years light pollution has increased so much that people in towns and cities now struggle to see them. The British Astronomical Society has set up a Campaign for Brighter skies, aiming to improve light direction so the same area can be lit to the same brightness, but with less powerful bulbs to reduce the impact on the sky. Better lighting not only helps with viewing space, but it saves energy and is better for the atmosphere. You can help the campaign by looking out for floodlights on advertising hoardings that are left on all night, and for cloud spotlights above nightclubs. If you see them, report them to your local authority. Such schemes have met with considerable success, such as in Milton Keynes. After hundreds of complaints from the local community, the skybeam above the Milton Keynes Shopping Centre was extinguished. Visit **www.dark-skies.org** and **www.cpre.org** for more information on how you can help.

★ **TOP TIP** – COUNCIL FOR THE PROTECTION OF RURAL ENGLAND
Don't waste light

Don't waste light outside your home. Angle outdoor lights downwards, fit hoods or shields to minimise light spill, use bulbs with minimal watts, and ensure lights are switched on only when needed.

Approach any neighbours including shops and businesses with overly bright security lights and politely ask them to angle them downwards, shield them or fit a passive infra-red sensor or a lower wattage bulb.

You can also contact local DIY stores and ask them to stock security lights that minimise light pollution. Visit **www.cpre.org.uk** for more information on their light pollution campaign.

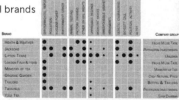

THINK BEFORE YOU BUY!

CLOTHES THat COSt tHE EARTH

Global warming, species extinction, animal testing, the arms trade and human rights abuses... all can seem way beyond our control. But as a consumer you DO have control, because many of these problems are either caused or perpetuated by corporations funded by the money that you spend on their products.

Every purchase you make has either a direct or indirect effect on the environment. When you exercise your power by choosing where and what to buy, and where and what NOT to buy, you help change the world for the better.

The first step is to become a better shopper, and find out the stories behind the shelves. *The Ecologist*, **www.theecologist.org**, *Ethical Consumer* **www.ethicalconsumer.org**, *Ethical Junction* **www.ethicaljunction.org** and *Get Ethical* **www.getethical.com** will keep you informed, and you can find all the background to ethical consumerism at One World's site: **www.oneworld.net**

THE ETHICAL CONSUMER

Shopping tips

In 1993, 188 workers were killed and 469 seriously injured in the world's worst factory fire in Thailand. The workers – impoverished women who made toys for Kader Industrial, were locked in to prevent stealing and hundreds were forced to jump out of upper floors rather than burn to death. Kader Industrial's factory never met minimum safety conditions – it was designed to be temporary as the company moved its operations taking advantage of low cost labour. And though global toy retailers had made millions profiting from the women's labour, they too showed little interest in safety, wages or working conditions and denied any responsibility for the circumstances surrounding the fire. Who is responsible? If the multinationals refuse to be, then it is us, the consumers, who buy products made in this way. Get informed, and think before you buy.

Your email can make a difference

When Polly Morgan noticed a 'Made in Myanmar' label on Kookai's clothes, she emailed the company to complain that they were supporting one of the world's most brutal military dictatorships by operating in Myanmar. The London buying director replied saying 'I agree with you that it is not ethical for us to produce our goods from Burma. I have stressed to Paris your concern and they have promised to eliminate production in Burma'. Write to retailers encouraging them to join the Ethical Trading Initiative (an umbrella group of companies aiming to improve workers' rights). Visit **www.ethicaltrade.org**, or call 020 7404 1463.

Wrest the power from the multinationals

Identify at least two multinational corporations (MNCs) with unethical environmental policies and boycott their products. You may be surprised at how many different products they sell. Visit **www.boycottbush.net**. Boycotting is an effective way of registering your disapproval and expressing your dissatisfaction towards a company. Even a 5% boycott can significantly affect profit. Consumers collectively have the power to change the world for the better. Success is not just limited to isolated cases. Stories range from the Save the Children campaign and trade unions that led to sports companies phasing out child labour for football stitching, to the hugely successful awareness campaign in Europe against GM foods. Visit **www.ethicalonsumer.org** for more success stores or contact Corporate Watch at **www.corporatewatch.co.uk** 01865 791 391.

You have a right to know

The International Right to Know (IRTK) Campaign is a coalition of more than 200 environmental, labour, social justice, and human rights organisations that have joined together to support international right-to-know legislation. IRTK is establishing guidelines that encourage companies to disclose their global policies and practices. The guidelines cover not only environmental impacts but also social impacts such as labour standards and human rights standards. Find out more from **www.irtk.org**

Avoid shopping in supermarkets whenever possible

In the UK, 60-70% of the food we buy comes from one of the four largest supermarket companies (Tesco, Sainsbury's, Safeway and Asda). This concentration of control forces farmers to accept lower prices for their products and means that food is often sourced from developing countries where supermarkets can profit from cheap labour and non-existent pollution laws. Transport pollution is probably one of the greatest threats to global warming – on average the item you buy in the supermarket has travelled 1,000 miles. Supermarkets act like giant vacuum cleaners, sucking money out of an area and putting it in the banks of distant shareholders, while hundreds of locals lose money as their jobs dry up.

If you can't find it locally and have to have it, buy from ethical or green shops online

Most ethical shops now have online stores where you can find lots of gifts, clothes, food and products for the home that are either fairly traded, or made ethically, without harm to the environment. Visit **www.naturalcollection.com** or **www.ethicaljunction.org** or **www.getethical.com** for information and products. Buying online is now more popular than ever, and it is beneficial to the environment and your purse. The companies tend to deliver to your doorstep, so you don't have to travel there, cutting down on exhaust emissions and traffic pollution and the number of cars on the road.

 TOP TIP – THE NATURAL COLLECTION
Bags of Trouble

Around 8 billion plastic bags are given away in Britain every year – that's more than 130 bags a year for every man, woman and child in the country. And as plastics are difficult and costly to recycle, many of them end up in a landfill tip. When you go shopping, take a bag with you, or re-use your shopping bags at home. Get an organic string bag for your vegetables or a fairly traded shopping basket made of palm leaf from Malawi – both from The Natural Collection **www.naturalcollection.com** (0870 331 3333).

 TOP TIP – FORUM FOR THE FUTURE
The disappearing bag trick

In 2003, Sainsbury's announced the launch of the first fully biodegradable shopping bags. Manufactured from the same starch used to make tapioca puddings, the bags break down within a month, and so are friendly to the environment. Unlike plastic bags that can remain in landfills for dozens of years and release harmful chemicals into the earth, the new tapioca bags quickly break down into harmless carbon, oxygen and hydrogen. The bags are only being used at three stores in London and Durham at present, but if you shop at Sainsbury's, ask your local store when they'll be introducing them. Only through lots of public support will the bags become widely used. For more information see Green Futures issue 40, **www.greenfutures.org.uk**.

Buy Locally

Just think of the resources wasted and the pollution created by shifting goods all over the world – and increasingly by air. Imported food and animal feed use 1.6 billion litres of fuel, and emit more than 4 million tonnes of CO_2 in the UK. Global transport costs can add as much as 16% to the price of food, while organic food that is locally grown is estimated to add as little as 3%. Other negative aspects of the global food industry are that it encourages farming mono-cultures, to the detriment of local biodiversity, and it has caused the closure of independent grocers, bakers, butchers and fishmongers – throughout the 1990s, around 1,000 independent local food shops closed each year. Investigate box schemes, farmers' markets, food co-ops and buy-local campaigns because we need to support and rebuild our local food systems!

Buy Recycled

If there was no market for recycled goods, recycling wouldn't happen. And it's not as hard as you might think to find recycled products – the National Recycling Forum has a database of all kinds of goods that started their lives as something else; visit **www.recycledproducts.org.uk/index.htm** or call 020 7089 2100 to find out more. Look for the Mobius Loop symbol which means that a product has been recycled. And remember, re-using is a form of recycling. Charity shops and jumble sales are full of second-hand goods with years of use still in them.

Buy from charity shops

Buying from charity shops is a really effective way of saving cash, donating money and picking up some unusual bargains. Some charities also sell a range of fair trade goods, many of which are available online; visit **www.avoidtherush.co.uk/shopping/2005/charities.htm** for more information. Do enquire before you donate, though, as charities can only sell books in good condition, won't sell cosmetics unless new, and can't sell second-hand mains electric goods. Tatty clothes and worn shoes can be recycled, but sort and bag them as such to save the volunteer workers time.

Support boycotts and shareholder actions

Support actions like the Nestlé boycott, which campaigns against all Nestlé brands and company subsidiaries to attempt to persuade the company to change its marketing of formula baby milk in the developing world. Boycotting products has a long history – in 1971 Britons boycotted Barclays bank over its investment policy in South Africa. Visit the Ethical Consumer's web page on Boycotts for information on current boycotts **www.ethicalconsumer.org/boycotts**

Shareholder actions can also force a public company to change its policies to become more ethical or environmentally friendly. If you buy shares in a company (even one share) you will be entitled to go to their AGM and question directors on their policies, and even force a vote on the issue. Successful shareholder actions have forced companies to change their policies on their impact on the environment, human rights issues and executive pay. For more information visit Friends of the Earth on **www.foe.org/international/shareholder**

Shop for jute

Jute – or hessian – is a plant related to European lime or linden, grown in Bangladesh and Western India for its fibre. This semi-wild monsoon-watered crop takes little from the land compared to cotton crops, which need prodigious amounts of water, fertilizers and pesticides. Over 4.5 million people in one of the poorest parts of the world are supported by the jute industry, which turns the fibre into woven bags and sacks. Jute shopping bags are a worthwhile alternative to plastic bags – practical, inexpensive, and good for the environment. For more information on jute, contact Canby **www.canby.co.uk** or call 020 8951 9325.

Go MAD! 2

FASHION VICTIM

The truth about clothes and makeup

Clothes are a necessity for most of us. But we rarely question the processes they go through before we put them on. It may be a divine little black dress that clings to all your curves, but how much energy, water and lowly paid fingers went into its construction?

Synthetic fabrics like polyester and nylon, made from non-renewable petrochemicals, use vast amounts of water and energy and take a very long time to biodegrade. Some cotton, too, may not be as natural as it seems, as it's the world's most pesticide-sprayed crop. In 1995 in Alabama up to 250,000 fish were killed after rain washed lethal concentrations of insecticides off the cotton fields into a nearby lake. The insecticides were used to deal with a budworm infestation which is thought to have been caused when the crops were sprayed with the insecticide malathion – designed to kill the boll weevil which also killed the budworm's natural predators.

Look for ecological or naturally made clothing materials instead. Visit Ethical Consumer's Green Clothing Directory for more ideas, **www.ethicalconsumer.org** *or call 0161 226 2929. Watch out for the Oeko-Tex label that guarantees the manufacture of clothes has met strict environmental standards.*

Who are the real fashion victims?

Our clothes are mainly made in factories in developing countries where labour and production costs are cheaper, and governments are less likely to regulate. Sadly only a few retailers respect their staff; many conglomerates believe workers rights are less important than maximising their profits. In such sweatshops staff may work up to 60 hours a week, in conditions that are rarely safe, where wages are unreasonably low, where children under 15 may be employed and unions are almost always banned. In these countries a single pair of trainers sold in the UK can cost more than the monthly wage of the person who made it. Visit **www.sweatshopwatch.org** for a list of 'dirty' companies whose products you should avoid and a 'clean' directory of companies whose products are made ethically, avoiding sweatshop labour. Join No Sweat, www.nosweat.org.uk where you can support the UK campaign to fight sweatshop bosses around the world.

Do you really need another T-shirt?

Many of us have wardrobes bursting with clothes we've bought on a whim but never worn. Before you shop for something new, look through your wardrobe – you'll probably find something you love but haven't worn for years, or a treasured item you put away for mending that hasn't been, or items destined for the charity shop. By the time you've finished sorting it out, you'll have found something 'new' to wear, mended some old favourites, donated your rejects, and saved money!

Care what you wear

Cotton plays a vital role in the economy of several dozen countries, but its environmental impact is hugely damaging. Close to US$3 billion-worth of pesticides are used annually in worldwide cotton production, and have resulted in cancer in humans, contamination of ground water, erosion and degradation of soil, decline of animal populations and the overall depletion of biodiversity. You can buy cotton that doesn't harm the planet – Gossypium **www.gossypium.co.uk**, is an ethical eco-cotton store selling garments, yoga wear and bed linen made from fairly traded organic fibre. The company uses its profits to support the farming communities involved in clothing production, helping to steer them towards a dynamic rural lifestyle.

Avoid over-packaging

Over 22% of the total product cost of perfumes and cosmetics come from packaging costs. Many cosmetics are double-packed unnecessarily, for aesthetic purposes. If you buy a product in plastic container and a box, leave the box at the checkout. And write to your favourite cosmetics company, asking them to set up a refill scheme.

Boycott animal-tested beauty products

100 million animals die in lab experiments each year, and a label that says 'not tested on animals' is not always telling the truth. The finished product may not have been tested on animals but this doesn't include individual ingredients. Look out for the Humane Cosmetics Standard 'rabbit and stars' logo. It's an internationally recognised guarantee that the product has not been tested on animals at any stage. A full list of HCS approved products is available free from the British Union for the Abolition of Vivisection.

★ **TOP TIP** – WWW.GREENCHOICES.ORG
Choose green shoes

Vegetarian credentials do not guarantee green credentials! Leather substitutes can include problematic materials such as polyurethane, nylon and even PVC. Leather-free environmentally friendly shoes are available from Green Shoes **www.greenshoes.co.uk** and the Vegetarian Shoes Online Store **www.vegetarian-shoes.co.uk**

Buy nothing on Buy Nothing Day

Buy Nothing Day is an effective way of having a break from consumerism and reminding ourselves how easy it is to become caught up in the 'shop till you drop' culture. Find out more at **www.buynothingday.co.uk** or visit the Canadian 'subvertising' site **www.adbusters.org/campaigns/bnd**

As a last resort...

If you really need to buy from one of the main UK chain stores, then there is a way of reducing the impact. UshopUGive is a new internet gateway to online retail outlets that donates a percentage of what you spend to a charity of your choice, without you paying an extra penny above standard retail prices. Visit **www.ushopugive.com**

WASTE NOT, WANT NOT

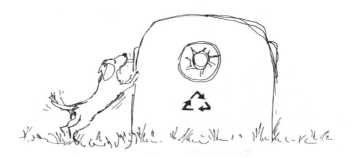

Nature has tremendously efficient ways of dealing with waste. Over time everything – plant matter, human and animal remains, ancient building materials and even rock – breaks down and is recycled. Our modern waste problems stem from technological proficiency – the earth just can't deal with the concentration of new chemical combinations in the quantities we're producing and dumping them. Each year, the UK generates 30 million tonnes of municipal waste – that's about 1.2 million tonnes per household – and currently 27 million tonnes of this is landfilled.

Rethink Rubbish **www.rethinkrubbish.com**, the national recycling campaign, is pushing to change this with better waste awareness. Over 60% of the contents of your weekly rubbish bin can be recycled, and if we just reduced the weight in our bins by 10%, in a year this would be a saving equivalent to 8,687 times the height of Blackpool Tower. So make a difference and think about your waste. Generate less, and recycle what you can.

RUBBISH SOLUTIONS

All about recycling

Here in the UK we're lazy about recycling waste, and only 11% of household rubbish is recycled. Yet the Zero Waste strategy in New Zealand has proved that by maximising recycling, incineration is unnecessary and the amount of rubbish going to landfill can be cut by 90%. Policy groups for Zero Waste strategies are slowly being introduced in Britain, such as by the Defenders of the Ouse Valley and Estuary www.dove2000.org. Wherever you live in Britain, you can do your bit to help recycle. Although you may already be recycling bottles, cans, and paper, consider recycling your oil, stamps, glasses, office equipment and mobile phones. Visit www.recycle-more.com to find out where your local recycling point is, and how to recycle the waste you want. Friends of the Earth believes that it's possible for us to recycle at least 80% of our waste. For tips on how to do this, visit www.foe.co.uk. For information on how to recycle electronic and electrical waste, as well as hazardous household waste, visit the Strategic Waste Management Services at www.swap-web.co.uk.

Ugly butts

A cigarette butt takes between one and 12 years to break down. So don't drop them. If you must smoke outdoors – and increasingly it's the only place you can smoke – carry a 35mm film canister to store discarded filters until you can dispose of them properly.

Make more use of it

Make sure you only use a product if there's no reusable alternative available. Try to reuse everyday items like paper, envelopes and paperclips. If each of the UK's 10 million office workers used one fewer staple a day by reusing a paperclip, that could save a staggering 120 tonnes of steel each year.

Go bare

Nowadays almost everything we buy comes swathed in layers of excess packaging. Indeed, 90% of the material used in the production of, or contained within consumer goods, becomes waste within just six weeks of sale. Shop with a critical eye, and avoid buying over-packaged goods. Also, reduce the amount of disposable products you buy, and always look out for alternatives that will last.

Find out more

Get informed, and find out about the recycling schemes run by your local council. Then campaign for them to be improved by writing to your local MP. Not only does recycling have environmental benefits, it also creates jobs. For every million tonnes of waste processed, landfill creates 40-60 jobs, incineration creates 100-290 jobs, and recycling 400-590 jobs.

Say NO to incineration

Some people see incineration as an attractive alternative to landfill for waste disposal. The UK government is planning the creation of 130 new waste incinerators, each one burning up to 250,000 tonnes of rubbish a year. But incineration plants release a number of toxic pollutants into the environment, including dioxins, furans, acid gases and heavy metals. These pollutants can pose serious risks to human health, including hormonal defects, reduced immune system capacity, and lung and kidney disease.

You can help by petitioning your local council to stop or reduce incineration in your area. The millions spent on incineration plants would be much better spent on setting up recycling schemes. Visit Friends of the Earth at **www.foe.co.uk/campaigns/waste** to find out the best way of sending letters to stop incineration in your area.

Give old clothes to a recycling scheme

Every year in the UK 1 million tonnes of textiles are thrown away, despite 75% of them being recyclable. 1.5 billion gallons of oil is used to manufacture this amount. If all the textiles discarded in one year were compressed, you could build a solid tower the width and three times the height of Cabot Tower, Canary Wharf.

Textiles can be valuable to somebody even if they appear worn out and useless to you. The fibres from most clothes can be shredded and rewoven to make new clothes; as long as they are clean, they are usable! High quality garments can be sold for reuse, whereas medium grade can be made into industrial rags, wiping cloths, and low grade filling and flocking for the furniture industry. Several charity shops run schemes that do this. Visit **www.oxfam.org.uk** (01865 312 610) or British Red Cross shops **www.redcross.org.uk** (020 7235 5454) to find your nearest shop.

Pick up one piece of litter a day

With the UK population standing at nearly 59 million, our streets would be a lot cleaner if everyone picked up one piece of rubbish a day.

★ **TOP TIP** – WWW.GREENCHOICES.ORG
Hi-tech recycling

Look out for full-on, hi-tech fleece jackets made from recycled drinks bottles. Outdoor gear company VauDe's Ecolog range (available in shops and mail order from Silvertrek, 01189 582 211) is both recycled and fully recyclable – everything, down to the zips and buttons, is 100% polyester. Worn out Ecolog garments can be returned either to your nearest VauDe stockist or direct to CDA Ltd, Unit 6C, Greensfield Park, Alnwick, Northumberland, NE66 2DE (01665 510 660).

Even some hi-tech waterproofs can potentially be recycled – if facilities exist. These include water-based coatings (applied without harmful solvents) and membranes such as Sympatex, which is 100% polyester. Avoid PVC, laminates and polyurethane.

CRYSTAL CLEAR

Recycling glass

Recycling just one glass bottle saves enough energy to power a TV set for an hour and a half. In every tonne of glass recycled, 135 litres of oil and 1.2 tonnes of ash, sand and limestone are saved. For more information and the location of your local bottle bank go to **www.recycle-more.co.uk**

Give milk bottles back to the milkman

Never put milk bottles in a glass recycling bottle bank, always return them to the milkman. And you can recycle the aluminium milk bottle tops, too. In 2000, 35,000 tonnes of household aluminium foil (worth around £12 million) was used in the UK, of which only 11% was recycled. Most recycled aluminium foil is used to make cast components for the automotive industry, such as cylinder heads and engine blocks. There are 189 local authorities collecting foil in the UK at present – check your local council's website or call them for information.

Sort before you bin

Successful glass recycling depends on you starting the process properly. Put different coloured bottles in the correct bank, and remove all metal and plastic tops, corks and rings from bottles or jars. Importantly, light bulbs, cookware such as 'Pyrex' or 'Visionware' and flat glass (as used in windows), should not be put in bottle banks. Find out more and what to do with these other types of glass from Recycle More at www.recycle-more.co.uk (08450 682572) and Waste Connect at www.wasteconnect.coluk (01743 343403).

Recycle your specs and sunglasses

Thousands of people in developing countries are hindered by poor eyesight, yet each year 4 million pairs of functioning glasses are discarded in the UK. By donating your old glasses you can transform people's lives for the better. Vision Aid Overseas has so far helped over 150,000 people with donations from the UK. Contact **www.vao.org.uk/specsort.htm** or call 01259 353 5016 for more details. Many local opticians support the scheme – if yours doesn't, then let them know. Alternatively, hand your glasses into any charity shop or high street retailer that runs a recycling scheme.

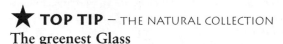

★ TOP TIP – THE NATURAL COLLECTION
The greenest Glass

Mail order company Natural Collection sells frosted tumblers made out of old wine bottles. The transformation does not involve any melting, making them more energy-efficient than normal recycled glass. For details, visit the Natural Collection website **www.naturalcollection.com** or call 0870 331 33 33.

PAPER CUTS

Recycling paper

Recycling paper can start at home and in everyday practices. Use waste paper as notepaper. Reload your printer with paper printed on only one side. Reuse envelopes. Cut up old cards to make gift tags. Wrap gifts in old wrapping paper or old newspaper, even put down old shredded newspaper as animal bedding, or put it on the compost heap.

No more junk mail

Around 1 million tonnes of junk mail and magazines get binned every year! To stop the onslaught, you can register with the Mailing Preference Service.

Visit its website at **www.mpsonline.org.uk**, email mps@dma.org.uk, call 020 7291 3310, or write to: The Mailing Preference Service, FREEPOST 22, London W1E 7EZ. Simply include your details and state that you would like to stop receiving unsolicited direct mail.

READER TIP – VIV CHAMBERLAIN-KIDD
No more junk mail II

Another alternative to the Mailing Preference service is: Door to Door Royal Mail, Beaumont House, Sandy Lane West, Oxford. OX4 6ZZ. There's also: The Facsimile Preference Service (a means to enable consumers to opt-out of receiving unsolicited sales and marketing faxes at home) **www.fpsonline.org.uk** and the Telephone Preference Service **www.tpsonline.org.uk**

Kids – Take old wallpaper to school

Old newspapers, magazines and even wallpaper can be easily recycled at school. They can be painted on, used to cover tables in craft lessons, or used for making papier-mâché. So don't just throw it, take it to school.

Recycle Yellow Pages

The Yellow Pages telephone directory is delivered annually to households and companies. The dye in the pages means they can't be recycled with other paper and newspaper. To recycle them you could either place them on the compost heap, shred them for animal bedding, or you could have them specially recycled by your local authority. Nine out of 10 local authorities now recycle directories.

Buy address labels from charities

Many charities sell labels you can stick over old addresses on envelopes – so you're saving paper and supporting a charity. For more tips on reusing envelopes and other paper-saving techniques, visit **www.conservatree.com**

Think hemp

Hemp produces up to four times more pulp per acre than timber, and produces higher quality paper. It recycles more times than wood pulp, and there are no environmentally damaging bleaching processes involved in its production. Unlike other fibre crops, it doesn't need the

intensive use of herbicides and pesticides to grow, so it's the perfect ecological crop for the 21st century. Commercial hemp growth has occurred in Britain since 1993, but the UK government has been unwilling to support hemp farmers because of the connection with cannabis. For more information and products visit The Hemp Shop **www.thehempshop.net** or call 07041 818 047.

Bind it

Think before you staple. For less than five sheets of paper use a clamp that makes the paper thread through itself, making its own paperclip, so there's nothing to remove before recycling the paper. For up to 35 sheets, use a paperclip. For large amounts of paper use a treasury tag.

★ TOP TIP – NATURAL COLLECTION
Turn it back into logs

Transform old newspapers into pulp logs – one newspaper will usually make one log, which will burn for up to an hour. For log-making machines visit **www.naturalcollection.com**, or call 0870 331 3333.

READER TIP – STEVE MCGRAIL
Keep those paper napkins

If you eat out at a restaurant or cafe, retain the paper serviettes (furtively or triumphantly, depending on your temperament). Cut up, they're perfectly good for toilet paper... but not if they've first had to deal with curry spills!

PVC IS NOT PC

Recycling plastic

We only recycle 15% of our plastic packaging. Councils will only invest in better recycling facilities if you show just how much you, as voters, care about it! A pioneering unit called Reclaim was set up in Sheffield in 1989, providing employment for people with mental health illnesses, and now recycling 100 tonnes of plastic film a year and 350 tonnes of plastic bottles. Make sure you write to both your local council and local MP to press for more recycling. To find out everything about recycling plastics and how set up schemes in your areas, contact RECOUP. Visit www.recoup.org, or call 01733 390 021.

A cooler glass of water

Always use a glass when you take a drink from the water cooler. This will save on the wasteful use of disposable plastic cups, and also save your company money!

Say no to unwanted bags (SNUB)

In total, UK shoppers use eight billion plastic carrier bags a year. That's 134 per person. When you're out shopping, consolidate all your purchases in one bag, rather than getting lots of new ones. And for the really organised, why not take old bags out with you when you go on a shopping trip?

READER TIP – MAGNUS F. SMYLY
Give your plastic bags to charity shops

Offer your used plastic carrier bags to local shops. This makes further use of the bags before they are recycled and therefore conserves energy. There is no central resource outlining all outlets that would like such bags, but if you ask local shopkeepers, you may find willing recipients.

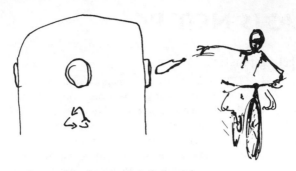

Reuse/recycle plastic drink bottles

If you buy a drink in a plastic bottle, don't just throw it away! In the UK, we use a colossal 15 million bottles a day, of which only 3% are recycled. Recycling just one plastic bottle can save the energy needed to power a 60-watt light bulb for 6 hours. If your bottle is made of PET, an easily recyclable plastic, take it down to your local plastic recycling plant. You can find out by looking for the number 1 (the symbol for PET) inside a triangle on the bottom of the bottle. To find out where your nearest plastic recycling plant is, call 0800 435 576.

Never use plastic in microwaves

Heat and cold speed up the rate of plastic degradation, accelerating the movement of plastic molecules into your food. Avoid using plastic in microwaves, otherwise you'll be eating plastic for dinner.

Avoid products containing PVC

PVC contains the softening agent phthalate, which leaks out during use. The most commonly used phthalate is DEHP, a possible carcinogen and a known cause of liver, kidney and reproductive damage. Wherever possible, avoid using products that contain PVC, such as Tupperware, garden furniture and window frames. For a list of all the products we use that contain PVC, visit **www.greenpeace.org**

PACK IT IN

What to do with packaging

Rethink Rubbish, the national recycling campaign, suggests you rifle through your rubbish to take a look at what you're throwing away. Next time you do your shopping, see if you can reduce your number of packaged purchases. And if you can't avoid packaging, dispose of it carefully. Visit **www.rethinkrubbish.com**, *and follow the tips below.*

Squash your rubbish

Squashing rubbish and packaging before you throw it away means it takes up less space in the landfill sites, and reduces the amount of land given over to these areas.

Reuse aluminium foil

Every year 26,000 tonnes of aluminium foil is used in the UK, but just 2,990 tonnes of this is recycled – that's only 12%! After using foil, where possible fold it and reuse it at a later date. Alternatively, use boxes with lids or cover food with bowls or plates instead of using foil, which can create unnecessary waste.

Avoid paper cartons

The 'paper' cartons containing milk and juice are not paper alone. They are 75% paper, 20% polyethylene and 5% aluminium foil. Subsequently they are a nightmare to recycle and all too often become incinerated or put into a landfill site. Avoiding them can help avoid these two environmentally damaging practices.

Buy refillables

Reduce landfill waste. Cleaning products such as dishwasher soap, floor cleaners and washing up liquid, or even personal toiletries such as soap, are now sold in refillable bottles. Make the effort and use them.

Say NO to bisphenol A

Ask your supermarket if it uses packaging that contains bisphenol A. Bisphenol A is a hormone disrupter, meaning it interferes with our daily bodily functions. Find out more about hormone disrupters from Friends of the Earth at **www.foe.co.uk/campaigns/safer_chemicals**. Some supermarkets can guarantee that their packaging is free from bisphenol A, especially for baby food, but others can't. Only through pressure from you, the consumer, will they take measures to stop its use.

READER TIP – DIANE BARNARD
Scrapstore it

Working in a playgroup, you can not only recycle your own packaging but use that provided by local businesses via Scrapstore, which provides novel craft resources for schools and other groups working with young people. There are several warehouses countrywide, many with their own websites, which you can link onto from the general website: **www.childrensscrapstore.co.uk**. Members may wheel supermarket trolleys down aisles containing shelves and barrels full of fabric, card and wood offcuts. If it's colourful and interesting it'll be in the warehouse!

Reuse cardboard boxes

It might sound obvious, but don't throw away those cardboard boxes. Next time you buy a pair of shoes, or something else that comes in a box, keep it to reuse, perhaps for mailing gifts.

GOOD ORE BAD

Recycling metals

Scrap metal such as copper, brass and aluminium is worth money and has a long recycling history, though most households don't generate enough to interest dealers. Domestic waste – batteries, tin cans and cars for example, can all be recycled, and aluminium cans could be recycled indefinitely. Find out more from Friends of the Earth **www.foe.co.uk**.

Cash for Cans recycling centres

Throwing away cans is incredibly wasteful, so bring your old aluminium cans to your nearest Cash for Cans recycling centre. To find out where this is, visit **www.cashforcans.co.uk** or call 0845 722 722. If there isn't a recycling centre in your local area, you can deposit your cans in an ordinary can bank. Remember to squash your cans before you put them in the bank to save on space.

Keep household batteries out of landfill sites

The average household uses 21 batteries a year, which adds up to around 650 million batteries throughout the UK. Of these, approximately 20,000 tonnes of batteries are landfilled annually. Batteries contain metals that can cause serious pollution problems, such as Cadmium which doesn't degrade and can't be destroyed. If it gets into the food chain it can damage the liver, kidney and brain of humans and fish. Some local councils and companies are beginning to develop ways of tackling this problem. In the meantime, using rechargeable batteries will reduce these problems. For more information go to **www.wasteonline.org.uk**

Recycle steel cans

Steel cans are found in every food service setting, from grocery stores to commercial and institutional kitchens. They are recyclable, but not enough is being done. The steel plate recovered from cans each year in

Western Europe weighs the equivalent of 132 Eiffel towers or 4,000 jumbo jets, but we could do better. For example, every year each Australian sends around 3.5kg of steel cans to refill – that's enough steel to make 40,000 fridges! So, make sure you're doing your bit, and take your cans to one of the 2,000 Save-a-Can banks across Britain. For more information, visit the Steel Can Recycling Information Bureau **www.scrib.org** or call 01639 872 626.

Abandoned cars

More than 2 million cars reach the end of their working lives every year in the UK. Of these, some 350,000 are illegally dumped – that's a staggering 994 cars every day. It's time for you to help with this growing problem of car dumping and flytipping. If you see an abandoned vehicle, you can report it to the Eco Salvage project at **www.rayzume.com/ecosalvage**. Eco Salvage is also keen for sponsorship from companies in the form of equipment to help its team operate. So, if your company produces any type of vehicle, outdoor clothing, climbing, recovery, safety or communication equipment, encourage them to sponsor Eco Salvage. For further details, visit the website or call 01404 831 071.

Recycle your old fridge

Every year 2.5 million fridges are thrown away – the average life span of a fridge is 11 years. If you buy a new fridge through Comet, they will collect your old one and deliver it to Ozone Friends. It will either be reconditioned and sold to someone unable to afford a new fridge, or the ozone depleting chemicals will be removed from it. Visit **www.ozonefriends.co.uk** for more information or for other alternatives visit **www.fridge-recycling.co.uk**. You can also advertise items like washing machines, freezers and fridges in your local paper – someone else can probably use them.

THE TAO OF POO

Sewage and stuff

*By 2005, only 25% of the UK's sewage will receive full tertiary ultraviolet radiation. Most of the rest only receives primary treatment, which means it still contains 10% of the faecal particles of raw sewage. Secondary treated sewage only contains 1% and tertiary just 0.0035%. When sewage is not properly treated, it prevents the use of water for irrigation, fisheries, recreation and drinking. Yet in the long-term, full treatment does not have to work out more expensive than secondary sewage treatment. To find out if your area is receiving full water treatment, contact your local water company or the Environment Agency online at **www.environment-agency.gov.uk** or by phone on 0800 80 70 60. Also, to help the campaigning group Surfers Against Sewage lobby for full treatment of sewage throughout the UK, visit **www.sas.org.uk** or call 01872 553 001.*

Think before you flush

Every time you flush the toilet, you use between 15 and 20 litres of water. So, next time you're about to flush, stop and think whether it's really necessary. You can help reduce your water consumption by placing a brick or hippo water-saver in your toilet cistern. In just one year, you could save over 3,000 litres of water. Visit **www.hippo-the-watersaver.co.uk** or call 01989 766 667 to order your water saver.

Spare a thought for exactly what you flush away, too. We flush an enormous number of chemicals and loose items, with an estimated three-quarters of blockages in water pipes being due to disposables such as sanitary towels, razor blades, syringes, even ladies tights and cotton buds. Last year over 75% of toilet debris on beaches was composed of the plastic sticks from cotton buds. Waste like this is not only unsightly, it's harmful to wildlife.

Filter your own water

When you turn on the tap, the water you are about to drink has passed through an ageing infrastructure of water pipes and been through various cleaning process which, when combined, can leave your water as more than just H$_2$O! It can contain chlorine, ammonia, bacteria, dissolved organic matter, suspended solids such as rust and dirt, and heavy materials such as aluminium, copper and lead. These can be removed using simple home water filtration methods. Find out how through the Fresh Water Filter Company **www.freshwaterfilter.org.uk**, 020 8597 3223 or the Pure H$_2$O Company **www.pureh2o.co.uk**, 01784 221 188.

If it's yellow let it mellow, when it's brown, flush it down

If you can, avoid flushing the toilet every time you visit – particularly at night. And try not to use the toilet as the bathroom rubbish bin as every flush will use 12 more litres of water.

Report incidents of water pollution

In order to be removed, sewage needs to identified. Don't assume that somebody else will report it! Even if they have, the pollution is clearly still there and has not been dealt with properly and the authorities still need notifying. If you see foamy scum or brown slick on the surface of rivers, lakes or sea, or smell sewage, get on the phone to the Environment Agency's hotline on 0800 80 70 60.

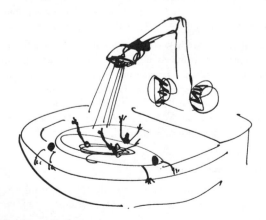

WWF - Buy With Your Heart & With Your Head

We're addressing the threats to ourselves and to global eco-systems such as global warming, toxic chemicals, freshwater and threats to endangered species and their habitats. We also believe in consumer power.

Everyone can make a difference but not everyone knows that WWF now offers a wide range of environmentally and socially responsible products.

If you'd like to shop with your heart and your head visit **www.wwf.org.uk/shop** or to find out more or make a donation visit www.wwf.org.uk/takeaction or call our Helpline on **01483 426333**

WWF Taking action for a living planet

GO WILD

In the 3.5-billion year history of life of Earth, there have been five major extinctions – events in which over 75% of all life disappeared. Today, experts from a whole range of fields – palaeontology, biology, climatology – in addition to statisticians are coming to the conclusion that we are on the brink of a sixth. 'Our activities have accelerated the rate of species extinction to hundreds – perhaps thousands of times the normal background rate,' according to the *New Scientist*, who reports Peter Raven, president of the International Botanical Congress, as predicting the extinction of about two-thirds of all bird, mammal, butterfly and plant species by the end of the next century.

This is not scaremongering. Since 1945, the UK alone has lost an estimated 95% of flower rich meadows, 30% of ancient woodland and 80% of lowland grassland. Fauna has fared little better: nearly 10% of our butterfly species, for example, became extinct in this country during the 20th century, and 50% more are on downward spirals. Various agencies are looking for solutions, among them CPRE, the Campaign to Protect Rural England **www.cpre.org.uk**, 020 7981 2800; and The Wildlife Trusts **www.wildlifetrusts.org**. Get involved with one, and you'll be helping make a difference.

CLOSE TO HOME

Wildlife in your garden

There's an immense pleasure to be gained from preparing your garden for wildlife: as the birds move in to nest, the butterflies are attracted by your nectar, the frogs make their home in your pond, and bats swoop the night sky above you, you realise that you have prepared a small oasis that nature now calls its own. There is no greater honour.

Build a wildlife pond

All wildlife needs water and countless species will benefit – you may find birds, badgers and dragonflies visiting your pond, and newts, frogs and toads making their home in it. If you're going to build a pond make sure it has shallow margins, deep areas and softly sloping sides for good access. Placing rock piles nearby will give shelter to frogs, newts and even toads. It also needs to be deep enough for wildlife to survive in winter. For more information visit **www.bbc.co.uk/nature/plants/charlie/howto_pond.shtml** or **www.beautifulbritain.co.uk/pond_pages.htm**

Save our hedgerows

The Department of the Environment estimates that between 1984 and 1990 121,000 km of hedgerows were lost. Hedgerows provide a rich and diverse natural habitat for plants, animals and birds, some of which are globally threatened. There is now less than 450,000 km of hedgerow left in the UK. CPRE – the Campaign to Protect Rural England, **www.cpre.org.uk**, can provide information on hedgerow management, or get advice from The National Hedge Laying Society at **http://members.lycos.co.uk/hedgelaying** (tel 01494 873980), BTCV (British Trust for Conservation Volunteers) at **www.btcv.org** and The Wildlife Trusts at **www.wildlifetrusts.org**

TOP TIP – BUTTERFLY CONSERVATION
Chemical warfare

More and more farmers are going organic and more and more of us want to buy organic food. It is, therefore, a shocking fact that our use of pesticides in the garden increased by over 75% between 1998 and 2001. Pesticides do not specifically target greenfly and vine weevil (regardless of what it may say on the tin!) and such poisons kill countless beneficial or harmless butterflies, moths and other insects in gardens every day. They can also have nasty knock-on effects on the garden birds, mammals and amphibians which feed on insects in your garden. Cutting down your use of pesticides will be of great benefit to your garden wildlife, will save you money and effort and will give natural predators a chance to sort those pests out for you! For more tips and information about butterflies and moths contact Butterfly Conservation at **www.butterfly-conservation.org**, or call 0870 774 4309.

Give an owl a home

Owls nest in hollow trees, old buildings or barns, and are often made homeless by modern developments. Encourage owls in your area by installing an owl box – it might just be the new des res an owl family is looking for. Contact the Hawk and Owl Trust for details **www.hawkandowl.org** tel 01582 832 182. Alternatively, the Trust will tell you how to 'Adopt a Box' to provide homes for owl families. You won't be told where your box is (because the birds are protected) but you will get news of what's been going on in your box, a certificate, an illustrated guide to Britain's owls, a sticker and a regular newsletter.

TOP TIP – BUTTERFLY CONSERVATION
Put your feet up for moths

You don't necessarily have to do extra things to attract
wildlife to your garden, doing less can also help. Planting specific
caterpillar foodplants can encourage butterflies to breed in your
garden, but your patch is already home to many moths.
An average garden will have scores of moth species breeding in it –
a large wildlife friendly garden in southern Britain might support
400 or more larger moth species alone.

Some of these common moths are declining rapidly, yet all
they need are the wilder, weedier parts of your garden or hedge.
Not being too tidy in the garden and not using pesticides will help
them to maintain their breeding colonies, which in turn provide vital
food for hungry Blue Tits, House Sparrow chicks and bats. Go out
with a torch on a summer evening to see moths drinking nectar from
flowers such as Buddleia, Honeysuckle, Evening Primrose and Red
Campion. For more tips and information about butterflies and moths
contact Butterfly Conservation **www.butterfly-conservation.org**,
0870 774 4309.

Gone but not forgotten

They may be long dead, but they're still precious. Fossils are in
constant danger from unscrupulous collectors who sell good specimens
for a hefty profit – some have even been known to dynamite the rock
in order to extract them. But even innocent collectors may inadvertently
damage the resource, which in the proper hands can tell us much
about the past – and therefore inform the present – life on Earth.

There are codes of conduct for collectors – by the sea they recommend
searching on the beach when the tide is going out, and in many places
it's necessary to seek the landowner's permission. Certain fossils need
registering, too. For more information visit the Discovering Fossils
website, launched in February 2003 as a non-profit making
information resource dedicated to British Fossils, at
www.discoveringfossils.co.uk/Code.htm

KIDS – count creatures

The UK Phenology Network is recording nature's calendar – seeking the first signs of spring and autumn by counting the numbers of individuals of different species in their local area. The results are entered onto an online database, which will help us to understand the effects of climate change on wildlife.

Recorders for the autumn 'count' should register in the summer for the following months and again in December/January for the spring 'flora and fauna census'. Volunteer opportunities are listed on the website: **www.phenology.org.uk** tel 01476 581 111.

Squirrel banquets

If you enjoy feeding squirrels remember they are actually hungriest in July, when their hidden stores are low and the new season's crop has yet to ripen. Try to provide food that approximates to their natural diet of tree seeds, tree flowers, tree shoots, mushrooms and fungi – they'll be grateful for peanuts, pine nuts, sunflower seeds, carrots and apples. Visit **www.overthegardengate.co.uk** for more wildlife tips.

 TOP TIP – BUTTERFLY CONSERVATION
Making hay while the sun shines

Long grass and wildflower 'meadows' are great for attracting more wildlife into the garden. Common visitors such as the Speckled Wood, Meadow Brown and Gatekeeper butterflies all lay their eggs on long grasses so it won't be long before they are breeding in your garden. The best way to look after such areas is to cut most of the long grass down in the autumn and take it off to the compost heap. If you cut in the summer, as soon as the grass turns brown (e.g. July/August), you'll be taking all the butterfly eggs and caterpillars away with the hay! Leaving the cut grass lying in-situ is also detrimental as it hinders the growth of wildflowers that provide vital nectar for butterflies. Leaving a few long tussocks over the winter will provide habitat for butterflies and other creatures during the winter. For more tips and information about butterflies and moths contact Butterfly Conservation **www.butterfly-conservation.org**, 0870 774 4309.

Leave wood to rot

Rotting wood is a common feature in the wild, and is an essential habitat for many species such as beetles. A log pile in an urban – or even city – garden will attract a wide range of creatures and makes a good nature museum for kids.

Batman...

Get a bat box to encourage bats to roost. Bats are an integral part of the ecosystem and – like many wild creatures – are suffering from the loss of their natural habitat. Of the 16 species left in Britain, six are endangered or rare and six others are vulnerable. Britain's commonest bat, the pipistrelle, is just 40mm long and weighs about 5 grams – less than a 2p coin. Despite its size it can eat up to 3,000 insects per night – so it's a real gardener's friend. You can find information on how to make or buy bat boxes at the Bat Conservation Trust **www.bats.org.uk**, 020 7627 2629. They also sell the Microbat, a tiny bat detector that enables you to identify bats in the field.

...and robin

The RSPB recommends you feed birds year round – twice daily when the weather is severe – and don't leave uneaten food lying around. Feeding areas and utensils should be kept clean to avoid disease – salmonella can break out at unclean feeding stations. Black sunflower seeds, pinhead oatmeal, sultanas, raisins, currants, mild grated cheese, seed mixtures without loose peanuts, soft apples and pears cut up are all recommended. Avoid giving peanuts, fat and bread in the summer as they're not good for nestlings. And always leave clean water out, changed daily. For bird feeding tips and much more visit **www.rspb.org.uk**

★ TOP TIP – BUTTERFLY CONSERVATION

Unmade bed

It's not only fans of modern art that like messy, unmade beds. Most garden butterflies and moths rely on dense vegetation, piles of dead leaves and grass tussocks as places to sleep through the inhospitable winter months. Most species spend the winter as eggs, caterpillars or pupae and not as hibernating adult moths or butterflies. By not tidying up all the fallen leaves, dead stems and long grass at the back of your flower beds, you'll be helping your garden wildlife to flourish for another year. For more information about butterflies and moths contact Butterfly Conservation **www.butterfly-conservation.org**, 0870 774 4309.

★ TOP TIP – BTCV

Go native!

The loss of valuable wildlife habitats has been severe owing to changes in agricultural practice, new housing and industrial development. If you buy and plant native trees, shrubs, wildflowers and bulbs you'll be helping to re-create some of these lost habitats and wildlife havens and you'll also be safeguarding the future of a significant part of our cultural and landscape heritage. For a wide selection of native trees, plants and wildflowers contact BTCV (British Trust for Conservation Volunteers) on 01302 572 200 or visit **www.btcv.org**

KIDS – Keep slow worms in the garden

Slow worms are the only legless type of lizard in the UK. They grow up to 50cm long and can 'lose' their tail when frightened and grow it again later. You can tell a slow worm from a snake by the size of its head – it's never bigger than its body. Slow worms feed on slugs, insects and spiders, hide in cool dark places during the day and come out at night to feed on their favourite meal, the slug. They're the perfect gardener's friend.

Kids – Hedgehogs don't like milk (or bread)

Nearly a quarter of the hedgehogs born into the world die before leaving their nest; probably a half of the rest don't survive their first hibernation, according to the British Hedgehog Preservation Society. They're inquisitive creatures and will eat almost anything, but that doesn't mean that they should! They've been found with their heads stuck in tins, yoghurt pots and plastic cups so keep your garden litter free of these items – especially if you live in a town. If you want to feed hedgehogs, give them tinned cat or dog food (not fish based), chicken leftovers, scrambled egg, chopped peanuts grated cheese and breakfast cereal. Don't give hedgehogs milk – they can't digest it. Visit **www.software-technics.co.uk/bhps** to find out more.

★ TOP TIP – MALCOLM TAIT, WILDLIFE EDITOR
Water tragedy

The average household uses 355 litres (79 gallons) of water a day, according to the Office of Water Services, all of which is leading to depleted rivers and wetlands. In England alone, 26 sites that are designated Sites of Special Scientific Interest are being affected badly by water reduction, and nearly 200 more are in danger. Reduce your usage by turning the tap on and off when you brush your teeth, using a bowl for your washing up, and running the washing machine only when you have a full load.

Wildlife Walks is a guide to over 500 of the UK's top nature reserves. Call 0870 101 9700 or visit **www.wildlifetrusts.org** for more information.

Gardeners – help increase the bee population

Since the 1960s certain species of native bumblebee have declined by as much as 95%, owing in large part to the loss of wild flowers in the countryside. Some have declined so much they are rarely seen – the Cullem's bumblebee was last seen in 1941, the short-haired bumblebee in 1999. As the principal pollinators of soft fruit they are essential to the eco-system – their loss would render many gardens sterile. English Nature and the National Trust are calling for gardeners to spurn modern hybrids such as petunias and plant traditional cottage flowers – rich in nectar – in their garden. There are 15 million gardens in Britain. If all gardeners planted bee-friendly flowers, it could make a big difference. Visit English Nature on **www.english-nature.org.uk** or call 01733 455 100.

Dead helpful

Graveyards, with their large expanses of open space, are the perfect havens for wildlife. With the help of the Yorkshire Living Churchyard's Project more than 1,300 graveyards in the York area are now thriving with native birds, mammals, insects, and rare plants. Find out what your local churchyard is doing to manage itself in an environmentally sympathetic manner. Not only will this add to the aesthetic appearance of the area, it will also benefit wildlife. For more information visit **www.yorkshire-wildlife-trust.org.uk/ylc** or call 01904 659 570.

A favour for foxes

If you leave your tin cans outside for collection, make sure you take the lids right off – don't leave them bent partially open for foraging foxes to cut their noses on. The National Fox Welfare Society **www.nfws.org.uk** provides information on the UK's foxes.

Keep your pond frost-free

Throw a tennis ball or rubber duck into your pond – it will bob about creating gentle movement that stops the pond icing over in all but the severest of frosts, and save your fish and frogs from a chilly death.

Don't remove pebbles from the beach

Removing pebbles from British beaches is prohibited, and you could face a heavy fine if you're caught. Clearing beaches of pebbles can deprive coastal plants and animals of their natural habitats and shelters. In addition, removing shingle can interfere with the natural beach processes and sediment cycling. Pebbles can act as natural defences against cliff and beach erosion, so depletion could start to increase the rate of erosion. If you want to use pebbles for aquariums or gardens, make sure you buy them from stone merchants.

Boxing clever

If you have nestboxes in your garden, clean them out once the breeding season is over to reduce the likelihood of infection and parasites next year. Meanwhile, if you plan to tie a nestbox to a tree, try using an old rubber inner tube, as it expands as the tree grows, causing no damage.

Wildlife Walks is a guide to over 500 of the UK's top nature reserves. Call 0870 101 9700 or visit **www.wildlifetrusts.org** for information.

Seeds of success

Although more woodlands are being protected than ever before, too many have already lost their carpets of wild flowers. Help repopulate them by simply helping transfer seeds from established woodlands. To join a project like this near you, contact Landlife on 0151 737 1819.

★ **TOP TIP** – WILDLIFE & COUNTRYSIDE LINK
Join in and help

If you want to help wildlife in the UK or around the world, join one of the charities which work to protect nature. Almost 7 million people are already members of wildlife and countryside organisations.
A list of charities is available from us at **www.wcl.org.uk**. Don't know which one to join? Can't afford to join them all? Support a different one each year!

WIDER WORLD

Do your bit for the world's wildlife

At present rates of extinction, 20% of the world's species of plants and animals could be gone within just three short decades. Habitat destruction is one of the key culprits, although climate change is not far behind. Faced with such daunting crises, can an individual really make much of a difference? You bet. Go MAD, and Go Wild.

Sponsor a cheetah

Your money could make a difference to some of the world's most endangered creatures. The Cheetah Conservation Fund (CCF) is working in Namibia to conserve cheetahs in their natural habitat. They have launched an 'adopt a cheetah' campaign which, while not tied to a specific animal, will help protect and care for cheetahs worldwide. Visit **www.cheetah.org** for more information.

READER TIP – JUSTIN FRANCIS
Volunteer for conservation research

There are many great trips where you can help conduct valuable field research on lion, elephant, cheetah, whales, dolphins and turtles and more. In addition to gathering vital data by staying with the conservationists some of the cost of your trip will support them and their work. Visit **www.responsibletravel.com** for conservation volunteering holidays.

Protect the whales' song

The song of a humpback whale is one of the most enigmatic and beautiful sounds of the natural world. These whales are extremely sensitive to noise and their ear drums can explode at 180 decibels. A new low-frequency submarine detection system being developed by the US and British navies together with NATO is blasting 240 decibels throughout the world's oceans. In areas where the system has been tested, huge numbers of whales have been beached with extreme auditory trauma. To find out more about the use of active sonar and add your voice to the growing protest, contact the Whale and Dolphin Conservation Society at **www.wdcs.org**

Stamp out illegal wildlife trade

Traffic in wildlife is second only to the trade in narcotics in its size and value. The Environmental Investigation Agency carries out undercover investigations into environmental crime, and exposes the horrific treatment we inflict on animals throughout the world. One of their current campaigns 'Species in Peril' focuses on species threatened with extinction because of the devastating impact of illegal trade in body parts. Bears in particular are highlighted, and the EIA is actively seeking to end the international trade in bear parts and derivatives. Visit **www.eia-international.org** tel 020 7354 7960.

Protest against the ivory trade

Despite the world wide ivory ban which has saved large numbers of African elephants from widespread slaughter, the illegal trade in ivory continues. In 2002, six tonnes of ivory – the equivalent of 600 elephants - was seized in Singapore on its way from Africa to China and Japan, where ivory is still highly prized. And in 2001 seven tonnes was seized in India. Despite this, at the last meeting of CITES, (The Convention on the International Trade in Species) delegates voted to allow three African countries to continue selling off ivory stockpiles even though evidence suggested this contributed to illegal poaching. China is becoming a major consumer of legally and illegally traded ivory. Support the Environmental Investigation Agency's campaign to ban the ivory trade. Lodge your protest with the Chinese ambassador – visit **www.eia-international.org** for details.

Save tigers' forests

In 2003 Friends of the Earth and the Environmental Investigation Agency discovered British cosmetic companies have been using talc illegally mined from a protected forest in India. These forests are home to endangered species including tigers – only 5,000 are estimated to

WILDLIFE

remain in the wild throughout the world. To find out more visit
www.eia-international.org

A lethal luxury

A shatoosh shawl, made from the fine wool of the Tibetan antelope
has become a 'must have' item among the rich and famous worldwide,
despite the fact that the antelope is in danger of extinction and only an
estimated 75,000 animals remain in the world. Unlike pashmina wool
which is shaved, shatoosh is plucked from the antelope, so it must be
killed first. For more information contact **www.traffic.org**

Support turtles

Six of the seven types of marine turtles are listed as endangered. In
the Pacific, the leatherback turtle is facing extinction and in the
Mediterranean numbers of green turtles are rapidly dwindling. Turtles
take decades to mature, mate and produce offspring but they have a
battle to survive from the very moment eggs are laid – from humans
who harvest turtle eggs, from long fishing lines and pollution in seas.
Visit the Caribbean Conservation Corporation **www.cccturtle.org** to
find out more.

Help stop whaling

Iceland has once again started to kill whales for 'scientific research'.
Iceland is exploiting a loophole in the world-wide moratorium
imposed by the International Whaling Commission (IWC) on
commercial whaling, by claiming its hunt has a scientific basis. Write
to the Icelandic Embassy in your country to voice your objection. If
you live in the UK, address it to Icelandic Ambassador to the UK,
Embassy of Iceland, 2A Hans Street, London SW1X 0JE.

CHANGE YOUR LIFE CHANGE OUR WORLD

Do you have a real appetite for change? Do you want to make our world a better, fairer place? Are you ready to live and work alongside people in some of the world's poorest countries?

If you are, you could use your skills to help local people to help themselves as a VSO volunteer. From midwives to marine biologists, from teachers to engineers, we need skilled and experienced professionals to live and work for two years as part of a community in countries such as Malawi, India and the Philippines.

As a volunteer, you will share your skills every day for the benefit of the people you are working with and for our whole developing world. When you go home, the skills you have shared will remain, so your work will last forever.

Even if the time's not right for you to become a volunteer yourself, you can still change your life – and our world. By taking part in activities like sponsored treks or challenge events you can make a real difference.

Either way, your life may never be the same again. So if you want to make a real difference, visit www.vso.org.uk and find out more about how you can get involved with VSO.

CHARITY NUMBER 313757

USE YOUR SKILLS TO CHANGE OUR WORLD
www.vso.org.uk
020 8780 7500   Ref: GOM

VSO
Sharing skills
Changing lives

AT YOUR LEISURE

'*When at leisure make preparations for a time of need*' warns an ancient Chinese proverb. Well, we're rapidly heading for a global time of need, so what can you do? The joy of leisure is that it gives you time to think – and therefore act – a little more carefully. Recycling is not just for bottles, cans and plastic – all sorts of other things, like books, can be exchanged and recycled, too. You can go green when entertaining, and if you really want to make a difference, volunteer. A whole host of organisations, at home and abroad, need your help now. So have fun, but go MAD too.

Meanwhile, American philosopher and naturalist Henry David Thoreau wrote in 1852: '*Haste makes waste, no less in life than in housekeeping*'. Take things slowly in your free time and you – and the world – will get more out of it.

IN AND OUT

Being green at home and on the town

To quote an old television programme, 'Why don't you just switch off your TV set and do something less boring instead'. Well, why don't you?

Detox from your TV

On average, children in the UK aged 6-16 spend three hours a day watching TV. That's higher than the European average of only 2 hours a day. Compared to their European counterparts, British children also do worse on other activities. Only 54% of British children read books in their spare time, compared to 90% of children in the Netherlands. In addition, while 89% of Swedish children read newspapers, only 33% of kids in Britain do the same. Having a TV-free week would free up 21 hours of time to spend with friends, playing sport, or reading a book.

> ## READER TIP – NICK HAY
> ## Turn it off
>
> Visit **www.whitedot.org** for details of an organisation dedicated to lessening the influence of TV in our lives.

Adopt a greyhound

Every year, tens of thousands of greyhounds are discarded by the ruthless racing industry. Of the 30,000 greyhounds bred for racing each year, 10,000 are killed before their first race, and a further 12,000 are injured during a race. You could boycott greyhound races, and encourage others to do the same. Alternatively, you could adopt an ex-racing greyhound. They make great pets, are suprisingly gentle, and don't even need much exercise. For information on how to adopt, visit **www.retiredgreyhounds.co.uk** or **www.adopt-a-greyhound.org**

 **TOP TIP** – CPRE

Join CPRE's letter-writing team

Letters really make a difference. The Campaign to Protect Rural England (CPRE)'s letter-writing team of members and supporters writes letters from time to time to key 'opinion formers' like local MPs, a Government department or a member of the House of Lords. The letters – about important environmental issues and concerns – are straightforward, politically balanced and don't take long to write. CPRE supplies suggested text highlighting key points, which you are free to amend. Volunteers also screen over 100,000 planning applications annually – raising the alarm when the countryside is threatened. Call 020 7981 2000 or visit **www.cpre.org.uk** for more information.

Join a green gym

Green Gyms are conservation projects involving regular outdoor work, such as cutting down shrubs, clearing paths and repairing walls and fences. Not only does this work help the local environment, it also helps improve the participants' physical and mental well-being. For more information on Green Gyms, and how to join your local gym, go to the British Trust for Conservation Volunteers website **www.btcv.org/greengym**.

Kids – Have fun and learn

There are Education Centres all over the UK, details of which can be found at: **www.schoolgovernment.co.uk/FSC/FSC.htm**. These are set up to help the public understand conservation issues and the natural environment, so what better place to take a day trip?

Get Festive

Go mad at WOMAD (World of Music Arts and Dance). The UK festival is in mid-summer, but festivals are held all year round in countries like Brazil, Australia, Italy and South Africa. Check out the website at **www.womad.org**. Festivals and performances are some of the best ways to help keep cultural diversity alive. Contact www.reclaimthestreets.net (020 7281 4621) for an agenda of the best street parties. *Festival Eye*, a magazine and a website, gives a comprehensive list of all festivals going on across the UK – visit **www.festivaleye.com**, or call 01568 760 492. Or try Efestivals' website: **www.efestivals.co.uk** for music festival listings and reviews.

Don't wake the neighbours

Noise is as much of an environmental pollutant as carbon dioxide or nitrous oxide, so do your bit to reduce its impacts. Some nightclub owners are starting to wise up to the problem, and now supply lollypops for exiting revellers to suck so that they don't make a noise. For more information and reports on the effect of noise pollution, check out **www.doh.gov.uk/noisepollution**.

 **TOP TIP** – FRIENDS OF THE EARTH
Question and badger

Decision-makers like MPs and Councillors are accountable to you. You have a right to know their position on an issue, and they want to hear from their constituents. They need your vote. Your troubles are their troubles.

The same is true for businesses. Friends of the Earth helped to organise people's opposition to GM foods and all of the major UK supermarkets U-turned their position to give their customers what they want.

Friends of the Earth could never have achieved successes such as doorstep recycling for all in England and Wales, and seeing the South Downs become a national park without people like you badgering decision-makers. Remember that trying to get a decent response is never pestering – it's lobbying!

For ideas and advice on questioning and badgering visit **www.foe.org.uk** or call the Friends of the Earth Information Service on Freephone 0808 800 1111.

Don't send that file

Email is subject to pollution too, so don't clog it! Be careful when
sending large attachments such as photographs. Large files can cause
havoc when they become looped between two mail servers on the net.
So, try to keep your photo files below 1mb, or simply stop and
question whether or not you really need to send that file!

Don't use disposables

When you're giving a party, don't take the easy option and use
disposable cutlery, plates and napkins. Just spare a thought for all
those bags of rubbish you'd be producing.

Turn down the heat

If you are having a lot of guests round, the chances are that their
combined body heat will be enough to heat the house, so turn the
heating off just before they arrive.

Have an eco-friendly evening

Take advice from the Organic Food and Cooking chapters and make
your party GM-free, organic and environmentally friendly! If you are
having a lot of guests, try to limit the waste created; buy a keg of beer
instead of bottles, for example. If it's a dinner party, practice portion
control to limit the food you waste.

WORD POWER

Eco reading

'To acquire the habit of reading is to construct for yourself a refuge from almost all of the miseries of life' *wrote Somerset Maugham. Why not go one step further and use reading to construct a means of TACKLING those miseries?*

Let your knowledge flower

Green Books, publishers of The Organic Directory, supply a huge range of books on organic living, business, economy, renewable energy, ecological building, literature and poetry. Visit their website www.greenbooks.co.uk or call 01803 863 260 for a catalogue. To order a copy of the Friends of the Earth publications catalogue, with books, briefings, reports and educational resources visit **www.foe.co.uk** or call 020 7490 1555.

For more on organic living, look at Green Guides. Published in nine regional editions, they contain listings of local shops, businesses, organisations and mail order services. Order a copy from **www.greenguideonline.com** tel. 020 8815 4730, email info@greenguide.co.uk. The company also publishes Pure, a magazine for the ethical consumer.

Ensure a greener read

The world's publishing industries remain vast consumers of paper. About 40% of the world's population uses hardly any paper at all: most of Africa and much of Asia use less than 10kg a head. But per capita consumption of paper in the more prosperous countries is massive – the table-topping USA uses 332kg while the UK and Germany are level in 13th place at 194kg. Responsible reading is an important way of cutting down deforestation, and ensuring the use of sustainable production methods in the paper industry. When choosing a book always ensure that it's produced from recycled or sustainable paper sources, or better still check for an NAPM (National Association of Paper Merchants) Recycled Mark **www.napm.org.uk**

Meeting of minds

Get informed. Set up a book club where you meet friends to discuss major environmental issues, choosing a few relevant books beforehand. Try books such as *Fast Food Nation* by Eric Schlosser, *Captive State* by George Monbiot, Lester R. Brown's *Eco-Economy*, and Andew Rowell's *Don't Worry, It's Safe to Eat*. Publishers which specialise in environmental books and will help you with more ideas include Green Books **www.greenbooks.co.uk** (01803 863 260) and Earthscan **www.earthscan.co.uk** (020 7278 0433). For background information visit the One World website **www.oneworld.net**, which brings you news and views from a network of over 1,500 organisations working for human rights and sustainable development.

Share the pleasure

Once you've finished a book, pass it on to someone else. This is especially useful when travelling as you can frequently exchange books with fellow travellers, making a single book purchase go a long way.

Become ecologically aware

Staying informed is one of the best ways you can help make a difference. To find out more about the world's environmental and social problems, and what we can do to help, get onto *The Ecologist* website. This monthly publication is the world's longest running environmental magazine, and is read by people in over 150 different countries. To take out a subscription to *The Ecologist*, fill in the form on page 274 of this book.

Green Metropolis

Rather than letting piles of old reads gather dust in your home, turn them into cash and receive £3 for every book sold. The website **www.greenmetropolis.com** specialises in the 'recycling' of paperbacks, from the latest releases to golden oldies. All books cost just £3.75 (including free delivery) and by selling them on you save existing trees. Better still, 5p from every sale goes to the 'Plant a Tree' scheme run by the Woodland Trust.

GET INVOLVED

Make a difference, volunteer!

Volunteering is easy, but to volunteer effectively requires a certain amount of commitment. Make sure that when you volunteer for something, you believe – or at least understand – the principles of the organisation you are working for. Not only will that encourage you to become more actively involved, it will also mean that you get far more out of it. Visit TimeBank – a national volunteering campaign – at **www.timebank.org.uk** *for details on how to volunteer and get involved in your local community.*

Change places

You can help change the places around you, by volunteering to work on local regeneration projects. Visit **www.changingplaces.org.uk** for details of schemes that transform derelict land into community gardens or playgrounds. You can also volunteer to work on sustainable development projects with Groundwork. This aims to build sustainable communities through joint environmental action between residents, businesses and other local organisations. At present 120,000 schoolchildren and 60,000 adults work on projects with Groundwork. Visit **www.groundwork.org.uk** for more information, or call 0121 236 8565.

Join the Woodcraft Folk

The Woodcraft Folk is an educational organisation for children and young people aged 6-20, and provides an original alternative to Scouts, Cubs, Guides and Brownies. It doesn't just involve woodcraft!

To find your local group, or to find out more information about the organisation, go to **www.woodcraft.org.uk**, or call 020 8672 6031.

 TOP TIP – GREENPEACE
Save it for the future

Greenpeace is an independent non-profit global campaigning organisation that uses non-violent, creative confrontation to expose global environmental problems and their causes. We research the solutions and alternatives to help provide a path for a green and peaceful future. Our goal is to ensure the ability of the earth to nurture life in all its diversity.

Greenpeace organises public campaigns:

- for the protection of oceans and ancient forest
- for the phasing-out of fossil fuels and the promotion of renewable energies in order to stop climate change
- for the elimination of toxic chemicals
- against the release of genetically modified organisms into nature
- for nuclear disarmament and an end to nuclear contamination.

To join Greenpeace call 0800 269 065 or visit the website, **www.greenpeace.org.uk**

Win a medal

The Duke of Edinburgh award scheme is run all over the UK, and offers young people the chance to achieve things that they would not normally be able to. The Award Scheme is open to boys and girls aged 14-17, and offers the opportunity to work towards bronze, silver and gold awards. In order to gain their award, children must learn a skill, carry out a physical activity, and volunteer to take part in community service. A great way of getting involved in the local community, visit **www.theaward.org** for more details.

Be excellent

The Millennium Volunteers Programme is aimed at young people aged 16-25. It gives young people encouragement and recognition for their volunteering achievements. The 'Certificate of Recognition' is awarded for 100 hours of volunteering and 'The Award of Excellence' is presented for 200 hours. The scheme pays travel and other expenses for those taking part in the awards, so you won't be out of pocket. Visit **www.millennium-volunteers.co.uk** for more information.

Get experience

Everyone has skills or talents that could be used to help others, and Experience Corps believes that these skills only improve over time. This scheme is thus aimed at people aged over 50, helping them to put their skills to use in their local community. The Experience Corps now has over 423,000 imaginative and innovative voluntary work opportunities on its database. And this number is rising every week. Visit **www.experiencecorps.co.uk** to discover how your skills can be utilised.

★ TOP TIP – MALCOLM TAIT, WILDLIFE EDITOR
Life's a beach

Many of Britain's beaches are a mess, but you can help clear them up. Every year, the Marine Conservation Society runs a September beach-cleaning weekend – although you can of course do your bit at any time of the year. For information, contact the MCS on 01989 566 017.

Wildlife Walks is a guide to over 500 of the UK's top nature reserves. Call 0870 101 9700 or visit **www.wildlifetrusts.org** for information.

Get active!

Anita Roddick founded the Body shop in 1976 – and started a consumer revolution. In her years at the helm she has travelled all over the world, meeting an incredible range of inspirational people and campaigning relentlessly for change on a huge variety of environmental and humanitarian issues. Now she is sharing her knowledge on **www.AnitaRoddick.com**, a website devoted to global issues with reports, updates and news of local action that people can participate in.

 TOP TIP – THE SOIL ASSOCIATION
Want a holiday with a difference?

The Organic Directory (**www.theorganicdirectory.co.uk**) lists holidays and weekend breaks on organic farms. Or visit Willing Workers on Organic Farms **www.wwoof.org** to find out about working on an organic farm in another country. **www.soilassociation.org.uk**

LOCAL HEROES

Working for the community

There are many ways you can do your bit for your community. Join the local Women's Institute, Working Men's Club, or simply shop at your local newsagent, grocers or petrol station, which are fast becoming endangered species, even though they are often a cheaper and better quality alternative. Your lack of effort may mean the death of local shops. Visit **www.pact.org.uk** *or* **www.impact-initiatives.org.uk** *to find out how you can do more.*

Take old magazines to your doctor

Doctors' surgeries don't have large budgets to spend on magazines, but we could all do with something to read while we're waiting for our appointment. So, whether it's *Cosmopolitan* or *The Ecologist*, take your old copies down to your local surgeries.

Fair exchange

LETS – Local Exchange Trading Schemes – are currently working to revitalise communities across Britain. They are local community-based networks, in which LETS members exchange goods and services with each other without the use for money. Using a special currency of LETS credits, people earn credits by providing a service, and can then spend the credits on whatever's offered by others in the scheme. For example, childcare may be exchanged for home repairs, or transport for the hire of tools and equipment. At least 40,000 people are involved in the UK's 450 LETS schemes at present, so visit **www.letslinkuk.org** to get involved yourself.

Aim to sustain!

Help your local area move towards a sustainable state. Local Agenda 21 was set up at the 1992 Rio Earth Summit, and is a comprehensive plan of action to help communities achieve sustainability through co-operation. Find out if your council is involved from the Improvement and Development Agency (IDEA). Visit **www.idea.gov.uk**.

You can get more involved by joining up to organisations such as Bio Regional. Bio Regional Development Group is founded on the green ideal of local production for local needs. Local production helps create employment and wealth in the local area, reduce waste, and limit our ecological footprint so we can live within the planet's resources. Visit **www.bioregional.com**, or call 020 8404 4880.

Get involved in local politics

Write to your MP and MEP on environmental issues. At election times, let the candidates know that you want environmentally friendly policies. Get involved in Local Agenda 21 – a community based organisation with the backing of the United Nations. Find out more at **www.scream.co.uk/la21**

Join a campaigning organisation

Join a campaigning organisation, such as the Appropriate Technology Association www.ata.or.th and then get involved. Just as you encourage your employer to do green things (recycling, composting waster, turn off unnecessary lights etc) get your church/youth club/social club to do the same.

PLAY ON...

Music

Music has been proven to make people happier, healthier, and smarter. Children who received music education in school have improved critical thinking and spatial-temporal reasoning, which resulted in better reading, language, and maths skills, as well as higher self-esteem. Statistics have also shown that kids involved with music are less likely to abuse drugs and alcohol, and are more likely to stay in school. **www.vh1.com/insidevh1/savethemus/you_can_help/research.html** *provides more information on music's many benefits.*

Buy used CDs

Sell your old music, and buy second hand CDs online at **www.amazon.co.uk**. Not only can you save yourself money, you're also limiting the wasteful use of resources.

Reject CD packaging

CD packaging can be extremely wasteful. CDs sometimes come in long boxes, cardboard packaging that is twice the size of the actual CD jewel case. This excess packaging was designed to stop shoplifting. Do your bit by refusing to buy CDs at stores that use the long box.

Go to charity concerts

Many artists donate proceeds from their concerts to a local or national charity, so you can give back to your community while enjoying a night out.

Recycle CDs

CDs are made from polycarbonate; a non-renewable, non-biodegradable petroleum-based product that usually ends up in landfills. Now there's a company – Polymer Reprocessors – that takes these CDs and turns them into items such as burglar alarm boxes, street lighting, and lenses. Visit **www.polymer-reprocessors.co.uk**

THE GREAT OUTDOORS

Our outdoors is popularly perceived as being in crisis. Infinitely varied sources of pollution, the effects of intensive agriculture, urban and industrial encroachment and exploitation means the picture looks bleak. But all this has brought the outdoors sharply into focus. Never before has there been more study, understanding and awareness of the state of the countryside and the effects of our actions. We're rediscovering the ecological and practical benefits of forgotten techniques of land management, we're developing greener methods of agricultural and industrial production, and finding more sustainable and less damaging ways of doing things. This goes right down to the nuts and bolts of what – and what not – to do when out and about. US President Theodore Roosevelt (1901-1909) said 'The nation behaves well if it treats the natural resources as assets which it must turn over to the next generation increased, and not impaired, in value'. Behave well as individuals, and we can affect the behaviour of nations.

PLAY FAIR

Green sports

It's not whether you win or lose, but how you play the game that counts.

Think where you drive

Off-road vehicles and motorbikes can do untold damage in the countryside if not driven with a bit of consideration. Deep ruts caused by tyres can scar green lanes – non-metalled routeways bounded by hedges – making walking and horse riding difficult. A survey undertaken in 2001 by JW Dover at the University of Stafford found that there are no accurate estimates for the UK stock of green lanes, which makes policy and conservation difficult, and that neglect is as much of a problem in certain cases as overuse. GLEAM (Green Lanes Environmental Action Movement) campaigns to preventing damage caused by recreational motor vehicles. Contact 0118 971 2103 for details. The Countryside Agency is compiling a national register of Greenways and Quiet Lanes – to help, visit **www.greenways.gov.uk**

Volunteer for sport

Be a sport and get involved in your local community! Without volunteers, there would be no sport and leisure activities as we know them in this country. As well as keeping us fit, sport can play an important role in tackling social exclusion and giving young people a good start in life. For more information and to volunteer, visit TimeBank, the national volunteering campaign at **www.timebank.org.uk**

The slopes are changing

If you're considering a skiing holiday, choose your ski resort on the basis of what it's doing for the environment. Global warming will have severe impacts on winter sports and recreation, so it's vital that resorts move towards the use of renewable energy resources. In February

2003, a new campaign was launched by the National Ski Areas Association to 'Keep Winter Cool'. This involves the promotion of simple, innovative efforts to reduce carbon dioxide and other heat trapping emissions using wind-powered ski lifts and car-pooling for guests and employees. Visit **www.nsaa.org**

Hitting greens

The Wildlife Trusts has long recognised that golf courses can make a significant contribution to wildlife conservation. For example, the Fynn Valley golf club in Suffolk has planted many native trees, such as the oak, and provides valuable habitats for dragonflies, barn owls and skylarks.

Friends of Conservation have set up a new campaign to stimulate golf courses to introduce wildlife friendly practices, such as restricting herbicide use, setting up bird-watching platforms, and training caddies to give wildlife talks. Visit **www.foc-uk.com** for details of how your local course can get involved. Also see **www.english-nature.org.uk** for 10 top tips on how to make your golf course wildlife-friendly.

Raise the standard of your local park

The Pesticide Action Network UK (PAN UK) **www.pan-uk.org** is aiming to raise the quality of local parks, making them cleaner, safer, more environmentally friendly, and better for the whole community. In 1997, they set up the PAN Green Flag Park Award, rewarding parks that are well maintained, sustainable, and do not use harmful chemicals and pesticides. Nearly 500 parks across Britain have expressed interest in the award, and are striving to improve the quality of their environment. Ask your council if your local parks are taking part in the scheme, and if not encourage them to join up today.

Cleaner swimming

There are approximately 100,000 swimming pools in the UK, and while swimming may be healthy, the stuff we put in them isn't. Pools are one of the best-established applications of solar water heating (visit Galeforce, the wind turbine and alternative energy company on

www.galeforce.nireland.co.uk tel 02879 659775 for information) so make pools completely green by using salt rather than chlorine. Australia is leading the world in salt chlorination systems, which are economical, environmentally friendly and safe. Visit **www.autochlor.com.au** for details.

 TOP TIP – GREENMATTERS.COM

Happy camping

The National Park System alone received over 10 million overnight campers in 2002. If you go camping anywhere, leave no trace that you have been there. Carry all trash out with you; don't burn or bury garbage without exception. Check your campsite carefully so as not to leave anything behind. If you are camping with a vehicle this is easy. If you are backpacking, plan wisely and take only minimally packaged items so as to reduce the volume of garbage you generate and to make packing it out easier. **www.greenmatters.com**

WOOD WORKS

Forests of the future

*Urgent measures are needed to save the remainder of Britain's ancient woodlands. Only 2% of ancient forests are left, and these are fast being gobbled up by urbanisation. Broadleaf forests are home to 50% of the UK's threatened species, so it's vital that we stop their destruction before it's too late. To get a copy of the Woodland Trust's free guide 'Is your local wood under threat?' Contact the Woodland Trust on 01476 581 135 or at **www.woodland-trust.org.uk**. You can also help axe illegal logging in the European Union and save global forests by writing to the UK minister for Europe. Visit Friends of the Earth's website **www.foe.co.uk** for a sample letter.*

Buy reclaimed wood

Ancient forests are being lost at a rate of one football pitch every two seconds, and every year the wood trade throws away thousands of tonnes of wood as waste. You can help by only buying wood that's produced sustainably, and by purchasing reclaimed wood. For more advice on how to buy second-hand furniture, and furniture manufactured from reclaimed wood, order a copy of the Good Wood guide from Friends of the Earth **www.foe.co.uk**, 020 7490 1555.

Bio-regional charcoal

Every year, Britain imports 60,000 tonnes of charcoal. This is despite the fact that our own woodlands could meet this demand many times over. About 90% of imported charcoal comes from the developing world, which leaves British woodlands uncoppiced and derelict. Bioregional **www.bioregional.com** is working to encourage British charcoal production, thus restoring our forests. At present 68 woodlands covering 4,000 hectares of land are certified by Bioregional and the FSC (**www.fscoax.org**). Not only do these provide local employment, the coppiced forests also provide habitats for endangered butterfly species such as the pearl-bordered fritillary. For more information on butterfly conservation and woodland, visit **www.butterfly-conservation.org**

Recycle wood as compost

The next time you have a pile of waste garden wood, don't take it to the local dump. You can recycle fallen branches, garden canes or any other type of wood in your compost heap. The larger the pieces, the slower they'll break down and the harder the pile will be to turn, so make sure you break them up into small pieces first. For more ideas on composting, and help on recycling projects, visit **www.diynet.com**.

Save wood by cutting up money

Did you ever wonder what happens to old money? It's recycled! You can now buy recycled pencils made out of denim, paper, and even money, instead of wood. By using a pencil made out of recycled money, you save a tree and create a new use for an old product. Learn about recycled products at **www.amazingrecycled.com**

Bring trees back into your local area

Trees can have enormous benefits for your local area. One hectare of woodland grown to maturity will absorb the carbon emissions of 100 family cars for a year. And a single large beech tree can provide enough oxygen for the daily requirement of 10 people. As well as these benefits, trees can make an enormous difference to the appearance of urban communities. You can help out by volunteering for a community tree planting scheme, or by joining the Million Trees campaign and sponsoring a tree for yourself or a friend. Contact Trees for London **www.treesforlondon.org.uk**, 020 7587 1320, or the Woodland Trust **www.woodland-trust.org.uk**, 01476 581 135 for more details.

Greenpeace Save or Delete Campaign

The world's ancient forests play a key role in the lives of people, are home to millions of plant and animal species and also help regulate the world's climate. This is why Greenpeace wants everyone to get involved in their latest campaign, Save or Delete, that aims to protect to save the world's forests from total destruction. Visit **www.saveordelete.com** to join the campaign. The site contains useful information on how to send letters to put pressure on the government to ban illegally logged timber imports to Britain.

Go MAD! 2

RESPONSIBLE RAMBLING

Walking, hiking and camping

There are 12 simple guidelines to remember when out and about:

- *Enjoy the countryside and respect its life and work*
- *Guard against all risk of fire*
- *Fasten all gates*
- *Keep your dogs under close control*
- *Keep to public paths across farmland*
- *Use gates and stiles to cross fences, hedges and walls*
- *Leave livestock, crops and machinery alone*
- *Take your litter home*
- *Help to keep all water clean*
- *Protect wildlife, plants and trees*
- *Take special care on country roads*
- *Make no unnecessary noise*

A new code is currently being drafted and will be available at the end of January 2004. For more in-depth information visit **www.countryside.gov.uk/access** *or call 01242 521 381.*

★ TOP TIP – THE RAMBLERS' ASSOCIATION
Spend locally

On a walking trip do all you can to support local business.

You might be staying in a village B&B anyway, but stock up on food in local shops rather than at your supermarket back home. Needless to say, visiting the local pub will also help! By the way, did you know that spending by walkers in England supports up to 231,000 full-time jobs? Visit **www.ramblers.org.uk** or call 020 7339 8500.

Country lovers unite!

Check out **www.countrylovers.co.uk**, which has details of various conservation organisations, as well as advice and information about several issues concerning the countryside across the UK. All of this is very relevant to hikers and campers, who will be passing through the countryside on their travels.

Hiking ethics

The Hiking Website **www.hikingwebsite.com** has a whole section devoted to 'Hiking Ethics' and how to behave out in the wild. Recommendations include not building another fire ring if one already exists, not digging trenches or building walls, and not cutting down plants or killing animals unless your survival depends on it. Visit the site for more details on hikers ethics. Also, try **www.campingresource.co.uk** for information about camping across the UK.

Blocked paths

If you come across a blocked path or other difficulty such as a broken style or field path that has been ploughed over contact your local highway authority (usually the local county council or unitary authority) or the local Ramblers' Association footpath officer. Call 020 7339 8500 to find out how to get in touch. Visit **www.ramblers.org.uk**

High performance, high impact

High-performance trekking and walking wear makes a real difference to our life in the outdoors – but how does it affect the environment itself? *Ethical Consumer* magazine conducted a survey of top brands in spring 2003. While manufacturing and production practices were found wanting in some cases, certain companies were found to be making an effort to reduce the environmental and humanitarian impact during manufacture. Patagonia **www.patagonia.com** came out top for waterproof jackets and rucksacks, and Ethical Wares **www.ethicalwares.com** were found to be best for boots. To find out more visit **www.ethicalconsumer.org**, 0161 226 2929.

 TOP TIP – THE RAMBLERS' ASSOCIATION

Use public transport to get to the start of your walk

As well as being better for the planet, not being reliant on a car enables you to do linear walks and these can be a lot more fun than the circular ones you have to do in order to get back to where you parked your car. For example, you can take a bus to somewhere, do your walk and come back on a different bus or train. You can do a far greater variety of walks this way. **www.ramblers.org.uk**

Get involved in footpaths week

Statistics from the Audit Commission on England's footpaths show that on average 31% of paths are difficult or impossible to use. This is a rise of 5% from 2000/1. If you want to make a difference to the accessibility of England's footpaths, take part in Footpaths Week on June 19-25 2004. Visit **www.ramblers.org.uk** or call 020 7339 8500.

A HEALTHY ATTITUDE

'*A wise man should consider that health is the greatest of human blessings*', according to the Greek physician Hippocrates, but how can you be healthy if your environment isn't? As a species we have been spectacularly successful, colonising the far reaches of the globe, but successful doesn't necessarily mean good.

For the individual, healthy living is mostly down to common sense and attitude, so think healthy, but think global. It's the health of our soils, rivers, forests and the very air we breathe that matters. Just one small action will make a difference.

GOOD VIBRATIONS

Healthier living

Humans are outdoor creatures, just like any other species. But we now spend at least 80% of our time indoors. The Environmental Protection Agency has found that outdoor air is often five times better and can be up to 100 times fresher than the stale air indoors. If you do spend a lot of time indoors, keep fresh air circulating. Studies have linked ill health – even cancers – to the quality of the air we breathe. So open the window and banish the musty air caused by a mix of fungi, bacteria, furnishings that give off carcinogenic chemicals and gas heaters and stoves that release carbon monoxide.

Eat fruit and vegetables every day

Eating 5 pieces of organic fruit or vegetables a day protects against coronary heart disease and some cancers, but people in the UK eat far less fruit and veg than other countries in Europe, and 1 in 5 kids in England eat less than one piece of fruit a week. Fruit and veg also provide essential minerals and vitamins, which are not available in other foods. Find out about Sustain's Grab 5 campaign at **www.sustainweb.org/grab5_index.asp**, 020 7837 1228, and if you have children, encourage their school to take part in Grab 5's activities such as breakfast clubs, playground markets and classroom games.

Go Barefoot

Your feet have a tough time of it. With each step you take, they absorb 3 times your body weight, so it's no wonder they like the chance to breathe. Going barefoot gives you a gentle foot massage, and because your feet contain thousands of nerve endings connected to different parts of your body, it keeps the rest of your body happy too.

Drink 2.5 litres of water a day

Our blood is 92% water, so if you're not drinking enough your complexion will look tired and dry: drink a litre of water a day and you'll be able to let your face speak for itself without foundation. But when you're exercising don't overdo it. Medical experts are increasingly concerned about the amount of water we consume during exercise – drinking too much can cause water intoxication, diluting the body's salts making people feel dizzy and, if serious, causing them to collapse. Drink a quarter of a pint of water for every hour of exercise you do.

KEEP IT CLEAN

Greener hygiene

Aggressive marketing shouts at us everywhere we look, promoting a supposedly cleaner lifestyle. However, the products we use to create this illusion of purity do so by damaging the environment we live in. This takes place at every stage of their life cycle – the manufacturing process pollutes, their usage gives off harmful chemicals into the atmosphere and when they are disposed of they are rarely recycled.

And getting dirty can be good for you! Scientists in Germany have recently discovered that children who grow up on farms are 50% less likely to suffer from hay fever, asthma and other allergies than kids who grow up in sanitised environments. This is because children who come into contact with dirt build up stronger immune systems, protecting them from illness later in life.

Buy recycled toilet paper

The average household uses 159 rolls – about three-quarters-of-a-mile of toilet paper per year. The amount of Andrex alone sold in a year is enough to wind round the M25 80,000 times. In Britain less than 10% of toilet paper is recycled - and while the paper may come from sustainably managed forests in Scandinavia, these forests are replacing ancient woodland that is home to thousands of endangered species.

Save the forests and use recycled toilet paper instead. It comes from office paper and wood pulp that has already been used at least once. It's nice and gentle too!

Take your shoes off!

Even the cleanest looking carpets can harbour a cocktail of toxic chemicals and pesticide concentrations brought in from outside off the soles of your shoes. When you whip round with a vacuum cleaner, most of these residues cling on tight to the carpet, building up over the years. Do yourself, your family and your pets a favour and leave your shoes at the front door.

Say no to aerosols

CFCs are no longer allowed to damage our environment but hydrocarbon propellants such as isobutane still do. Used in aerosols, they contribute to air pollution and are thought responsible for respiratory diseases. Say no to aerosols and use pump dispensers or roll-on alternatives instead.

Avoid deodorants containing aluminium

If you use a commercial deodorant, the chances are it has got aluminium in it. Daily exposure to aluminium can be harmful. When absorbed through the skin it can pass into the liver, kidneys, and brain, cartilage and bone marrow, increasing the risk of blood poisoning.

Aluminium-containing anti-perspirants can also block our pores and prevent us from sweating. A deodorant stone is a healthier alternative, based on natural mineral salts and free from aluminium chlorohydrate. Find out more from **www.deodorant–stone.co.uk**, or call 01666 826 515.

Switch to non-bleached sanitary products...

... a big step when we're used to the easy-to-use sanitary products on the shelves. Women have been convinced that bleached disposable pads and tampons are the only option and few consider the risks to their health. A woman can use up to 11,000 tampons in her lifetime, increasing exposure to dioxine, a chemical by-product of bleaching, linked to cancers and immune system depression. Tampons also have additives to increase absorbency such as surfactants, which may also pose health risks. Ask your doctor about the risks of toxic shock syndrome, which can be caused by tampons and opt for unbleached organic cotton pads and tampons, which are healthier for you and less damaging to the environment. For more information contact Spirit of nature at **www.spiritofnature.co.uk**, 0870 7250 9885 or FemCare Plus at **www.femininehygiene.com**

READER TIP – ESMAY SLATOR
Buy biodegradable or reusable hygiene products

Biodegradable sanitary products are kinder to the environment – they don't get flushed into the water system or pile up in landfills. Boots the Chemist offers a line of sanitary products that biodegrade within a month. Alternatively, you can avoid creating extra rubbish by opting for washable menstrual pads, available from The Carrying Kind at **http://pacificcoast.net/~manymoons** or call 0116 257 1897.

Choose safe toothpaste

Many commercial toothpastes contain polishing agents and whitening chemicals, which can be directly absorbed into the body through the teeth, the tongue and the gums. Sodium lauryl sulphate can irritate the skin and cause ulcers, while Triclosan, a synthetic anti-bacterial agent, has been linked to cancer, decreased fertility and immune suppression. Toms of Maine has a selection of natural toothpaste for sensitive teeth and gum disease with strawberry flavour for kids, **www.tomsofmaine.com**. Kingfisher sells natural toothpaste in lemon, mint and aloe vera flavour as well as toothpaste without fluoride, **www.kingfishertoothpaste.com**

Campaign for water coolers in schools

Dehydration affects health, well-being, performance and learning. Long terms risks include constipation, continence problems, kidney and urinary tract problems, and some cancers. A child should have 4-5 glasses of water a day at school, but access to drinking water in some schools is insufficient. Visit **www.wateriscoolinschool.org** to find out if your school has joined the campaign to ensure drinking water in school.

Use real handkerchiefs

Every person in the UK uses an average 215kg of paper or card a year. That's the equivalent of 426 cornflake boxes, or over 8 boxes per person per week. You can help reduce the amount of paper you use by switching from paper tissues to real handkerchiefs. Paper tissues come in a bewildering array of types, colours, textures, thicknesses and shapes, so using handkerchiefs will also reduce the energy and expense involved in their production and packaging.

A SPOONFUL OF SUGAR

Medicine that's good for the planet

The average Briton spends £137 on medicine per year. Much of it is necessary and life-enhancing, but all too often we seek short-term answers from our pills which can cause long-term problems. We need to make sure that our drive to make ourselves feel better not only does the job, but looks after the health of the planet too.

Support your local pharmacy

Supermarket pharmacy counters have threatened the future of 12,000 local pharmacies, which are essential to the well-being of a local community. Groups that will be particularly affected by their loss are the elderly, disabled and young mothers, who rely heavily on the free advice and range of services offered by local pharmacies. When the pharmacies go, you will have no choice but to go to the supermarket for medicines.

Alternative medicines

If you're stressed, can't sleep, or are simply feeling under the weather, try an alternative treatment before reaching for the pills or ringing the doctor. Homeopathy works by stimulating a person's immune system and resolving problems from within. People have turned to homeopathy for almost 200 years as a natural alternative and a specialised treatment. To find your local practitioner visit The Society of Homeopaths at **www.homeopathy.soh.org**

READER TIP – MELANIE DANIELS
Make your own everyday medicines

Be your own doctor when it comes to the simple needs of your body. Homemade natural remedies can often reduce or prevent symptoms. Tea Tree Oil is excellent to gargle with when you have a sore throat, or to massage on sunburnt skin and insect bites! A few drops of lavender oil on your pillow will help you sleep, and eucalyptus oil dabbed on a tissue will help clear out stuffy noses. Make sure your ingredients make suitable medicines and before experimenting consult a good book for expert advice. Check Herbal Safety News **www.mca.gov.uk/ourwork/licensingmeds /herbalmeds/herbalsafety.htm#john** if you are unsure of any ingredients. If you want to consult a professional, the National Institute of Medical Herbalists can provide you with a list of herbal medicine practitioners in your area. Visit **www.nimh.org.uk**

Chuck out old medicines

Open your bathroom cabinet, and chances are, you'll find some old medicine – an out-of-date painkiller or a nasal spray. Don't leave them lying around – medicines can be dangerous if they find their way into little hands – or flush them down the loo where they'll poison the water supply. Take them to your local pharmacist where they can be disposed of safely, without harm to others or the environment.

SKIN DEEP

Real beauty tips

*Women (and men!) can absorb up to two kilos of chemicals through toiletries and cosmetics each year. If you can reduce the amount of creams, moisturisers and make-up you use or switch to natural and organic products the benefits will be more than just skin-deep. Clear out your make-up bag, throw away the old products you haven't used and choose ones that are kind to your body as well as the environment. Visit **www.organicaj.co.uk** for details.*

When natural is not natural

A product that claims to be 'natural' may be far from it: the ingredients might have been natural at first, but by the time they reach your skin they may have been processed. In fact, for a commercial product to be called 'natural', it only has to consist of 1% of that natural product. Anita Roddick of the Body Shop has said that the marketing blurb on cosmetic labels often amounts to 'a scandalous lie'. Are you buying it? Find out more from Kim Erikson's book *Drop Dead Gorgeous*. Protecting yourself from the hidden danger of cosmetics and support the campaign to end the cosmetics cover-up. Details are available at the Women's Environmental Network **www.wen.org.uk**

Buy pure soap

We all need soap but we don't have to poison our world in the process! Commercial soaps often come bearing overpowering artificial scents and many layers of wrapping. Various brands of pure, organic soap are sold in health food shops and chemists, without additives and without wasteful packaging. Choose these over commercial brands.

Make up your own make-up

Many cosmetics are made in science laboratories from chemicals, which can cause harmful side effects, such as skin irritation and allergic reactions. But women have been making their own cosmetics for thousands of years – in ancient Greece women used harmless berries and seeds to create beautiful blushers. Check out **www.makeyourcosmetics.com** for recipes and information on ingredients that are kind to your skin. For tips on natural facemasks go to **www.womenexcel.com/ecowatch/ecobeautytips.htm** and for more general natural beauty products information visit **www.happyhippie.com/directory/beauty.htm**. For a more extensive selection of natural cosmetics tips and recipes check out *Natural Beauty at Home: More than 200 Easy-To-Use Recipes for Body, Bath, and Hair* by Janice Cox and *Recipes for Natural Beauty* (Neal's Yard Remedies) both available on **www.amazon.co.uk**

Use natural fragrances

An extravagant bottle of perfume could contain a mixture of 600 synthetic chemicals. Over 95% of chemicals are made from petroleum and many are designated hazardous. As an alternative use essential oils, plant extracts or aromatherapy oils which can be applied to the skin. Find out more from Culpeper at **www.culpeper.co.uk** or call 01223 891 196. A directory of aromatherapy suppliers and practitioners is available at **www.fragrant.demon.co.uk/ukaromas.html**

Choose your hair-dye carefully

You may be dying to colour your hair, but have you thought how the chemicals in the dye may harm you? Hair dye uses harsh chemicals – ammonia, peroxide, p-Phenylenediamine (PPD) or diaminobenzene, and repeatedly dyeing hair, especially dark brown or black, can increase the chances of developing some cancers, such as non-Hodgkin's lymphoma, multiple myeloma, and cancer of the bladder. Henna, made from the leaves of the desert shrub lawsonia is a safer alternative. It can also be customised using natural ingredients: coffee to darken, tea to lighten and apple cider vinegar to cover grey hairs. Your salon may also use natural alternatives. Visit **www.cfsan.fda.gov/~dms/cos-hdye.html** and **www.emagazine.com/july-august_2002/0702gl_consumer.html** for other suggestions.

Buy Phthalates-free products

Make sure you are not buying any products containing DBP (dibutyl phthalate) or any ingredients ending with -phthalates. Used in some makes of hair spray, perfume, body lotion, deodorant and nail varnish, animal studies have linked this chemical to damage to the lungs, liver, kidneys and the testes of unborn offspring. Manufacturers aren't required by law to list this product on their labels. To find out if the products you are using are safe visit **www.wen.org.uk** or **www.nottoopretty.org**. Recent studies have shown women aged 20-40 are especially at risk of multiple exposure from beauty products.

If a fragrance says 'musk' on the bottle, don't touch it!

Artificial musks are 'bioaccumulative': they build up in body fat, blood and breast milk, and in the environment. Other side effects can be headaches, dizziness, rashes and respiratory problems. Some are also hormone disrupters, interfering with the hormones, which regulate our daily bodily functions. They are found mainly in perfumes and cosmetics, but also in laundry detergents – to find out more, visit **www.foe.org.uk**, or call 020 7490 1555.

Boycott animal-tested beauty products

A label that says 'not tested on animals' is not always telling the whole truth. Just because the finished product hasn't been tested on animals, it doesn't mean that the *individual* ingredients haven't been tested on animals. Look out for the Humane Cosmetics Standard 'rabbit and stars' logo. It is an internationally recognised guarantee that the product has not been tested on animals at any stage. A full list of HCS approved products is available free from the British Union for the

Abolition of Vivisection. Visit **www.buav.org** or call 020 7700 4888.
Beauty without Cruelty can also send you a list of companies,
which produce cosmetics without causing harm to animals. Visit
www.bwcindia.com, or write to Beauty without Cruelty, 74 Oldfield
Road, Hampton, TW12 2HR or call 020 8979 8156.

Choose electric razors

Our obsession with smooth skin is having devastating effects on the
environment. Every day, Bic sells 10 million disposable razors, which
end up in landfill. Once there they don't biodegrade, and can even
release toxic chemicals into the ground, contaminating soil and water.
Avoid disposables and buy electric or traditional razors instead. And
when you are shaving, avoid foams, gels and depilatory creams that
contain alkylphenols and potassium thioglycolate. The former is a
hormone disrupter, while the latter is a derivative of thioglycolic acid,
which is listed in the US as a highly toxic material.

FOOD FOR THOUGHT

The pursuit of cheaper, readily available 'food for all' that began after WWII has been astonishingly successful and has led to us getting whatever we want, whenever we want – for which we ought to be truly grateful. It's what lies beneath that is a little less palatable. Methods of production range from unsavoury to cruel. Traditional British farming is on its knees as it no longer pays in this cost-cutting climate. Over-processing and lack of sensible eating is causing a frightening range of health problems – to the point that nutrition has now entered the political arena. Measures taken to counteract our slide into crisis are at best ineffectual: The words 'healthy food' are shamefully over-used by the food industry.

But it's not all bad. The response has been a flowering of the organic movement – according to the Soil Association 80% of British households now shop organic – and there are now 450 thriving farmers' markets with a turnover of over £1.5 million selling all kinds of produce from cheese to flowers.

As consumers we are in a position to make food a pleasure, both to eat and to produce. Exercise your choice and the whole world will be a healthier place!

GREEN GROCERIES

The world of food

The average item of food in a supermarket travels over 1,000 miles. Assisted by free trade, with no tax on aviation fuel, supermarkets transport food all round the world – Tesco lorries alone travel 224 million kilometres a year distributing food. Are the costs in transport emissions and packaging worth it?

One kilo of New Zealand apples accounts for its own weight in CO_2 transmissions by the time it arrives in the UK, while 10 litres of orange juice need 1 litre of fuel (for processing and transport) as well as 220 litres of water for irrigation and cleaning. The food in a typical Sunday lunch could have been transported 49,000 miles – equivalent to twice round the world – releasing 37 kilograms of carbon dioxide. Buying locally is one of the most important things you can do to improve the environment. Support local agricultural communities and avoid food miles. Find out more at **www.mcspotlight.org/media/reports/foodmiles.html**. *You can also visit* **www.soilassociation.org** *and Cultivating Communities at* **www.cuco.org.uk**

Protect children from junk food marketing

In the UK 9% of boys and 13.5% of girls are overweight. Between 1984 and 1994 the prevalence of obesity rose by 140%. Type II diabetes, closely associated with obesity and previously only found in adults, is also making an appearance in children. But despite these alarming figures, UK children face the heaviest onslaught from TV ads that market junk food directly to them. In 'TV Dinners', a report published in 2001, Sustain (The Alliance for Better Food and Farming) found that 95 to 99% of food advertising aimed at children was for fatty, sugary and salty food. Join the growing call to ban junk food ads aimed at children. For information on how you can help visit Sustain at **www.sustainweb.org/index.asp**

Grow your own

Don't buy it from a supermarket – grow your own! Home-grown food contributes to the reduction of CO_2 emissions caused by transporting food around the world, minimises packaging that ends up in landfill, composts green waste effectively, and enables you to try out a whole range of non-commercial organic varieties which challenges the supermarket mono-culture. Tending a garden also relieves stress, and reduces environmental pollution – particularly in cities. It can also be a great educational tool for children. Better still, it's cheap and the feeling you'll get when you see your first tomatoes on the vine, or apples on the tree will surpass any sugar high!

A slim chance

According to The Alliance for Better Food and Farming, 88% of slimming advertisements make claims which are in breach of the British code of Advertising and Sales Promotion put out by the Advertising Standards Authority. Watch the diet products you buy. Are their claims realistic or just hype?

Say no to GM crops

GM crops are now grown in 16 countries worldwide. Bio-tech companies insist on the benefits, claiming that they will significantly increase food production in areas of scarcity – such as Africa. GM crops are developed either to tolerate herbicides enabling farmers to use a broad spectrum herbicide that kills off every other plant in the field, or imprinted with a toxin that kills off pests that feed on the crop. But concerns about contamination of non-GM crops are mounting, as experience shows GM crops contaminate far more widely than the 50–100 metres the biotech companies claim. In 2000 British farmers were sold rape seed that had been contaminated by GM crops over 4 kilometres away. We can only speculate what could happen to disturb our ecosystem if wild plants or weeds were contaminated, as not enough research has been carried out. But if GM continues to contaminate, it will threaten organic farming and reduce consumer choice. Moreover, it will concentrate the world's food supply in the hands of 5 bio-tech companies, with one, Monsanto, owning 90% of the business.

To find out more visit Friends of the Earth at **www.foe.co.uk**. They will tell you whether your local council has declared itself a GM-free zone. Many councils have already – if yours hasn't, write to them to ask why.

'Beggars can't be choosers...'

... according to one US official approached over the policy of linking GM food aid with assistance for famine and HIV-inflicted countries in Africa. Many feel that food aid is being used as a marketing tool to force the African continent to accept GM food so that US agri-business giants can capture new markets. To date Zambia has succeeded in rejecting all GM crops, but both Mozambique and Zimbabwe were forced to accept milled GM corn – even though non-GM food was available. To find out more about GM food and food aid visit **www.farm.org.uk**

Support farmers

In 1991 the farm gate price for a kilo of potatoes was 9 pence and the retail price 30 pence – a mark up of 233%. In 2000, the farm gate price was still 9 pence a kilo but the retail price was 47 pence – an increase in the mark-up to 425%. Farmers can do little against the global profiteering of supermarkets – if they don't like the terms the supermarkets offer, the multinationals will simply source elsewhere. Farmers are forced to accept crippling farm gate prices or go out of business, and they are also frequently made to supply supermarkets without the security of contracts, to pay for food wasted in-store, packaging, in-store promotions and buyers' expenses.

As a result agriculture in the UK is in crisis. We are losing 11 farmers every day, largely because on average farmers earn £11,000 a year – compare that with Tesco's Chief Executive who was paid 2.8 million in 2003. Agricultural charities are paying out record amounts to farmers to help them make ends meet. To arrest this decline, support rural farmers and buy from farmers' markets, independent shops and market stalls. You'll be doing yourself a favour too – according to Sustain, fruit and vegetables are 30% cheaper bought this way. Farmers' markets provide good quality, locally grown produce, and by cutting out the middle man prices can be reduced by up to 40%. In just 5 years farmers' markets have multiplied – there are over 450 in the UK today. Contact the National Association of Farmers' Markets at **www.farmersmarket.net** to find the nearest one to you. You can also find out more about local foods from **www.cpre.org.uk**

Campaign for more responsible supermarkets

It's been estimated that the opening of a supermarket will result in the loss of 276 jobs in the area and the closure of all village shops within a 7 mile radius. Friends of the Earth is campaigning to hold supermarkets to account for their negative environmental and social impacts. Visit **www.foe.co.uk/campaigns/real_food/resource/retailers.html** to find out what they are doing.

Eat seasonal produce

All fruits and vegetables have seasonal lifecycles – vast amounts of land on the other side of the world have been deprived of growing the crops their people need, so that they can produce mange tout for our Sunday roasts and satsumas for our summers. Having given up their land to produce export crops, the farmers are then forced to spend the money they earn growing crops they don't eat, just to buy back the crops they once grew for free. Seasonal fruit and vegetables haven't been hanging around for a few months, they taste fresher, and they save on food miles and pollution. Find out more from **www.thefooddoctor.com**

Preserve biodiversity

Of all the 7,000 species of plant that are edible, only about 100 are considered essential to feed the global population! And 50% of the world's dietary energy comes from just four crops – rice, maize, wheat and potatoes.

We don't help our environment by eating in this limited way. Agricultural biodiversity sustains diverse ecosystems, maintains food security and promotes genetic diversity. But this is all threatened by industrialised agriculture production.

Annual seed fairs across Africa help to keep diversity alive, but more can be done to encourage diversity. Buy food that is specific to an area or country. Try to eat a wide variety and if you are growing food, plant a wide variety of seeds too. Also look out for rare types of food, such as purple carrots, and buy produce local to you. Visit **www.itdg.org/html/advocacy/web_of_life.htm** for more information. HDRA, the Henry Doubleday Research Association run a scheme to adopt a vegetable – visit **www.HDRA.org.uk/adopt.htm** to find out how you can help.

Avoid chocolates with lindane residues

Lindane is a dangerous pesticide that was banned for use in the UK in 2002. In the same year an 8-year-old girl died after swallowing a tiny amount of lindane in ant powder. Lindane is extremely hazardous to those who use it as well as those who are exposed to it – both in the environment and food. But it is still used in Africa especially in the cocoa industry and there may be remnants of it in your chocolate bar. Join the Ban Lindane Campaign – visit **www.pan-uk.org/banlindane**

Beastly genes

In a few years' time we could be eating salmon that has been genetically altered to grow at twice the rate it does normally, or sheep that have had medicine added to their genes. Is this safe? Environmentalists concerned about whether genetically modified animals may produce poisonous proteins, or the impact on wild animals if GM herds escape are battling against bio-tech companies who claim their products are safe, even though there is insufficient research to prove it.

Equally concerning are the efforts to clone animals – such as Genesis the cow cloned from the Dairy champion Zita in the USA. There are over 1,000 cloned farm animals in the USA and the agri-cloning lobby is eager to sell genetic material from them, which may mean we will be drinking cloned milk in the future. Cloned animals appear to be more susceptible to obesity and diabetes – so should we be concerned about drinking cloned cows milk? To find out more visit **www.organicconsumers.org/patent/clonedmilk720.cfm**

Avoid pesticides in food

A recent government study found that 1 in 3 pieces of fruit or vegetables contained pesticides. More than 300 different chemicals have been found in our bodies, but since there has been little research on the effect of such chemicals we don't know how they will affect us in the long term. Some chemicals known as hormone disrupters can interfere with hormones, while others accumulate within our bodies.

In many cases, washing or peeling the fruit or veg won't make a difference. If you're concerned, Friends of the Earth's campaign to phase out risky chemicals will give you all the information you need – and take a look at their 'risky chemicals supermarket league table'… Visit **www.foe.co.uk/campaigns/safer_chemicals**

Buy fair trade chocolate

We spend £700 million extra on chocolate at Christmas. In the last 10 years the price of cocoa beans has halved while the price of a bar of chocolate in the UK has increased by two-thirds – so it's definitely not the farmers who are making the extra money. The Day Chocolate Company, which makes 'Divine' and 'Dubble' chocolate bars, ensures that cocoa farmers are paid a fair price. In fact the cocoa bean farmers from Ghana own a one-third share of the company. Flavours include plain, milk, white and hazelnut. Chocoholics take note!

Buy fair trade food

Next time you shop, look out for the fair trade logo. Fair trade ensures producers in developing countries get fair prices for their goods. With fair trade 4.5 million growers and 500,000 workers across 36 countries are currently being paid a living wage for their produce. By buying fair trade products you can help more farmers to survive, and not put more dollars in middlemen's pockets.

The UK is the second largest consumer of fair trade produce in the world, we drink 1.7 million cups of fair trade tea, coffee and cocoa each day, and eat 15 million fair trade bananas a week. Find out more at **www.fairtrade.org.uk** or call them on 020 7405 5942.

Buy better bananas

The banana industry is dominated by five international companies whose operations are so huge they dwarf the export revenues of all the banana-producing countries combined. But few benefits are passed onto the plantation workers. On the contrary, the social and environmental cost of producing bananas is huge, and has brought misery to thousands. Indigenous people have been driven out of their lands to make way for new uncontaminated plantations, workers earn as little as US$1 a day in some countries, unions are banned and unionised labour blacklisted. Worse, thousands of tonnes of toxic pesticides have been poured on the plantations – often sprayed from planes overhead, drenching workers still in the fields. Currently 24,000 plantation workers are bringing a law-suit against the companies for a range of severe health problems including sterility and birth defects. To learn more, and find out where to buy fair trade bananas visit **www.bananalink.org.uk**

Go without meat for a week

Meat production consumes vast amounts of resources – 10,000 litres of water are needed just to produce one kilo of beef, compared with only 500 litres of water needed to produce one kilo of potatoes. The less meat we as a population eat, the better the conditions under which the animals are reared will become. Go without meat for a week and see how many other options there are. To make sure everything you eat is meat free, look for the vegetarian society logo, which guarantees food is free of animal products and genetically modified organisms. Visit **www.vegsoc.org** for details.

Also look out for the Vegan Society logo – this ensures products haven't been developed using animal products, by-products or derivatives. Visit **www.vegansociety.com** for details.

Be kind to animals

Did you know that a battery hen often has no more space to stand on than the size of an A4 sheet of paper? Or that a broiler chicken's muscles grow faster than their skeletons making it difficult to walk? Or that dairy cows are normally forced to give birth every year to keep them producing milk? Or that pigs are kept in such crowded conditions they often can't turn around? Or that animals often journey over 2,000 km to slaughter and their throats may be insufficiently cut to cause a quick and painless death. Support Compassion in World Farming. Visit **www.ciwf.co.uk** to find out more. And look for the Freedom Food scheme set up by the RSPCA, to ensure welfare standards are followed. Check out the RSPCA website for more details: **www.rspca.org.uk**

A fishy business

Globally, we eat 91 million tonnes of seafood a year and more than 200 million people depend on fishing for their livelihood. But our seas are being over-fished – of the world's commercial fishing stocks, 15% are over exploited and 10% are either severely depleted or recovering. Better managed fish stocks would contribute to better ecosystems. Don't buy fish unless you know it's been caught by environmentally responsible fisheries. You can also buy fish that has been caught using methods that don't harm dolphins or whales. Visit the Whale and Dolphin Conservation Society **www.wdcs.org** for more information.

NATURE'S WAY

Organic food

We often read that organic is better, but we often find that it's costlier too. Is it worth the hassle?

The answer is a definite yes. In order to be registered organic, a farmer is allowed to use only 7 natural pesticides on a restricted basis. Conventional farms, however, can use as many as 450 registered pesticides, as well as fertilisers. The full health implications of this vast range of chemicals lingering around our food are still being studied but it is now accepted that neurological disorders, a lowered sperm count, and certain cancers are caused by exposure to pesticides. The World Health Organisation estimates that 20,000 deaths are caused worldwide each year by pesticide exposure.

In addition, pesticides damage soil structure and destroy organisms living naturally within. They also disrupt the food chain. Pesticide contamination of drinking water supplies in the UK costs £120 million annually. For more information on pesticides visit **www.pan-uk.org**. *And for more information on how organically grown food benefits the environment visit HDRA, the Henry Doubleday Research Association, at* **www.hdra.org.uk**, *0247 630 3517. To learn more about how organic food can benefit you, visit* **www.organicfood.co.uk**

Choose one organic product to buy regularly

The more people demand organic products, the more farmers will decide to produce organic food and the cheaper they will become. Choose to buy one organic product such as milk, bread or eggs regularly. It's a good way of getting into the organic shopping routine.

Look at the labels

Although many shops, stores and supermarkets have organic sections for fruit and veg, other products, such as organic baked beans, may not be so easy to find. Look for the European Authority Certifying code number UK1, which means the food has met the organic standards laid down by the Government. The code UK5 means the product has met the more exacting standards of the Soil Association, which certifies 70% of UK organic food. For information on the many types of food labelling, see **www.foodstandards.gov.uk/foodlabelling** or contact the Soil Association **www.soilassociation.org**, 0117 929 0661. Check products' origins, too – if the item you want has been transported from the other side of the world and local alternatives exist, put it back and buy local.

Don't just eat organic, drink organic!

The alcoholic drinks industry uses as many pesticides as the food industry. Hops, for example, are sprayed 12-14 times a year with an average of 15 different pesticides. The sprays are intended to minimise weed growth in hop fields but they also kill off the wildlife living within them. Vinceremos Wines and Spirits **www.vinceremos.co.uk**, 0113 244 0002, deliver organic alcohol countrywide, as do several online organic food companies.

Join a box scheme

Box schemes and organic delivery companies save you the effort of searching out organic products – they deliver fresh local vegetables straight to your door. Box schemes source most of their produce from local farmers and consequently invest more into the local economy than supermarkets. There are over 350 box schemes in the UK. Visit **www.simplyorganic.net**, the **www.organicshop.co.uk**. If you live in London, contact Farmaround **www.farmaround.net** or the Organic Delivery Company **www.organicdelivery.co.uk**, 020 7739 8181.

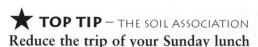

★ TOP TIP – THE SOIL ASSOCIATION

Reduce the trip of your Sunday lunch

The food in a typical Sunday lunch could have been transported 49,000 miles – equivalent to twice around the world – releasing 37 kilos of carbon dioxide. You can reduce food miles by buying local produce. To find out about your nearest box scheme, farmers' market, local farm shop or independent shop, visit the Organic Directory online **www.organicdirectory.co.uk**. Visit **www.soilassociation.org**, 0117 929 0661.

Turn Britain organic

The demand for organic food is high – almost 80% of households buy organic products, and the amount of land given over to organic production almost doubled between April 2001 and 2002. But although many more UK farmers want to convert to organic farming, many can't afford to without government assistance. As a result of this, 70% of organic food comes from abroad.

Join the Organic Targets Campaign and help turn Britain organic. In 2000 it was estimated that if 30% of the land was organic, 16,000 new jobs would be created, the bird population would increase by 10%, the butterfly population would increase by 25%, and 11.5 million hectares of arable land would no longer be sprayed with pesticides. Contact **www.sustainweb.org** to add your voice, or call 020 7837 1228.

Save seeds with Greenpeace

Proposed amendments to the EU's Seed Directives would allow GM contamination of seeds by thresholds of 0.3-0.7% without labelling them as genetically modified. But Greenpeace and other organisations feel that any detectable GM contamination is unacceptable, and are arguing for 'zero tolerance'. Support this campaign by logging onto **www.saveourseeds.org** and signing the online petition.

HINTS FOR THE HOB

Greener cooking

*Life used to revolve around the kitchen. Now we often rush in, pop a
pre-prepared meal in the microwave, wolf it down and then hurry off
to the rest of the day's activities.*

*Taking the time out to cook not only creates a peaceful and relaxing
interlude in the day, which you can share with other people, but it
means you can eat better too. It enables you to select ingredients,
which are locally produced where possible, and which you know
haven't been processed.*

KIDS – Get cooking

Next time you go to a birthday party, how about taking some biscuits
you've made? If you just learn to cook one dish a month, in a year's
time you'll have 12 different dishes you can prepare for your friends
and family.

Plan your meals and save

When you cook, plan ahead so everything is in the oven at the
same time. Where possible, cook things in the oven rather than over
the hob; oven cooking is more efficient because the heat stays in
the oven. And if you can, avoid opening the door to take a sneaky
peek. Every time you do, the blast of cold air from the kitchen can
cause the temperature in the oven to drop by as much as 24°C. Then

the cooker needs to use more energy to bring the oven back to its original temperature. Instead, be satisfied and look through the door.

Buy a pressure cooker

Improve energy efficiency by investing in a pressure cooker. They're not just easier to use, they can decrease cooking times by one-third. Pressure cookers can be used for meats, beans, fruits and vegetables, and they have greater vitamin preservation than ordinary cooking, which makes them a great choice for today's healthier lifestyle.

READER TIP – GAVIN BUTTERWORTH
Conserve water when you cook

When cooking vegetables or pasta on the hob, don't overfill the pan with water and always use a pan with a lid. This way, the water doesn't vapourise into steam and it cooks more efficiently, heating the whole pan rather than just the bottom – so you use less energy. If you're boiling meat or vegetables, don't throw the water out, use it to flavour soups, gravies and jus. Alternatively, steam vegetables – you'll use less water, and conserve vitamins.

Invest in a slow cooker

A slow cooker uses little more electricity than a light bulb – and makes delicious slow cooked energy-efficient meals.

Take your time!

The SlowFood campaign started in Italy, and spread all over the world, with 77,000 members in 48 different countries. SlowFood is a movement that tries to bring the pleasure back to eating by taking your time. That doesn't just include the time involved in cooking and eating the food, but also in growing and preparing it – giving the control over what we eat back to us! And with slowness comes diversity.

Mass production means we have less choice. For instance, in Italy in 1900 there were 200 species of artichoke, but now there are only a dozen. The SlowFood movement is a reaction against this reduction of variety. For more information on SlowFood initiatives all round the world, visit **www.slowfood.com**

READER TIPS – ANDREW FISHER
Release the heat

When you've finished using the oven in the wintertime and turned it off, leave the oven door open to allow the remaining warmth into the room. This saves having to switch on the central heating for some time, as the extra heat keeps the room nice and warm.

Steam and save

If you're boiling pasta or rice, and you want to steam some veg, remove the saucepan lid, place your vegetables in a colander on top of the saucepan, and put the saucepan lid back over the vegetables. This works just like a steamer, but saves plugging in an extra electric gadget.

Peel before you cook

Friends of the Earth estimates that half of all UK fruit and vegetables sold contain pesticide residues, some of which can accumulate in our bodies and harm our hormone systems. Recent pesticide studies have revealed that pesticides found in unpeeled potatoes can exceed the safety level for toddlers by a staggering 21 times! So when you're preparing fruit and vegetables for children, make sure you peel them first.

Organic advice

To encourage your kids to eat organic food, **www.organics.org** has recipes and a Kids' Club.

If you're searching for gluten-free products and recipes visit **www.dovesfarm.co.uk**. Alternatively, to learn more about organic food in general visit **www.greencuisine.org** where you'll find details of organic cooking courses on the Welsh borders.

FINE DINING

Eating out

There's little more frustrating than having to compromise your organic standards when you eat out. You can search for organic restaurants and pubs in your area by visiting **www.gustoguide.co.uk**, *or* **www.aboutorganics.co.uk,** *01386 871 384. The Organic Directory also has details of organic restaurants throughout the country; visit* **www.theorganicdirectory.co.uk**

Choose cod and tuna carefully

Since 1972 there has been a seven-fold increase in tuna catches in the South Pacific and, since the price of tuna is so high, a dramatic increase in the incidence of illegal fishing. Bluefin tuna is now listed on the WWF Endangered Seas Campaigns needing immediate action to avoid extinction. Cut down on your tuna consumption, especially in Japanese sushi bars, where raw bluefin is a speciality.

And it's not just tuna that's under threat. Cod and chips could be off the menu too unless cod consumption is restricted. A recent warning from the International Council for the Exploration of the Sea says UK cod stocks are so low that fishing should be suspended indefinitely or until stocks recover, and that may take several years.

Choose your fish carefully. When you're eating out, ask where the fish is sourced from. If buying fish to cook at home, consult your local fishmonger or choose environmentally friendly brands such as Fish4Ever, sustainably-fished tuna (and the only sustainable tinned fish on sale in the UK) available from Organico **www.organico.co.uk**

Does your restaurant recycle?

Britain's pubs, restaurants and hotels use about 350,000 tonnes of glass each year, and 80% of this goes to landfill. Ask if your local café or restaurant recycles its glass and, if not, find out why. If it's because the local collection schemes are inadequate, suggest that they team up with other restaurants to lobby the council to set up a better scheme. Visit **www.wasteconnect.co.uk** to find out about the schemes that are currently available.

Support restaurants with small menus

The larger the menu, the more likely it is that more food will go to waste each day because the restaurant has to have a greater number of foodstuffs ready for consumption. If choosing between eateries, go for the one with the smaller menu. While you're choosing restaurants, try too to eat in an independent restaurant or café. You'll help preserve the individual nature of your community, and support local people.

Visit McSpotlight

2003 was a bad year for McDonalds, with dwindling profits and outlets closing, but there have been other setbacks too. First, scientists declared food high in fat and sugar to be as dangerously addictive as tobacco – paving the way for more obesity lawsuits against the company; then a policeman was hospitalised after glass was found in his burger; a restaurant was shut in Buenos Aires after bacteria was found in food samples – the second time this year; an outlet in Greece was set on fire by anti-capitalist marchers; a man in America claimed he found chewing gum in his salad; and residents have successfully campaigned against having new McDonalds outlets in the UK, the USA and Australia. In 2002 the company were forced to pay out US $6.85 million to Hindu and vegetarian groups after meat flavouring was found in 'vegetarian' fries. Find out more about the activities of the global hamburger giant that everyone loves to hate. Visit **www.mcspotlight.org**

CHEERS!

Better ways to drink

While water used to be the only drink available – and still is in most parts of the world – many of us are now substituting it with fizz – flavoured, coloured and in fancy packaging. They may keep our taste buds happy but not our bodies, the environment or local economies.

Two companies control 77% of the soft drinks market: Coca-Cola and PepsiCo. They have swept their way through the developing world flooding the market of locally produced drinks and replacing healthier drinks in children's diets. Coke's active ingredient is phosphoric acid, which can dissolve a T-bone steak in two days, or a nail in four.

Back in 1969, 54% of babies who were hospitalised for malnourishment in Ndolo in Zambia had the diagnosis 'Fantababy' written at the food of their beds. Their parents had fed them Coke and Fanta believing it to be the best drink for their children – a problem reflected all across the developing world. The chairman of Coca-Cola is on record as saying: 'The only business we don't want, is the business that does not exist.' Do you want to drink to his health?

Tap is top!

Bottled water isn't better and it costs us and the environment more, too.

In 1997 the Food and Agricultural Organisation said that bottled water was not any cleaner or more nutritious than ordinary tap water. Bottled water costs twice as much as petrol, 3 times as much as milk and 10,000 times as much as tap water. Add to that the 1.5 million tonnes of plastic used every year to make water bottles – each of which could take untold years to biodegrade. And when you think that water companies pay nothing to extract water, while 1.1 billion people are living without adequate water supplies – doesn't it make you want to turn on the tap again?

Not worth a bean

In 1992 the global coffee economy was worth US$30 billion –
US$8 billion of which went to producers. In 2002 the global market
had risen to US$50 billion, while producers only received US$8 billion
– a drop of 24%. In fact the farm gate prices of tea, coffee
and cocoa have not risen in real terms for 40 years. Moreover the
international prices of these products are so low that frequently they
fall below the cost of producing them, forcing farmers into a spiral of
debt and destitution.

At the same time coffee companies make huge profits – between
1997 and 2000 Starbucks' profits tripled to 181 million. Buying
fair trade coffee, tea and cocoa will ensure that the producers are
paid a living wage. At the moment fair trade schemes only account
for about 1% of the market, although they are now widely
available. For more information visit the Fairtrade Foundation
www.fairtrade.org.uk or **www.cafedirect.co.uk,** or contact Oxfam
www.oxfam.org.uk/fairtrad/food.html or call 0870 333 2700.

Use a thermos

Make coffee in a thermos flask. This will save you boiling the kettle
every time you need a drink.

Make your own

Squeeze your own fruit juices and invent flavours never experienced
before. Make your own lemonade. By using locally grown, organic
fruits you can make a drink that's cheaper, healthier and much,
much tastier than any you can buy.

Rip up the plastic ring holders from beer cans

If these rings get into the sea or other ecosystems they pose a
real danger to wildlife. Animals can get their heads caught in the
near-invisible rings, and they either choke or starve to death. Small
birds can get their wings trapped, and larger aquatic birds can catch

the rings around their bills when they dive for food. So, get ripping and do your bit for wildlife.

Choose wines with natural corks

Between 5% and 8% of wine becomes corked when sealed with a traditional cork stopper and the wine industry has increasingly turned towards plastic corks in an effort to improve quality. But the move away from traditional corks is having devastating effects on the unique habitat of the oak cork woodlands in Spain and Portugal. Falling demand has meant forest owners are increasingly turning to more profitable but less environmentally friendly methods of agriculture and the wildlife is suffering. The forests are home to the critically endangered Iberian Lynx – an estimated 150 remain in the wild of which only 30 are breeding females. Visit **www.sos-lynx.org**

For centuries cork stoppers have been an effective, environmentally friendly method of corking wine – why change to plastic with its associated health concerns and problems of disposal?

Support local breweries and pubs

In the UK we consume an average 95 litres of beer per person per year, but 83% of it comes from just four multinational brewing companies. The ingredients in a locally produced beer might travel a total distance of 600 miles during production, but beer from a large brewery can be transported as many as 24,000 miles, belching out CO_2 all along the way. In addition, small breweries suffer from having to pay the same level of duty on alcohol as large ones, so their production costs are higher making it harder for them to survive.

In Germany, a Progressive Beer Duty system to help smaller breweries has been operating for a number of years, and in the UK the Society of Independent Brewers is trying to impose a similar duty. For more information see **www.siba.co.uk** or call 01845 565614. The Campaign for Real Ale also has details on supporting small breweries in order to stimulate local economies. Visit **www.camra.org.uk** or call 01727-867201 for more information.

Get milk delivered in bottles

Get your milk delivered in bottles. Unlike plastic bottles and cartons
from corner shops and supermarkets, bottles are used up to 60 times
before being recycled. Each time a bottle is reused, the energy used to
make a new one is saved – so by changing you can help reduce the
amount of CO_2 released into the environment too!

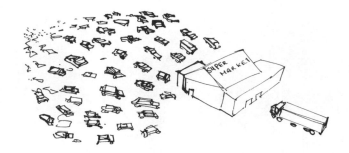

RESPONSIBLE TRAVEL

Tourism accounts for as much as 4% of the world economy. In 2002 almost 700 million people travelled worldwide, and according to research by the UK charity Tearfund, that figure is expected to double in the next 20 years. With CO_2 emissions, airport expansion issues, archaeological damage and threats to world ecology in the news, critics might argue that the only green traveller is the one that stays at home. However, the industry provides income, jobs and foreign exchange to countries and communities that badly need them, and can make a difference in other areas, too. Many developing countries, for example, can't afford the luxury of conservation funding. Without tourists – and the money they bring – many national parks would probably cease to exist. So get out there and travel – but travel thoughtfully. Think about where you go, and what you do when you get there. Plenty of organisations can offer you help and advice – the online travel company **www.responsibletravel.com** provides holidays that give the world a break; and the charities Tourism Concern **www.tourismconcern.org.uk**, 020 7753 3330 and Tearfund **www.tearfund.org**, give up-to-date information.

DO NOT DISTURB

Hotels that don't harm the planet

*It is estimated that five million people worldwide opt for all-inclusive holidays each year. In some destinations, such as the Bahamas, all-inclusive holidays account for up to 80% of UK bookings, and the sector is growing at a rate of 22% per year. But tourists in these resorts spend very little money outside the resorts, making them exclusive, rather than inclusive, for the local economy. Such resorts also swallow up large areas of land, often in the most beautiful parts of the country, restricting access for local people. So think before you book – your holiday should benefit you, but it's best if it benefits local people **and** the environment at the same time.*

Always think local

Of each US$100 spent on a holiday in a developing country by a tourist, only around US$5 actually stays in the country's economy. This 'leakage' may be as high as 80% in the Caribbean, with money spent by tourists leaving the countries via tour operators, airlines, hotels, and imported food and drink. Always use local tour operators, stay in locally run hotels, and only buy locally produced goods. The Special Places to Stay series by Alastair Sawdays provides travel choices across Britain and Europe that emphasise local food and environmental and social awareness. For more information, visit **www.sawdays.co.uk** or call 01275 464 891. For holidays further afield visit Conservation Corporation Africa at **www.ccafrica.com**.

No change

The majority of hotel guests are willing to use their sheets and towels for more than one day. The largest chunk of a hotel's energy use – 42% – is for heating water, and much of this goes on laundry operations. If each room had a sign for guests to leave out for the chambermaid requesting that they don't change sheets or towels, it's estimated hotels would reduce their energy use by at least 5%. If the hotel you're staying in doesn't have a 'no change' policy, try writing your own no change request note.

Don't use the freebie minis

Mini they might be, but the impact on the environment is far from small. The production of mini bottles and containers causes significant waste of resources and energy. Hotels could save on thousands of bags of waste each year by using refillable dispensers for shampoo and skincare lotions, and by recycling soaps.

Look out for the Green Globe sign

Green Globe 21 is the travel and tourism industry's only global environmental programme. Initiated by the World Travel and Tourism Council, it is based on Agenda 21 and principles for sustainable development agreed at the Rio Earth Summit in 1992. The programme gives certification to hotels, airlines and travel agents that meet their standards for the responsible and sustainable development of world tourism. For more information on the Green Globe members in over 100 countries, view **www.greenglobe21.com**

 TOP TIP – WWW.RESPONSIBLETRAVEL.COM

Ask your tour company or hotel for their written policies with regard to the environment and local people. If they don't have one, ask them why not. For some of the world's best responsible and ecotourism holidays from tour companies and hotels with responsible travel policies visit **www.responsibletravel.com**

Take an organic holiday

Both in the UK and abroad, there is an increasing number of organic hotels, guesthouses and B&Bs which provide organic venues for catered and self-catered holidays or short breaks. With their organic lifestyle standards, not only would you be eating healthier, but you would also be supporting the local areas' businesses and economy. For more ideas, and a list of organic holiday destinations in Britain and worldwide, visit **www.organic-holidays.com** or call 01943 870 791. For information on holidays just in the UK, try About Organics at **www.aboutorganics.co.uk/organic_holidays**

Hostel it!

Hostelling has moved on – it's no longer just about dormitories and boy scouts. Today, many hostels are not unlike budget hotels where the only significant difference is the price. For the biggest hostel database on the internet, visit **www.hostels.com**. As well as offering online booking, the site gives in-depth advice on what makes a good hostel.

Save water

Conserve water when you're in areas with limited supply. When abroad, the average tourist can use over 800 litres of water in 24 hours. That's more than a villager in the Developing World would use in 100 days. Encourage hotels to become water efficient by harvesting rainwater, fixing leaks, and switching to low-flow showerheads, sink aerators and toilets. Installing inexpensive tank-fill diverters in older toilets can save 4 litres of water on each flush. British tour operators take note!

BROADEN THE MIND

Tips for the eco-traveller

'Tourism' is derived from the Hebrew word 'Tora' meaning to study. Travelling shouldn't just take us to see new horizons, but should also expand them. Do a bit of background reading on the places you plan to visit, and always remember that your holiday destination – no matter how remote – is someone else's home.

Use small, location-specific tour operators

Around 80% of British package holidays are booked through the big tour operators. With a tendency to undercut prices and use mass-purchased, imported goods, they may destroy the livelihood of local hotel owners and tour operators. Instead, use small, location-specific travel operators that either serve a specific market, or cater to a specific interest group or activity. Visit **www.responsibletravel.com** for a comprehensive list of eco-aware operators.

Offset your carbon

Each year, aviation produces nearly as much CO_2 as is produced by all human activities in Africa. One long-haul return flight can produce more CO_2 per passenger than the average UK motorist produces in a year. As a result, scientists have predicted that, by 2015, over half the annual destruction of the ozone layer will be caused by air travel. If you're travelling from Luton airport, pay your voluntary tax of 0.2p per mile. This helps fund a tree-planting programme around the town, to soak up carbon emissions pumped out from the planes. For more information on how to join tree-planting schemes to offset your carbon emissions and become carbon neutral, visit **www.futureforests.com**

READER TIP – LOUISA RADICE
Avoid air travel for short journeys

Over distances of less than 500km, air travel generates around three times more CO_2 per passenger than rail. For alternatives to air travel, check out The Man in Seat 61 **www.seat61.com** for information on how to travel to destinations in Europe, Africa, Asia and America by train and boat.

Calculate the real cost

For more information on aircraft emissions, and to work out the greenhouse warming effect of any flight, visit **www.chooseclimate.org**

Walk, bike or take the bus

When you travel, try to use public transport whenever possible – or better still, walk or hire a bike. You'll see your destination in a completely different light.

 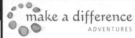

Leave nature where it is

Natural souvenirs made of wood, coral, shell or ivory can be tarnished with environmental damage. Plant and tree life is also under threat from the souvenir trade. Between May 2002 and April 2003, 419 seizures were made by customs officials under legislation relating to the Convention on International Trade in Endangered Species (CITES), many of them live animals, others animal and plant products. So buy your souvenirs with a critical eye!

Dive responsibly

Coral reefs are the foundation of marine life and possess extremely high levels of biodiversity. For example, the Great Barrier Reef in Australia is home to more than 400 species of coral, 1,500 species of fish, 4,000 types of mollusc and 200 species of birdlife. Yet all over the world reefs are dead or dying. Already 10% have been lost, and it is estimated that 70% of all corals will disappear by 2040 unless they are properly protected. When you go on diving holidays, you can reduce the tourist pressures on reefs by following a diving code of practice. This includes not touching the corals or sea life, not removing anything you didn't bring with you, being careful not to brush against the reefs and watching where you kick with your fins. For more information, visit **www.responsibletravel.com**. Also, consider booking an eco-friendly diving holiday, such as those run by Baobab Travel **www.baobabtravel.com**, 0870 382 5003.

 TOP TIP – TOURISM CONCERN
Stop child sex tourism

Large numbers of children from countries such as China, Cambodia and Burma are being forced to work as prostitutes in China. More than a million children aged 7-17 enter the sex trade each year, and many end up in brothels frequented by sex tourists. You can help by not turning a blind eye – if you see anything suspicious when abroad, tell your hotel or guesthouse manager immediately. For more information on the fight against sex tourism, contact HM Customs and Excise at **www.hmce.gov.uk**, 0845 010 9000 or Tourism Concern at **www.tourismconcern.org.uk**, 020 7753 3330.

Spend culturally

Local and traditional values are being subsumed by globalisation. When travelling abroad, be sure to eat in local restaurants and buy local produce. You'll support not only the regional economy and culture, but also provide counterweight to the growing influence of the multinationals.

 TOP TIP – TOURISM CONCERN
Respect the local cultures

When you travel, give consideration to the fact that you're often going into a culture completely different from your own. If you think carefully about what is appropriate in terms of the clothes you wear and the way you behave, then you'll be more welcomed and respected by the local people. Drug and alcohol laws can vary in different countries, and the effects of travellers taking drugs can be dramatic. For example, if travellers take drugs when visiting the hill tribes of Thailand, it encourages the local people to start selling drugs and then become addicted themselves. This is especially true of the younger people, who are keen to emulate western tourists. The result can devastate local communities, so think before you act. For more information, contact Tourism Concern at **www.tourismconcern.org.uk**, 020 7753 3330.

 TOP TIP – WWW.RESPONSIBLETRAVEL.COM
Use local guides

You will get an amazing insight into local cultures and places, and they will get an income. Agree a fair price BEFORE you set off, and remember that in developing countries what is a little to you might help feed or educate their families.

'Take only photographs, leave only footprints'

As a tourist, you are directly responsible for the environment in the places that you visit. So, if you notice environmental damage, be sure to report it to local tour operators, and if you booked through an operator in the UK tell them on your return. Ethical tourism organisations publish their own Travellers' Codes of Conduct for you to follow. Familiarise yourself with them, and try and follow them wherever you go.

Travel to work

Want a working holiday? The National Trust organises them, and has many other volunteer positions on offer. For more information visit **www.nationaltrust.org.uk/volunteering**. And if you want a real cultural experience, consider taking a course in Teaching English as a Foreign Language (TEFL). With opportunities to teach in places such as Indonesia, China and Turkey, you can really get to know the place and the people. Courses are easily organised through the TEFL website **www.tefl.com**

Exchange it

Exchange programmes involve staying with a family in your chosen country, while someone from the exchange family comes to live with yours. Under the ERASMUS scheme, undergraduates from the UK can study in another EU state for 3-12 months, giving them the opportunity to learn a new language, experience a new culture, and gain a new perspective on their study course. Have a look at **www.studystay.com/htm/Courses/Exchange_programs.htm** for more information.

Porters' rights

When enjoying your adventure holidays abroad, don't neglect the importance of fair trade in tourism. Porters are an essential part of trekking in the Himalayas, Peru and Pakistan, but their working conditions are often appalling. Nepalese porters suffer four times as many accidents and illnesses as western trekkers, and in the UK the majority of operators are not addressing the issues of porters' rights. They are not superhuman, and cannot carry heavy loads improperly dressed and shod. So, if you're going on holiday, check that your tour operator has policies on porters. Find out more at **www.tourismconcern.org.uk/campaigns**

Malaria control

When you travel to malarial areas, don't rely solely on insect repellent. Use it in combination with other less environmentally harmful methods to gain better overall protection. Cover up in the morning and evenings when mosquitoes bite, and wear dark clothes. Sleep under a mosquito net during the night and if you're roughing it make sure you aren't sleeping near stagnant water or banana trees where mosquitoes like to breed.

 TOP TIP – TOURISM CONCERN
Minimise your environmental impact

When you're abroad, give extra thought to what happens to your rubbish. Try to take biodegradable products and a water filter bottle with you when you go out. Some places can often have limited water, fuel and electricity resources, so be sensitive and restrict your use of these. Protect the local wildlife and habitats by respecting local rules and codes of conduct, such as keeping to footpaths, not touching coral and not buying products made from endangered species. By following these simple rules, you can reduce your ecological footprint and your negative impact on the areas you visit. For more information, contact Tourism Concern at **www.tourismconcern.org.uk**, 020 7753 3330.

 **TOP TIP** – BTCV
Take a conservation break

Try a holiday with a difference and have the experience of a lifetime! By taking part in practical hands-on conservation projects either in the UK or around the world you can do your bit to contribute to a sustainable future. You can also benefit from some stunning scenery, a sense of achievement and a new bunch of friends! BTCV organises holidays from taster conservation weekends in rugged North Yorkshire to 6-week bird census and beach survey holidays in the Caribbean. Visit **www.btcv.org** or contact customer services on 01302 572244.

A WHEEL EFFECT

With global warming currently the greatest environmental threat, our streets grid-locked, choking pollution and road traffic predicted to increase by up to 50% in 2025, there has never been more reason to abandon your car and walk. Road transport is currently the third largest source of carbon dioxide emissions in the UK, which is directly contributing to the earth's increasing temperature. And as if global warming was not enough reason to leave the car in the garage, up to a fifth of all lung cancer deaths in cities are caused by tiny particles of pollution; the majority of which are from vehicle exhausts. The convenience of car travel also means that the population is increasingly suffering from health issues. A 10% increase in the number of people walking regularly would lead to a 4% reduction in the numbers of people with heart disease, thereby saving the NHS £200 million a year.

REVERSING THE TREND

Cars and the planet

Current studies show that 71% of road trips by motor are under five miles and 46% are less than two miles. So, the best thing you can do for the environment – and for yourself – is to leave those car keys at home. However, if you do need to get into your car, there are all sorts of ways to make that journey less damaging.

Take public transport

Traffic delays cost the country around £15 billion each year. One litre of fuel can carry a person 4 miles in a large car, 5.5 miles in a small car, 31 miles in a bus with 40 passengers and 34 miles in a train with 300 passengers. A double-decker bus can carry the same number of people as 20 full cars, yet takes up just one seventh of the road-space.

 **TOP TIP** – THE ENVIRONMENTAL TRANSPORT ASSOCIATION

National Car Free Day

Sacrifice your car on September 22nd for the European National Car Free Day – you might just be surprised at how easy it can be! In 2002, the Car Free attracted over 1,300 participating cities across the world, and more than 40 local authorities across Britain closed town centre streets to cars and lorries and opened them up for people to enjoy walking, cycling and dancing. Visit **www.eta.co.uk** for further information on alternative eco-friendly transport solutions.

Join a car-sharing pool

Every day more than 10 million empty seats clog the roads, with one-person car trips accounting for 60% of all journeys. If just half of all UK motorists received a lift one day a week, congestion and pollution would be reduced by 10% and traffic jams by 20%. There are other benefits, too. The air quality is often poorer inside the car than out, especially in heavy traffic, and car users regularly suffer up to 3 times as much pollution than pedestrians. Lift sharing also contributes to social inclusion, helping many socially excluded people access facilities such as healthcare, shops or social activities. Visit **www.carclubs.org.uk**, 01132 349 299 and **www.liftshare.org**

Choose a low-impact vehicle

In a journey of 6,000 miles, the average car produces its own weight in carbon dioxide emissions. And it's not just CO_2 that's the problem – other exhaust emissions, oil and noise also create pollution. You can help by buying a car which has the fewest environmental impacts and is the most fuel-efficient. For a guide to cars, contact the Environmental Transport Association (**www.eta.org.uk** or call 01932 828 882) and visit **www.vcacarfueldaa.org.uk** to help you find out your car's pollution emission and help you to choose a better car in the future.

Get a lift

If you're heading off on a long journey with space in your car, offer that space to someone who needs it. Freewheelers links drivers and passengers to share the cost of travel. It saves you money, helps other people and reduces pollution. Visit **www.freewheelers.com** to search an online database of people offering or requiring lifts. Hook up with people travelling to work, festivals, gigs and sporting events.

Choose your fuel wisely

Air pollution as a result of traffic fumes is a serious problem in Britain. Three times as many people in Europe die from the health-damaging effects of vehicle emissions as die in road accidents. Although leaded petrol has now been banned, exhaust fumes still contain carbon monoxide, nitrous oxides, benzene and particulates – minute particles of matter – that can negatively impact on human health. Benzene, which accounts for 5% of the output of a car, is a known cause of leukaemia, while nitrous oxides are respiratory tract irritants that can cause emphysema. You can help by buying ultra low sulphur petrol where possible, which produces 45% less nitrogen oxide and is lower in benzene. Finally, join *Ethical Consumer* magazine's campaign to boycott Esso. Esso is the oil company most strongly involved in the Bush administration's anti-environmental policies, and the StopEsso boycott aims to stop the company through consumer action. Visit **www.ethicalconsumer.org** for more information.

Fit a fuel saver – cut emissions by 40%

Simply fitting a fuel-saving device into the fuel line that feeds your car engine can reduce harmful emissions by 40% saving you at least 10% on fuel costs. Devices can be easily fitted to any hydro-carbon fuelled vehicles or energy-efficient cars, and will last for ever. They can even be transferred from vehicle to vehicle, so no excuses! For information on fuel savers, visit **www.powerplus.be** (01323 417 700) or **www.ecotekplc.com**. And more good news – the less your car pollutes, the less car tax you pay. Brand new fuel-efficient cars, and existing cars with engines up to 1200cc pay a special lower rate.

More haste – less speed

Stick to the speed limit! Rapid acceleration and harsh braking leads to greater fuel consumption; smooth driving can use 30% less fuel and makes for a more pleasant journey. Driving at 50mph uses 25% less fuel than 70mph, so improve your efficiency and decrease your speed.

Go electric

Become a green driver and make your friends green with envy. It costs from £7-10,000 to convert a small local runabout and £20-35,000 for a car that travels over 100 miles. Visit the Electric Car Association on **www.avt.uk.com**, or call 01823 480 196 for details. Alternatively, hybrid cars (run on petrol and electricity) produce 75% less pollution than standard ultra-low-emission vehicles, and they can be charged in the comfort of your own home; simple! The Environmental Transport Association has a car buyers' guide full of data for various models, and is the only company involved in the scheme. Visit **www.eta.co.uk** or call the ETA on 01932 828 882.

 **TOP TIP** – UNIT[E]
No local emissions – no global emissions!

Buy an electric vehicle and power it with renewable power. And in London's Westminster area you'll get no parking charges, no road tax and no congestion charges. Make a difference and lobby your local authority to provide charging bays for electric vehicles. Visit Scoot Electric Ltd **www.scootelectric.co.uk**. For more information on renewable power, visit **www.unit-e.co.uk**

Recycle used motor oil

Every year, 13,000 tonnes of car oil are improperly discarded, contaminating the country's rivers, lakes and streams and threatening aquatic life. The toxic metals contained in oil such as lead, nickel and cadmium can poison the soil and lead to infertility and poor crop yields. Used oil which has been properly handled can be easily re-refined into lubricants, processed into fuel oils and used as raw materials for the refining and petrochemical industries. Many petrol stations or recycling depots will recover your oil for you. For details on schemes near you contact the Oil Bank on 0800 663 366 **www.oilbankline.org.uk**. Find out more from the Environment Agency's Oil Care Code campaign **www.environment-agency.gov.uk**

★ **TOP TIP** – GREENPEACE
Don't buy Esso!

The Stop Esso campaign is calling on the public not to buy any Esso products until the company changes its stand on global warming and stops interfering in international negotiations to tackle climate change. Join over 1 million people in the UK who are boycotting the world's biggest climate villain. StopEsso is a coalition of Greenpeace, Friends of the Earth and People and Planet. To find out how you can join the boycott visit **www.stopesso.com**

Don't leave it idling!

As well as wasting fuel and costing you money, idling also prevents the catalytic converter from working efficiently and removing pollution in the exhaust. Idling also creates noise pollution; you may not be aware of it but others certainly will be!

More car don'ts...

Don't use the A/C!

Why use the air conditioning, open the car's air vents instead?

Don't open windows unless you need to!

Opening windows just increases wind resistance and thus efficiency.

Don't buy enormous cars!

Just buy the smallest car that fits your needs.

Don't neglect your car!

Old plugs, leads on their last legs and clogged cleaners are the main culprits for lost gallons with modern fuel injected systems.

 **TOP TIP** – FORUM FOR THE FUTURE
Running on jojoba

Most people have heard of jojoba in relation to beauty products such as shampoo, moisturisers and massage oil. But now you could be using jojoba to run your car! Recent research has shown that mixing a small amount of methanol with raw jojoba oil produced a mixture with similar properties to diesel. However, the new product is far more environmentally friendly than diesel, as it's lower in carbon and contains no polluting sulphur. Jojoba is just the latest plant oil, following rapeseed, sunflower and soybean oil, to be successfully tested as a diesel alternative, and now British farmers are lobbying the government to reduce the duty imposed on biofuels. You can do the same, to help encourage the use of alternative fuel sources and cut down on fossil fuel consumption. For more information see *Green Futures* magazine issue 40 online – visit **www.greenfutures.org.uk**

★ TOP TIP – CPRE
Airport expansion

The Government has forecast that air travel could almost triple by 2030 – from 2000's 180 million to 500 million passengers a year. To provide for this level of activity, the Government is considering building new airports and expanding current ones. This would result in an increase in noise pollution, air pollution and greenhouse gases, land and special sites would be lost, new roads would be built, rural economies could be hurt and water supply could be put at risk.

The solution lies not in expansion, but in managing demand for air travel, so write to your MP with your concerns. If you'd like more information, CPRE (the Campaign to Protect Rural England) has leaflets for distribution – *Flying to Distraction* and *Expanding Airports Destroy the Countryside*. Visit **www.cpre.org.uk** for copies.

Running on cooking oil

If you're seriously thinking about recycling cooking oil to use to run your car, the Low Impact Living Initiative – **www.lowimpact.org** – can give you all the information you need. They run weekend courses on producing bio-diesel, from home-made plant to commercial production, including environment agency and VAT issues. Alternatively you can buy bio-diesel from Ebony Solutions **www.ebony-solutions.co.uk**, where it is taxed at source and apparently gives off the pleasant odour of French fries!

Beware the dangers *inside* your car

A little known fact is that the interior of car can give off high levels of toxins. For example, interior plastics can leech an ammonia gas that has been linked with foetal abnormalities, and so pregnant women in America are now advised to drive with their car windows open. Textiles and leathers used inside cars can also emit up to 60,000 different allergens, which may have harmful effects on human health. Write to your car manufacturer to ask them what they're doing to assess these risks, and demand they subject all their car components to rigorous testing.

PEDAL POWER

Tips for cyclists

Traffic jams getting you down? It's understandable when we spend on average nine days a year in the car. The UK has the worst traffic congestion in Europe, costing the economy £20 billion each year. 70% of us choose to travel to work by car, each of which cost on average £2,400 a year to run. Bikes outnumber cars in the UK, yet most of them are unused because of the sheer danger and unpleasantness of cycling in traffic, yet in London cycling is often twice as fast as cars. Cycling is the most environmentally sound means of transport after walking. So save your money, time and the environment and get on your bike today.

Set cycling goals

Aim to cycle once a week to work or to see your friends. Start with small achievable journeys and gradually increase the distance, as you become more accustomed to it. The British Medical Association believes that cycling for 30 minutes a day can increase your life expectancy and can even give you a fitness level equivalent to a person ten years younger.

KIDS – Ride your bike to school

Cycling to school is good for the health of your kids and the environment. If you wish to provide an escort, you might bicycle to the school with your kids and then ride the rest of the way to work.

But make sure that your children are aware of road safety and wear helmets and reflective strips every time.

KIDS – Go on a family bike ride

Parents, arrange annual family cycling trips! Challenge your kids to cycle from an early age and improve their confidence through teaching them a lifelong skill. Cycling can also encourage environmental participation from young children to provide further Eco-friendly choices later on in life. Studies have found that obesity figures among children have doubled in the last ten years. Cycling for just 15 minutes can provide the daily moderate activity needed to promote health in children, and it can be fun!

Use your bike for short journeys

On short journeys, the catalytic converter which help cuts down a car's carbon monoxide emissions does not become effective until you have driven 2 miles. Road transport is responsible for 70% of all carbon monoxide emissions in the UK. 58% of all car journeys are less than 5 miles long and 25% less than 2 miles. Make a difference by using your bike for all journeys under 1 mile. If a third of short car journeys were made by bike, national heart disease rates would fall by 5-10%.

And when you tire of the roads, try something a bit more challenging and start mountain biking! **www.mbuk.com** and **www.bikinguk.net** are both dedicated to mountain biking and provide plenty of information for all budding enthusiasts.

Recycle your bicycle

Got a new bike? Don't discard your old one, by recycling it. Bike Recycling projects can even find a use for bikes destined for the scrap heap! The schemes are usually community run and help provide jobs for people out of work. Look for your nearest project at **www.wastecollect.co.uk**. Alternatively donate your bicycle to ReCycle. This charity helps people in developing countries, who use the bikes to cut water collection journey times by up to 3 hours in places, and helps travel to towns and farms. Contact them on **www.re-cycle.org**

Get an electric bike

Make cycling a more realistic option with an electric bicycle. Electric bikes are the cleanest motorised vehicles on the road, and costing just 1.5p a mile to run they're the most affordable solution for yourself and the environment. Visit **www.powabyke.com** or call 01225 443 737.

Reclaim the streets

Use Pedal Power! With 25 million cars on the roads of Britain, cyclists, runners, walkers and other road users are being pushed off the roads to make way for even more cars and even more pollution. Critical Mass is an international protest which uses 'pedal power' to encourage people to stand up and reclaim the streets. For information on rides near you and abroad see **www.critical-mass.org**

Make cycling easier

Join a campaign. Several organisations are pioneering cyclists' rights – contact them and find out how to get involved. Sustrans **www.sustrans.org.uk**, 0117 929 0888; CTC – the UK's national cyclists' organisation **www.ctc.org.uk**, 0870 873 0064; London Cycling Campaign, **www.lcc.org.uk**, 020 7928 7220.

TREAD CAREFULLY

Tyres and what to do with them

How many tyres will you make use of in a lifetime? Whether it's 20 or 200, consider that those tyres will sit in a landfill for around 400 years before beginning to decompose. 40 million scrap tyres are discarded in the UK each year – in Europe it's 200 million. When you return old tyres to the garage, ask if their tyre collectors are members of the Responsible Recycler Scheme. The scheme ensures the members recycle wherever possible, rather than dumping. It's not a small organisation either – 80% of all tyres are currently recycled in this way, so there's

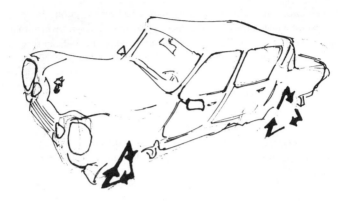

*no excuse for your retailer to be dealing with the remaining 20%. For details of this scheme visit **www.tyredisposal.co.uk**. For more on tyre recycling try REG Tyre and Automotive Recycling: **www.reguk.com**, 01895 444 714.*

Tyres in your garden

Tyres are made from rubber, oil, sulphur and zinc oxide, which makes them almost obscenely durable. Put this durability to good use in the garden. Use old tyres to grow potatoes; put a potato seed in the centre of the tyre and cover with 1cm of compost. As the plant grows, add soil to just below the tip of the shoot and add more tyres as required. Similarly tyres can be used to protect newly planted trees or make a frame for climber plants. You can also use tyres for garden steps, compost heaps, animal feed containers, or raised garden platforms. There are countless uses for tyres, just Go MAD and use your imagination.

Tyred kids

Kids – make a tyre swing or playground area. Tie them to secure branches or get your parents to set them securely in a sandpit.

Pump up your tyres

For every 6psi that a tyre is under-inflated, fuel consumption can rise by 1%. Michelin have produced special energy saving tyres which they claim are 20% freer rolling over a conventional design and can save 6% in fuel use over 12,000 miles – which equals £70 in your pocket.

Buy re-treaded tyres

Re-treading is the most environmentally friendly method of dealing with used tyres. Re-treading only uses half the amount of energy needed to replace the whole tyre, and doubles the life span of car tyres. Truck tyres can be retread twice further and aeroplane tyres 7 times.

Eco-friendly tyres

As tyres wear, they release polyaromatic hydrocarbons into the atmosphere, which can cause allergies, breathing problems and may be carcinogenic. Several companies are taking steps to remedy this with more eco-friendly ranges. Goodyear's GT3, for example, uses a substance derived from maize starch instead of chemical compounds, and JK Tyres, India's largest domestic producer and exporter has a coloured eco-friendly radial tyre range. It's a move in the right direction...

Buy products made from recycled tyres

With a total worldwide production of tyres exceeding 800 million per year, there's some hope for tyres after a life on the road. With hundreds of products including stationery, mouse mats and coasters there's no need for tyres to end up on the scrap heap. Find out more at Remarkable Technologies Ltd. Visit **www.remarkable.com** or call 020 8741 1234.

Recycled rubber from old tyres can also be used in mats, soles and heels of shoes, bike pedals, and tips for walking sticks and crutches, and even conveyor belts and inner tubes for bicycles. A by-product of old tyres is granulated rubber powders or crumb, which can be used for sporting or athletic tracks, playground flooring and general road surfaces. Find out more at **www.bir.org/aboutrecycling/tyres.asp**

Say no to tyre energy plants

Tyres have a high calorific value, and are therefore often burnt to provide energy. The fumes emitted are poisonous and can pollute water supplies. Fires can also become impossible to control, devastating the environment further. But such plants give off toxic dioxins, which are recognised carcinogenics, affecting fertility and the immune system, as well as particulates and toxic emissions. Plants such as these are found in cement kilns and should not be used due to the long-term damage they inflict on the environment. Find out more from Friends of the Earth, **www.foe.co.uk** (020 7490 1555).

MAKE IT WORK

Businesses waste resources. Lighting, heating, paper, computers that constantly need updating, refurbishment, office moves... the list of waste-generating activities goes on. But this also means that changing wasteful practices will make a big difference. The Government has set a target to reduce greenhouse gas emissions by 60% by 2050, and increased energy efficiency in homes, businesses, schools and industries was identified as the best way to meet that target. Pioneering businesses have already proved that corporate social responsibility works. Friends Provident is the first company to get virtually all of its electricity from renewable sources at no extra cost to the company or shareholders, helping to reduce energy-related CO_2 emissions by 80%. They have introduced measures to reduce inter-office travel and have a campaign to reduce paper use year-on-year.

But no matter where you work, or what kind of business you're in, there are things to be done. Even one recycling bin will make a difference...

OFFICE EFFICIENCY

Making your work environment greener

For businesses, becoming more energy-efficient and environmentally aware has all sorts of rewards, including financial gain and enhanced reputation. If your company is thinking of relocating or doing building work to its current structure, just stop and think about the materials that'll be used, the building methods that'll be employed and the resulting environment that'll be created.

www.greenbuildingstore.co.uk *and the Association for Environment Conscious Building* ***www.aecb.net*** *have plenty of information about how to create a more environmentally friendly working environment. Finally if you are refurbishing your old office and want to give it a makeover, why not consider recycling your old furniture, computers and phones.* ***www.recycle.mcmail.com/shop.htm*** *lists outlets that sell and buy used office goods.*

Save paper!

An office worker uses an average of 20,000 A4 sheets a year. Most of this gets thrown away. But every tonne of paper recycled will save approximately 17 trees, 462 gallons of oil, and 5 cubic metres of landfill. With just a few simple steps you can reduce the amount of paper your office uses. If you print and photocopy on both sides, send emails and faxes rather than letters and memos, circulate documents by intranet rather than hard copy, cancel unwanted publications and use transit envelopes, it will all help. You can also reuse paper for notes and envelopes for sending internal documents. And if you haven't got one install an office recycling scheme that includes all types of paper – including post-it notes! Finally, by using recycled paper you will strengthen the long-term market in recycled paper.

Turn scrap paper into notepads, and use both sides of the paper when photocopying or producing reports. And think before you photocopy. First, do you need that copy? Second, are the settings correct? Recycling bins beside photocopiers are full of wrong-size copies.

Put a spider plant on your desk

Indoor plants are a natural air conditioner and can remove up to
87% of indoor pollution in 24 hours.

Don't print your emails

Avoid printing out your emails if you can. And when you send an
email, include a reminder at the top, such as: 'Don't print! Save
trees!'

Recycle or refill your ink cartridges

Over 7 million toner cartridges and 40 million ink jet cartridges are
used every year. Almost 90% of them could be recycled. The
Cartridge Company collects and delivers cartridges – contact for
details on 0800 080 808. Charities also collect cartridges and some
shops have facilities where you can throw your empty cartridges
away in store. **www.essexcc.gov.uk** provides useful information in
the site's waste and recycling section. You can also refill your own.
Find out how at **www.refilltoner.com**

Use green stationery

In the UK 5 billion disposable plastic cups are thrown away each year. If you are one of the guilty drinkers you can redeem yourself by using pencils made from recycled plastic cups. You can also use colouring pencils made from sustainable wood or mouse mats, pencil cases made from recycled tyres, and pens made from plastic bottles. Visit **www.remarkable.co.uk**

You could also encourage your office to buy recycled stationery. For more information, visit the Green Stationery Company website at **www.greenstat.co.uk**, or call 01225 480 556. Alternatively, try Recycled Paper Supplies at **www.recycled-paper.co.uk**

Think durable

Try to avoid buying disposable products such as pens and pencils. Make sure your company buys refillable pens and propelling pencils in preference. Where disposable pens are necessary, ensure that their barrels are made from recycled material. Use solvent-free correction fluids and paints in the office, and choose locally produced goods and materials to reduce the energy and pollution involved in their transportation. For green office equipment, ranging from eco-friendly marker pens to stapleless staples, visit **www.naturalcollection.com**

Fair tea breaks

Make a stir in your office by asking for fair trade tea and coffee. Over the past three years, the world price of raw coffee has fallen more than 50%, and the market price of commodities has frequently dropped below the price of producing them, forcing farmers to work harder and longer for less. Since the prices of tea and coffee haven't been reduced by the same amount – where's the money going? Fair trade buys direct from the farmers at higher prices. Visit **www.coffee.uk.com** to buy a range of fair trade coffees, teas, herb teas and cocoas.

Save energy in the office

With a bit of planning you can save energy too. Position desks and workstations to exploit natural light. Check the plumbing regularly and repair leaks and dripping taps quickly. Only heat work areas that are being used and fit controls to radiators to regulate individual room temperatures. Be sure to switch off lights and machines when not in use! **www.actionenergy.org.uk** has information, tips and ideas for the workplace, and can provide free onsite energy services to identify energy saving opportunities. And for further advice on reducing carbon emissions and moving towards a low carbon future, contact the Carbon Trust at **www.thecarbontrust.co.uk**, or call 020 7170 7000.

Don't dump the furniture

Don't throw out your old office furniture into the landfill – it can be recycled too! Greenworks is a not-for-profit organisation that recycles unwanted office furniture to schools, charitable organisations and businesses in need. Apart from reducing landfill, they support projects based in deprived inner city areas and provide employment and training to the disadvantaged and disabled. For more information visit **www.green-work.co.uk** or call 020 7981 0450.

 TOP TIP – RETHINK RUBBISH
Don't be a mug!

Rediscover the real taste of tea and coffee by drinking your cuppa out of a real mug. It will taste better than if it were in plastic, you won't burn your hands, and you'll cut down on the use of plastic cups. If your office does use a vending machine, however, and there isn't a viable alternative, contact Save-A-Cup on 01494 510 167 or visit **www.save-a-cup.co.uk** which offers a collection and recycling service. Your used plastic cups can be made into a whole range of products, such as pens, rulers and cup coasters. Visit **www.rethinkrubbish.com** for more information.

Share facilities and reduce overhead costs

If your company shares an open-plan office space with another company, think about setting up a sharing scheme. By sharing equipment such as printers and copiers you could help reduce their energy consumption and reduce overhead costs.

Companies – rethink your role in the future

How does your company's products and the way they are produced impact on the environment and the people who live in it? Are they contributing to society or functioning at society's expense?

Key questions to ask yourself – are the materials sourced and the production methods used sustainable? Does it follow fair trade principles? Are its investments ethical? Does it invest in its workforce – both at home and overseas? Does it support its local community or charities? And what, apart from its products does it do to contribute to society? For more information visit the Centre for Sustainable Urban and Regional Futures at Salford University: **www.surf.salford.ac.uk**.

 TOP TIP – WWW.GREENCHOICES.ORG
Reduce water waste

Water bills could be costing your company over 1% of business turnover, and many organisations are paying more in water and associated costs than they need to. Investing a little time and money in implementing a simple water management plan could reduce water consumption releasing money to be invested in other parts of your business. As part of its commitment to 'greening the business world' the Environment Agency **www.environment-agency.gov.uk** has produced a series of free publications to help your organisation become more water efficient.

Ask your business to send an energy management email to every employee

When Rover sent an energy management newsletter to its employees at its Longbridge car plant, with simple energy saving tips, total energy savings worth £1 million were achieved in just six months. For a good example look at Co-operative Bank's paper management, air conditioning and recycling policies on Save Waste and Prosper's website. **www.swap-web.co.uk**. The bank's guidebook The Green Office Manual is available by email from sales@wastebusters.co.uk

Make your company sustainable

Get advice on making your workplace practices more sustainable and environmentally friendly. Contact Business in the Environment at **www.business-in-environment.org.uk** or call 0870 600 2482, or the National Centre for Business and Sustainability at **www.thencbs.co.uk**, 0161 834 8842. Make sure the advice reaches the right people and is acted on. Friends of the Earth also publishes a Green Office Action Plan. Get your copy from **www.foe-scotland.org.uk**

Publish environmental and social accounts

Encourage your company to publish its environmental and social accounts – to take a detailed audit not only of its financial progress but also of its effect on the environment and society. A number of high-profile companies have already done this, including The Body Shop, Camelot, Traidcraft and Ben and Jerry's. To find out more visit the New Economics Foundation, (NEF) **www.neweconomics.org** or the Institute for Social and Ethical Accountability at **www.accountability.org.uk**

Keep an eye on the world's multinationals

Your office may have a glowing social environmental record but what about those that don't? Find out why Indians are accusing Coca-cola of polluting their water supply, or what happens in Nike sweatshops in China – visit **www.corpwatch.org**. Keep informed by taking out a corporate subscription to *The Ecologist* [see page 274]

★ TOP TIP – THE NATURAL COLLECTION

Don't use poison pens

Conventional marker pens are filled with chemicals. But there are pens that don't intoxicate – Friendly Markers are Swedish, with a barrel made of waxed recycled paper and inks that contain no heavy metals or xylene or toluene solvents. For whiteboard or flipchart – water-based or permanent – they are effective and eco-friendly.
www.naturalcollection.com, 0870 331 3333

TECHNOLOGY BYTES

Computers, phones and more

We can now link up across the planet, so let's try and link with the planet. Computers are all around us, and we're upgrading and replacing them all the time. But it takes a lot of natural resources to make a computer. Seven litres of crude oil are used to make the plastic inside just one system. So what can you do...?

Donate your old computers

Each year over 100 million computers are sold and 1 million computers end up in landfill sites. If your computer has ended its life in one situation, it can still work in another. Finding a new home will extend its life and provide someone with a computer who can't afford a new one. Sell it on ebay on **www.ebay.co.uk** or donate it to computer aid international who will pass it onto an organisation in need – visit **www.cit.org.uk/computeraid.org** or call 020 7281 0091. You can also donate it to Bytes Twice – The Association of Community Computer Re-use Projects; contact them on 020 7248 0242. And if you are buying a computer for the kids, think about buying a recycled computer rather than a new one. UK Computer Recycling sells refurbished equipment to schools and charities. Visit the website at **www.uk-cr.org.uk** or email enquires@uk-cr.org.uk to find out more.

Use mobile phones carefully

It is predicted that there will be 1.6 billion mobile phones in use by 2005, yet we know little about how they affect our health. Computers and mobile communications have promised, and provided, an incredible technological revolution. But while they have become a part of life they have also become another environmental problem.

Mobile phones made in the UK emit a low level of radio waves that are considered safe for us. However there is evidence that phones can stimulate changes in brain activity, but the reason for this is not clear and not enough research has been done. In the absence of further research, use your phone cautiously – keep calls short, use a hands-free set and when buying a new phone take account of its SAR values that monitor radio waves.

If indoors, use your mobile by a window

Signal strengths can be up to 10 times greater by a window, so standing near one means the handset needs less power to connect with the mast. Make sure you have the handset on the window-side, too, so that less of the signal passes through your head.

Say NO to mastheads by schools

One in every two people in Britain owns a mobile phone. And there are now 20,000 base stations and 82,000 cell sites in the UK, which permanently emit signals that may be harmful. Some evidence suggests that the radio waves emitted from mastheads may provoke headaches, disrupt sleep and cause short-term memory loss. Find out more at **www.mastaction.org**, or write to Mast Action, PO Box 312, Hertfordshire, EN7 5ZE, or ring their advice line between 1pm and 8pm: 08704 322 377.

Change your charger

Here are some phone rechargers that are good for both you and the environment. The Green Shop – **www.greenshop.co.uk** sells solar-powered mobile phone chargers. They're a convenient power supply for charging your mobile phone at no cost when you have no access to a power point. Alternatively, you could charge up your phone using pedal power. For more information on this nifty little gadget that attaches to your bicycle visit **www.edirectory.co.uk**. And if cycle charging sounds a bit too active, get a wind-up charger for a more leisurely way of generating power to talk. Three minutes of wind-up provides 8 minutes of conversation – from The Green Shop.

Recycle your old mobile

There are over 20 million potentially toxic mobile redundant phones lying abandoned around our houses. Laid out together they would cover an area 4,950 kilometres square. Imagine how much noise they all would make if they were still ringing? Donate your old phone to a charity so that someone else can make use of it. Contact CRUMP – the Campaign to Recycle Unwanted Mobile Phones on 0800 083 2103 or visit **www.childadvocacyinternational.co.uk** or **www.mobilephonesforcharity.com**

Look for the Energy Star

The Energy Star System is a US-developed rating system that also applies to goods sold in the UK. When you buy a printer, modem, scanner or monitor with the Energy Star sign on it you know it will be one of the most efficient models. If you use Energy Star Computer equipment you could save up to £25 per year per computer. Find out more about Energy Star products at **www.energystar.gov**

Screensavers don't save energy

In fact sometimes they use more energy than when the computer is in use. If you are going to be away from your computer for over an hour, switch it to sleep mode or turn it off. A computer monitor left on overnight wastes enough energy to laser print 800 A4 pages.

Turn off your computer when you leave work

Employees who didn't turn their computers off when they went home at night cost their companies £90 million in 2002. Worse, throughout the night those computers pumped a staggering 2.8 million tones of CO_2 into the environment. Always turn your computer off when you go home, and if you work at home, turn it off when you're not working.

Recycle your compact discs

Don't throw away old CDs. Donate them to a charity shop or a local school so that they can be re-used. Or string them up in fruit trees if you wish to keep birds away from your fruit.

Recharge your batteries

Every year over 15 billion batteries are produced and sold worldwide. The majority are non-rechargeable alkaline or lithium batteries. No battery is biodegradable, so all wasted batteries will simply gather in the rubbish dumps around the world. Rechargeable batteries can be used up to 1,000 times, and the technology is always improving. Some rechargeable batteries are even recyclable – that's good news for the landfill. For more information, visit **www.greenbatteries.com**.

Do you really need that new gadget?

Gadgets make useful small presents, they're ingenious and fun to use. But when we lead such busy lives how often are they really used after the novelty has worn off? Try to limit the amount of gadgets you buy or make sure they benefit the environment. Visit **www.greenchoices.org** or **www.naturalcollection.com** for solar-powered and wind-up devices, energy and water-saving products for the home.

Sustainable Returns with Social Responsibility

QUADRIS Group specialise in investing in projects or businesses which are related, directly or indirectly, to the production, processing, marketing and selling of hardwood.   As practitioners of strict, dark green investment criteria, **QUADRIS** ensure that all projects in which the Group invests are based on positive selection criteria to ensure that investments are ethical, sustainable, environmentally sound and socially proactive.

If you are looking for an investment which, in addition to a realistic financial return, can offer truly positive contributions to the environment and in particular the precious natural rain forests of the world, then call us to find out more.

QUADRIS Environmental Investments Limited
Regent House, 19-20 The Broadway
WOKING, Surrey, GU21 5AP
Tel: 01483 756800
Fax: 01483 776800
invest@quadris.co.uk
www.quadris.co.uk

WISE INVESTMENTS

If you invest your money in a savings scheme, pension or insurance policy, that company has your money to do what they will with for the duration of the scheme. Most large UK fund managers, for example, include BAE Systems in the stock market portfolio of their ISAs or PEPs. This British company is among the top suppliers of military equipment to the developing world. Do you want your hard-earned cash to finance a war? Or drug testing on animals? Or child labour? In fact, most of the companies listed in the FTSE 100 are off limits, but you can make a profit and be ethical, as many companies have found. So think before you invest, borrow or buy. Ask questions, read the small print – a small investment of your time could save an awful lot of pain in a lab, sweatshop or distant country.

BANKING ON THE FUTURE

Ethical money

Switch your money to an ethical bank. The Co-operative Bank –
***www.co-operativebank.co.uk**, 0161 832 3456, and the Triodos Bank*
***www.triodos.co.uk**, 0117 973 9339, provide a wide range of*
accounts, loans and savings schemes, as does the Ecology Building
Society, which offers savings schemes as well as mortgages. Ethical
banks don't encourage trade with oppressive regimes or support the
distribution of arms. They discriminate in favour of companies with
sound environmental policies, so your money is working for – not
against – the world. When you close existing accounts, banks usually
ask why. Make sure you tell them.

Learn the lingo

Investment is traditionally filled with phrases that are designed
solely so that Bankers and Traders are kept in a job, otherwise there
would be no need for the middleman, and ethical investment is no
different. However, it does help to know the criteria that investment
companies use to decide whether a company is ethical or not. They
have the best of sector, where investments are made in companies that,
although not 100% environmentally friendly, are leading the field in
their area and are still striving to improve. Similarly there is thematic
investment, which invests directly in companies that are believed to be
improving the world, such as health or education organisations.
Another method is positive and negative screening, which a company
is compared to a positive or negative list of ethical standards, and if it
fulfils enough positive criteria, or too many negative criteria, then it
will pass or fail respectively.

Renovate when you relocate

If you're looking to move house, consider renovating a derelict
building. These can traditionally be hard to get mortgages for as most
building societies and lenders tend to shy away from such an
investment, but the Ecology Building Society actively encourages such

borrowers. They only give mortgages to buyers purchasing derelict buildings, energy-efficient homes or people looking to build new homes from reclaimed or sustainable materials. That way you can create your own energy-efficient dream home from scratch. **www.ecology.co.uk**, or call 0845 674 5566.

Insure in the future

Car insurance is essential, but when you join the AA or the RAC you are indirectly supporting the despoilment of the countryside, as these organisations lobby the government to increase the number of roads being built. But there is an alternative. The Environmental Transport Association, an organisation that campaigns for alternative methods of transport and a reduction in car use while fully recognising our need for cars – provides insurance and breakdown services at competitive rates. Visit **www.eta.co.uk** or call 01932 828 882 for details. To insure your home and your travels ethically, contact Naturesave Policies Ltd, **www.naturesave.co.uk**, 01803 864 390.

Cool communications

The Phone Co-op is making communication greener. Owned and controlled by its customers, it offsets all the carbon dioxide generated by its activities and the telecoms services it supplies through payment of a voluntary levy to Climate Care which, in turn, invests in renewable energy and re-forestation projects. They purchase their electricity from a green source, and have a strong recycling policy. They offer a good low-cost phone service plus flat rate internet services and a low-cost pay-as-you-go service. Visit **www.thephone.coop**, or call 0845 458 9000 for more details (and a human at the end of the line!).

Take out a green mortgage

Borrowing money ethically is just as important as investing ethically. Before you take out a mortgage with any of the big players, check out the policies of the Co-operative Bank, **www.co-operativebank.co.uk**, 0161 832 3456. They also offer a free energy survey. The Norwich and Peterborough Building Society **www.norwichandpeterborough.co.uk**,

0845 300 6727, offers mortgage products linked to reforestation schemes. The Ecology Building Society, **www.ecology.co.uk**, 0845 674 5566, grants mortgages on properties which give an ecological payback, encouraging energy efficient housing and ecological renovation.

Retire ethically!

Pension funds control more than a third of the shares in the UK stock market – so everybody who has a pension can do their bit. Make the effort and read the small print – notably your pension fund's Statement of Investment principles. If you don't have this, ask to be sent a copy. Research by the Campaign Against the Arms Trade (CAAT) **www.caat.org.uk,** 020 7281 0297, shows that the pension funds of many local authorities, trades unions, NHS Trusts and even charities are being invested in the arms trade. What contributes to a long and happy retirement in one part of the world could be causing misery in another.

Proof of the pudding

Friends Provident **www.friendsprovident.co.uk**, 0870 607 1352, has been providing ethical investment schemes for 19 years, proving you can make a profit with sound ideals. Take a look at what it has to offer – they'll be only too glad to tell you what your money would be used for.

Use your investor-power

The Ethical Investment Research Service (EIRIS) provides the independent research needed by investors to make responsible investment decisions. With research covering over 2,600 companies across the globe EIRIS can tailor-make 'acceptable lists' of the companies that most fit an individual investor's social, environmental and ethical priorities. EIRIS has also produced a number of guides on ethical investment, including ones on funds, banks, pensions and charities. Visit **www.eiris.org** or call 020 7840 5700.

Green credit cards

Affinity – or charity – credit cards give a small percentage of your spending (usually around 0.25%) to charity. There is an enormous range to choose from, including The Wildlife Trusts, National Canine Defence League, and NSPCC among others. They are an easy, popular way to make a difference, and though they may attract a higher rate of interest on spending, customers think it's worth it. A standard credit card – the Smile credit card **www.smile.co.uk**, is available from the Co-operative Bank. Visit **www.charitycard.co.uk** for a full list of charity credit cards available.

And finally, forget money altogether...

The New Civilization Network Alternative Money System team **www.newciv.org/ncn/moneyteam.html** was founded to discuss the prospects of doing away with money systems and using a resource-based system instead. Its website features information on schemes and ideas, including Letslink UK, the umbrella organisation for Local Exchange Trading Schemes. LETS promotes the exchange of goods and services so individuals, groups and businesses can function in the community without money. Visit **www.letslinkuk.org**

Schumacher COLLEGE
An International Centre for Ecological Studies

Schumacher College runs residential courses which aim to explore the foundations of a new world view. Taught by leading environmental thinkers and activists, the courses offer a combination of intellectual inquiry, meditation, physical work and aesthetic experience, thus creating a sense of the wholeness of life. Course participants find refreshment and often new direction – they find they have touched a source of inspiration and are reminded that there are others who share their deepest values about life and its meaning.

"Schumacher College is simply one of the finest teaching and learning environments to be found anywhere in the world."

David Abram, author of *Spell of the Sensuous*

College teachers include: Vandana Shiva, Fritjof Capra, Amory Lovins, Thomas Moore, Ann Pettifor, and Jonathon Porritt.

For further details please contact: **The Administrator, Schumacher College, The Old Postern, Dartington, Totnes, Devon TQ9 6EA, UK**
e-mail: admin@schumachercollege.org.uk Tel 01803 865934 Fax: 01803 866899

website: www.schumachercollege.org.uk

On our website you can find the full text of the College prospectus, current course programme, and application form. Additional material such as student profiles, articles of related interest and scholarship details is also available.
A department of The Dartington Hall Trust, a registered charity. 279756

Schumacher Schumacher Schumacher Schumac

FIND OUT MORE!

All the organisations mentioned in Go MAD! 2 are
listed here – so make that phone call, send that email
or write that letter!

Go MAD is all about interaction, so please let us know of any
organisations or initiatives you feel should be mentioned in the
book, as well as any new environmental tips. Send your idea
by post or email and if we use your suggestion we'll send you
a free copy of the next edition of Go MAD!

Go MAD! 2 Tips
Think Publishing Ltd.
The Pall Mall Deposit
124-128 Barlby Road
London W10 6BL

Email watchdog@thinkpublishing.co.uk

Don't forget to include your address.

Go MAD! 2 is published by Think Books, part of Think Publishing, the UK's leading environmental publisher

Working towards a more sustainable future

Environmental perceptions are changing in Britain. Where once the ecologist or conservationist was seen as a breed apart, in today's post-modern age environmental concerns are fitting into our daily lives. Recycling, charitable donations and organic farming are becoming part of the British culture, and millions of people are joining in.

These people are often called green consumers but, in reality, most of them are like you or me: they want the right to take walks in the countryside, to eat unpolluted food, to visit unspoilt regions of the world, and to ensure that their children can enjoy these pleasures in the years to come. We call them the conscientious consumers.

Think Publishing firmly believes that this group is growing every day and that protection and understanding of the world around us is built in to what we all do. Through the magazines and books that we publish, we constantly try to develop this ethos. We already reach over 400,000 conscientious consumers through our titles, and are increasing this circulation. In just three years, we have become the largest environmental publisher in the country.

If you would like to know more about Think Publishing, please call Tilly Boulter on 020 8962 3020 or email tilly@thinkpublishing.co.uk

THINK
BOOKS

www.thinkpublishing.co.uk

ABOUT ORGANICS
Organic hotels, guesthouses and B&Bs that provide organic venues for holidays or short breaks.
www.aboutorganics.co.uk/organic_holidays/organic_holidays.htm

ACCOUNTABILITY
Promotes social, ethical and overall organisational accountability, for achieving sustainable development.
Institute of Social and Ethical Unit A, 137 Shepherdess Walk, London N1 7RQ, United Kingdom • 020 7549 0400
www.accountability.org.uk

ACTION ENERGY
A site dedicated to helping companies save energy.
08707 870776
www.actionenergy.org.uk/

ADBUSTERS
Campaign set to topple existing power structures and forge a major shift in the way we will live in the 21st century.
1243 West 7th Avenue, Vancouver, BC, V6H 1B7, Canada • 1 800 663 1243 Toll free worldwide.
www.adbusters.org

ALTERNATIVE CEREMONIES
Offers an alternative to traditional wedding, baby naming and funeral ceremonies and rituals.
www.alternativeceremonies.co.uk

AMAZING RECYCLED PRODUCTS
An American company specialising in innovative products made from a wide variety of recycled materials.
www.amazingrecycled.com

AMNESTY INTERNATIONAL
Worldwide movement of people campaigning for internationally recognised human rights.
99-119 Rosebery Avenue, London, EC1R 4RE • 020 7814 6200
www.amnesty.org

ANITARODDICK.COM
The founder of the Body Shop campaigns for change on a variety of environmental and humanitarian issues.
www.anitaroddick.com

ANTIQUES WORLD
The best internet guide to markets and fairs throughout the UK.
www.antiquesworld.co.uk/

ARCANIA GREEN TECHNOLOGY SPECIALISTS
The first UK company to offer services powered by 100% solar power.
www.arcania.co.uk/greentree/features/clean.htm

ASSOCIATION FOR ENVIRONMENT CONSCIOUS BUILDING
The UK's leading independent environmental building trade organisation.
PO Box 32, LLandysul, SA44 5ZA
www.aecb.net

AURO ORGANIC PAINT SUPPLIES LTD
Organic paints that don't pollute the environment.
Unit 2 Pampillions Farme, Purton End, Debden, Saffron Walden, Essex CB11 3JT
01799 543 077
www.auroorganic.co.uk/

AUTOCHLOR
A high-performance salt chlorination system for swimming pools that doesn't use harsh chemicals.
www.autochlor.com

AVEDA
For environmentally-friendly hair, skin, makeup and lifestyle products.
www.aveda.com

AVIAN ADVENTURES
Birdwatching and wildlife holidays organised worldwide.
49 Sandy Road, Norton, Stourbridge DY8 3AJ • 01384 372 010
www.avianadventures.co.uk

AVT
Electric cars, conversions & components
Blue Lias House, Station Road, Hatch Beauchamp, Somerset, TA3 6SQ
0182 348 0196
http://www.avt.uk.com/

BABY MILK ACTION
A non-profit organisation to promote safe and appropriate infant feeding.

CONTACTS

23 St. Andrews Street, Cambridge, CB2
3AX • 01223 464 420
www.babymilkaction.org

BABY ORGANIX
Manufacturers of organic baby food.
Knapp Mill, Mill Road, Christchurch,
Dorset, BH23 2LU • 01202 479 701
www.babyorganix.co.uk

BABY THINGS
For buying and selling used or unwanted
baby's and children's goods.
www.baby-things.com

BABYNAT ORGANICO
Importers of high-quality organic food at
fair prices.
60-62 Kings Road, Reading, RG1 3AA
01189 510 518
www.organico.co.uk

BACKYARD BIODIVERSITY DAY
A website encouraging young people to
appreciate nature in their own back yard.
www.biodiversityday.org

BAN LINDANE CAMPAIGN
see Pesticide Action Network
www.pan.uk.org/banlindane

BANANA LINK
Supporting sustainable production and
trade in bananas.
38-40 Exchange St. Norwich NR2 1AX
www.bananalink.org.uk

BAOBAB TRAVEL
Promotes sustainable tourism in Africa, to
benefit local communities and the natural
environment.
Old Fallings Hall, Old Fallings Lane,
Wolverhampton WV10 8BL
08703 825 003 or 01902 558 316
www.baobabtravel.com

BARN OWL TRUST
A charity dedicated to conserving the barn
owl and its natural habitat in the UK.
Waterleat, Ashburton, Devon, TQ13 7HU
• 01364 653 026
www.barnowltrust.org.uk

BAT CONSERVATION TRUST
A UK organisation devoted to the
conservation of bats and their habitats.

15 Cloisters House, 8 Battersea Park
Road, London, SW8 4BG • 020 7627 2629
www.bats.org.uk

BATTERSEA DOGS' HOME
An organisation that rescues and re-homes
stray and ill-treated dogs and cats.
4 Battersea Park Road, Battersea,
London, SW8 4AA • 020 7622 3626

BBC MAKES AND BAKES
A web site with ideas and instructions to
accompany the Blue Peter.
www.bbc.co.uk/cbbc/bluepeter/makes

BEANTREE ORGANICS
Specialists in quality organic foods.
663A Ecclesall Road, Sheffield, S11 8PT
01142 662 972
www.beantreeorganics.com

BEAUTIFUL BRITAIN
A website dedicated to outdoor living,
with tips on introducing wildlife to ponds,
gardens, canals etc.
www.beautifulbritain.co.uk

BEAUTY WITHOUT CRUELTY
An International Educational Charitable
Trust for Animal Rights.
Visage International, 3 Phoenix Square,
Wyncolls Road, Colchester CO4 9AS
01206 752 722
www.bwcindia.org

BEETROOT ENVIRONMENT
Provides ideas on environmental and
sustainable development education to
pupils in out-of-school hours.
www.beetroot.org.uk/environment_reso
urces.htm

BEST FOOT FORWARD
A company set up to assist individuals
and organisations to become
environmentally sustainable.
The Future Centre, 115 Magdalen Road,
Oxford OX4 1RQ • 01865 794 586
www.bestfootforward.com

BHOPAL MEDICAL APPEAL
A campaign site providing information
about the chemical leak in Bhopal and its
ongoing consequences.
www.bhopal.org

BICYCLE BEANO
Offers cycling tours of the Welsh countryside, combined with quality accommodation and vegetarian cuisine.
Bicycle Beano Cycling Holidays, Erwood, Builth Wells, Powys, LD2 3PQ, Wales
01982 560 471
www.bicycle-beano.co.uk

BIO REGIONAL DEVELOPMENT GROUP
A group founded on the ideal of local production for local needs, that promotes sustainable development.
BedZED Centre, Helios Road, Wallington, Surrey, SM6 7BZ • 020 8404 4880
www.bioregional.com

BLUEPET
Delivers supplies for cats and dogs, including healthy food, natural remedies and pet accessories.
Peckleton Lane, Desford, Leicester LE9 9JU • 0845 330 6451
www.bluepet.co.uk

BODY SHOP INTERNATIONAL PLC
International retail chain renowned for its environmentally friendly and naturally inspired beauty products.
Watersmead, Littlehampton, West Sussex, BN17 6LS • 01903 731 500
www.thebodyshop.com

BORN
Provides information and alternative products, enabling parents to make informed choices about their babies' welfare.
64 Gloucester Road, Bishopston, Bristol, BS7 8BH • 01179 245 080
www.borndirect.com

BOYCOTTBUSH
This site is where Ethical Consumer charts the campaigners' progress and lists the brands for consumers to avoid.
www.boycottbush.net

BRITISH ASSOCIATION OF FAIR TRADE SHOPS
A network of independent Fair Trade or World Shops, aiming to promote fair trade retail in the UK.
TDA House, 211 Clapham Road, London, SW9 0QH • 020 7737 5156
www.bafts.org.uk

BRITISH COMPLEMENTARY MEDICINE ASSOCIATION
Provides information on complementary therapies, for practitioners, clients and students, aiming to promote high standards throughout the country.
PO Box 5122, Bournemouth, BH8 0WG
0845 345 5977
www.bcma.co.uk

BRITISH FILM INSTITUTE (BFI)
A registered charity that promotes film, television and the moving image.
Stephen Street Office/bfi National Library, British Film Institute, 21 Stephen Street, London W1T 1LN
020 7255 1444
www.bfi.org.uk

BRITISH HEDGEHOG PRESERVATION SOCIETY
A UK Charity dedicated to helping and protecting hedgehogs.
Hedgehog House, Dhustone, Ludlow, Shropshire, SY8 3PL • 01584 890 801
www.software-technics.co.uk/bhps

BRITISH KITE SURFING ASSOCIATION (BKSA)
An association providing information on this radical sport and other extreme activities.
British Kite Surfing Association, P.O. Box 101, Keynsham, Bristol BS31 1ZR
01179 161 380
www.kitesurfing.org

BRITISH TOY AND HOBBY ASSOCIATION
Represents the interests of British toy manufacturers and works to raise standards of practice in the industry.
80 Camberwell Road, London, SE5 0EG
020 7701 7271
www.btha.co.uk

BRITISH TOY MAKERS GUILD
Promotes British craft toys for children and grown-ups.
www.toymakersguild.co.uk

BRITISH TRUST FOR CONSERVATION VOLUNTEERS
An organisation that works with volunteers to bring about positive environmental change.
36 St Mary's Street, Wallingford,

Oxfordshire OX10 0EU • 01491 821 600
www.btcv.org

BRITISH UNION FOR THE ABOLITION OF VIVISECTION

Britain's anti-vivisection organisation that campaigns to end all animal experimentation.
16A Crane Road. London, N7 8NN
020 7700 4888
www.buav.org

BRITISH WATERWAYS

Promotes, manages and conserves Britain's inland waterways.
Willow Grange, Church Road, Watford, WD17 4QA
www.britishwaterways.co.uk

BRITISH WIND ENERGY ASSOCIATION, (BWEA)

Aims to promote wind energy in the UK.
British Wind Energy Association, Renewable Energy House, 1 Aztec Row, Berners Road, London, N1 0PW, UK
020 7689 1960
www.bwea.com/about/index.html

BUSINESS IN THE ENVIRONMENT

137 Shepherd's Walk, London, N1 7RQ
0870 600 2482
www.bitc.org.uk

BUTTERFLY CONSERVATION

Protects native butterflies, moths and their habitats from a range of threats.
Manor Yard, East Lulworth, Wareham, Dorset. • 0870 774 4309
www.butterfly-conservation.org.uk

BUY NOTHING DAY

A day celebrating simple living and no spending.
www.buynothingday.co.uk

BUY RECYCLED

Guide to products available in the UK containing recycled materials.
www.recycledproducts.org.uk

BYTES TWICE

The Association of Community Computer Re-use Projects
The Niven Suite, The Mansion, Ottershaw Park, Surrey, KT16 0QG • 01932 874 066
www.free-computers.org

CAFEDIRECT

Sells fairly traded tea, coffee and cocoa that provides producer partners with a living wage.
Cafédirect Ltd, City Cloisters, Suite B2, 196 Old Street, London, EC1V 9FR
020 7490 9520
www.cafedirect.co.uk

CAMPAIGN AGAINST ARMS TRADE

Campaigns for the reduction and ultimate abolition of the international arms trade.
11 Goodwin St, London, N4 3HQ
020 7281 0297
www.caat.org.uk

CAMPAIGN FOR DARK SKIES

Highlights the problem of light pollution.
38 The Vineries, Colehill, Wimborne, Dorset, BH21 2PX
www.dark-skies.org

CAMPAIGN FOR REAL ALE, (CAMRA)

Helps safeguard the future of British beer.
230 Hatfield Road, St Albans, Hertfordshire AL1 4LW • 01727 867 201
www.camra.org.uk

CAMPAIGN FOR REAL FOOD

Campaign to promote real food, supporting local producers and independent retailers.
PO Box 132, Sutton, SM3 8WQ
0800 328 3750
www.thecarf.co.uk

CAMPAIGN TO PROTECT RURAL ENGLAND

Campaigns for the protection and enhancement of the countryside.
CPRE national office: 128 Southwark Street, London SE1 0SW
020 7981 2800
www.cpre.org.uk

CAMPAIGNS OF THE NATIONAL LABOUR COMMITTEE

Promotes and defends workers' rights on a global scale.
275 Seventh Avenue, Suite 1503 New York, NY 10001 • +1 212 2423002
http://www.nlcnet.org/campaigns/shahmakhdum

CANBY

Provides jute bags and environmentally

friendly packaging.
BO4 Acton Business Centre, School Road, London NW10 6TD • 020 8951 9325
www.canby.co.uk

CARBON TRUST
Promotes the development of low carbon technologies to support the transition to a low carbon technology in the UK.
Carbon Trust, 9th Floor, 3 Clement's Inn, London, WC2A 2AZ • 020 7170 7000
www.thecarbontrust.co.uk

CARE, REHABILITATION AND AID FOR SICK HEDGEHOGS
A charity dedicated to care for sick and injured hedgehogs, with the aim of returning them to the wild.
45 Culliford Crescent, Canford Heath, Poole, Dorset BH17 9ET •01202 699 358
www.hedgehogs.org.uk

CARIBBEAN CONSERVATION CORPORATION
Campaigns for research into and preservation of sea turtles.
Caribbean Conservation Corporation, 4424 NW 13th St. Suite #A1 Gainesville, FL 32609
www.cccturtle.org

CARTRIDGES 4 CHARITY
Funds small charities by recycling printer cartridges and mobile phones.
Bachilton, Crieff, PH7 4DZ 0870 991 4070
www.cartridges4charity.co.uk

CASH FOR CANS
Promotes local level aluminium recycling in the UK and abroad, offering incentives to individuals and organisations.
www.cashforcans.co.uk

CATS PROTECTION
A feline welfare charity that rescues and re-homes cats and promotes responsible cat ownership.
Cats Protection, 17 Kings Road, Horsham, West Sussex RH13 5PN 08702 099 099
www.cats.org.uk

CENTRE FOR ALTERNATIVE TECHNOLOGY
Environmental charity that aims to inspire, inform, and enable people to live more sustainably.
Centre for Alternative Technology, Machynlleth, Powys, SY20 9AZ, UK 01654 705 950
www.cat.org.uk

CENTRE FOR SUSTAINABLE URBAN AND REGIONAL FEATURES
Promotes urban regeneration and renewal.
The SURF Centre, University of Salford, 113-115 Portland Street, Manchester, M1 6DW • 0161 295 4018
www.surf.salford.ac.uk

CHANGING PLACES
Tackles the legacy of post-industrial decay to breathe new life into derelict and neglected land.
www.changingplaces.org.uk

CHARITY CARDS
Provides a selection of charity cards.
PO Box No. 777 Kings House, Forth Banks, Newcastle upon Tyne NE99 2UD 0191 261 6263
www.charitycards.co.uk
www.christmas-cards.org

CHARITY COMMISSION
A government organisation aiming to increase public confidence in the integrity of charities in England and Wales.
20 Kings Parade, Queens Dock, Liverpool, L3 4DQ • 0870 333 0123
www.charity-commisson.gov.uk

CHEETAH CONSERVATION FUND (CCF)
Research into and preservation of cheetahs in their natural habitat.
PO Box 1380, Ojai, CA, USA 93024
www.cheetah.org

CHEMICAL BODY BURDEN
Provides information on synthetic chemicals and heavy metals that build up in our bodies.
PO Box 8743 • Missoula, MT 59807
www.chemicalbodyburden.org

CHILD
Information on all aspects of pregnancy, childcare and parenting.
www.child.com

CHILDRENS SCRAPSTORE
Recycles clean and safe waste products from industry to create resources for children's art and play activities.
O'Shed, Welsh Back, Bristol, BS1 4SL
01179 252 229
www.childrensscrapstore.com

CHOOSE CLIMATE
Calculates the cost of your flight to the environment.
www.chooseclimate.org

CLIMATE ARK
Offers news and information on climate change and renewable energy.
www.climateark.org

COALITION TO STOP THE USE OF CHILD SOLDIERS
2nd floor, 2-12 Pentonville Road, London N1 9FP
www.child-soldiers.org

CODA
Aims to organise educational and social development activities with disadvantaged groups in Southern Africa and Central America.
129 Seven Sisters Road, London N7 7QG
020 7281 0020
www.cit.org.uk/

COMMUNITY COMPOSTING NETWORK
Provides advice and supports community composting projects across the UK.
67 Alexandra Road, Sheffield, S2 3EE
01142 580 483
www.othas.org.uk/ccn

COMMUNITY RECYCLING NETWORK
A membership organisation promoting community-based sustainable waste management.
Trelawny House, Surrey Street, Bristol, BS7 9JR • 01179 420 142
www.crn.org.uk

COMMUNITY REPAINT
A scheme to collect and distribute paint to people who can't afford it.
www.communityrepaint.org.uk

COMMUNITY SHARE CAR NETWORK
A non-profit organisation to promote and support the development of car clubs.

The Studio, 32 The Calls, Leeds, LS2 7EW • 01132 349 299
www.carclubs.org.uk

COMPASSION IN WORLD FARMING
Campaigns to end factory farming and improve transport of animals.
Charles House, 5A Charles Street, Petersfield, Hampshire
www.ciwf.org

COMPOST ASSOCIATION
Promotes good practice in composting and the use of composted materials.
Avon House, Tithe Barn Road, Wellingborough, Northamptonshire, NN8 1DH • 01933 227 777
www.Compost.org.uk

COMPUTER AID INTERNATIONAL
Charity that refurbishes computers from the UK for re-use in developing countries.
433 Holloway Road, London, N7 6LJ
020 7281 0091
www.computeraid.org

COMPUTERS FOR CHARITY
A voluntary organisation that campaigns to improve access to IT for community groups, through the recycling of computers.
PO Box 28, Bude, Cornwall, EX23 8BL • 01288 361 199
www.computersforcharity.org.uk

CONFRONTING COMPANIES USING SHAREHOLDER POWER
Handbook for socially-conscious investors.
www.foe.org/international/shareholder/

CONSERVATREE
Promotes recycled paper products within the paper industry.
100 Second Avenue, San Francisco, CA 94118
www.conservatree.com

CONVENTION ON INTERNATIONAL TRADE IN ENDANGERED SPECIES (CITES) SECRETARIAT
The United Nations secretariat that monitors the trade in endangered animals and plants.
www.cites.org

COOPERATIVE BANK
Ethically guided banking facilities,
encouraging business customers to invest
in environmentally conscious companies.
Head Office, PO Box 101, 1 Balloon
Street, Manchester, M60 4EP
08457 212 212
www.cooperativebank.co.uk

CORAL CAY CONSERVATION
Not-for-profit organisation that sends
volunteers to survey endangered coral
reefs and tropical forests.
The Tower, 13th Floor, 125 High Street
London SW19 2JG • 020 8545 7717
www.coralcay.org

CORPORATE WATCH
Investigates corporate crime, and
monitors corporate power.
16B Cherwell Street, Oxford, OX4 1BG
01865 791 391
www.corporatewatch.org.uk

CORPWATCH
Counters corporate-led globalisation
through education, networking and
activism
2288 Fulton St., #103, Berkeley, CA
94704 USA
www.corpwatch.org/

COUNTRY LOVERS
Information on visiting, living or working
in Britain's countryside.
www.countrylovers.co.uk

COUNTRYSIDE AGENCY
The statutory body working to improve
the quality of the countryside and life for
people in the countryside.
London Office, Dacre House,19 Dacre
Street, London, SW1H 0DH
0207 340 2900
www.countryside.gov.uk

**COUNTRYSIDE FOUNDATION FOR
EDUCATION**
An educational charity that works to
bring the countryside into the classroom.
PO Box 8, Hebden Bridge, HX7 5YJ
01422 885 566
www.countrysidefoundation.org.uk

CRITICAL MASS RIDES WORLDWIDE
An organised coincidence of cyclists who

resist the problem of car culture
throughout the world.
www.urban75.com/Action/critical.html

CTC
A one-stop shop for everything to do with
cycling.
PO Box 186, Portsmouth, PO5 1WE
08708 730 061
www.ctc.org.uk

CULPEPER HERBALISTS
Manufacturers of herbal medicines,
aromatherapy products and fine foods.
Hadstock Road, Linton, Cambridge CB1
6NJ.• 01223 891 196
www.culpeper.co.uk

CURTAIN EXCHANGE
For recycling and buying curtains.
Unit 3, Bull Lane Industrial Estate,
Acton, Nr. Sudbury, Suffolk CO10 0BD
01787 319 099
www.thecurtainexchange.net

CYCLIST'S TOURING CLUB HQ
Technical advice and information on
insurance, organised tours and events.
Cotteral House, 69 Meadrow, Godalming,
Surrey, GU7 3HS • 08708 730 060
www.ctc.org.uk

DAKINI
A fair trade organisation specialising in
stationery, soft furnishings and gifts.
00 353 9177 6747
www.dakini.ie

DAY CHOCOLATE COMPANY
Manufacturers of fair trade chocolates
produced from Ghanaian cocoa.
4 Gainsford Street, London, SE1 2NE
020 7378 6550
www.divinechocolate.com

**DEFENDERS OF THE OUSE VALLEY AND
ESTUARY**
Zero waste strategy policy group in the
UK created to address major
environmental interests in the area.
www.dove2000.org

DEODORANT STONE (UK)
Range of natural body deodorants that do
not contain aluminium chlorohydrate and
are not tested on animals.

Caerdelyn, Dolgran, Pencader,
Carmarthenshire, SA39 9BX
01559 384 856
www.deodorant-stone.co.uk

DEPARTMENT OF HEALTH, CENTRE FOR NOISE POLLUTION
A site dedicated to combating the effects
of noise pollution.
Room 693D, Skipton House, 80 London
Road, Elephant and Castle, London
SE1 6LH • 020 7972 5028
www.doh.gov.uk/noisepollution

DIRECTORY RECYCLING PROJECT
Telephone directory recycling scheme
C/o Resource Base, Meridian TV.
Southampton, SO14 0PZ • 02380 236 806
www.integra.org.uk/wastedirectory

DISCOVER THE WORLD
An environmentally responsible travel
company that specialises in Arctic
holidays.
29 Nork Way, Banstead, Surrey, SM7 1PB
01731 218 800
www.discover-the-world.co.uk

DISCOVERING FOSSILS
An educational resource dedicated to
British fossils, fossil collecting locations
and the geology of the UK.
www.discoveringfossils.co.uk

DISCOVERY INITIATIVES
Travel company that supports
conservation worldwide.
The Travel House, Cirencester,
Gloucestershire GL7 1QD
01285 643 333
www.discoveryinitiatives.com

DO-IT-YOURSELF NETWORK
A site dedicated to DIY information
including tips on personal recycling
projects and composting.
www.diynet.com

DOVES FARM FOODS
Gluten free organic food manufacturer.
Salisbury Road, Hungerford, Berkshire,
RG17 0RF • 01488 684 880
www.dovesfarm.co.uk

DRIVE ELECTRIC
The electric vehicle specialists.

08707 443 006
www.drivelectric.com

DUKE OF EDINBURGH AWARD SCHEME
National award scheme open to young
people aged 14-17, with a focus on
physical activities, learning skills, and
community service.
Gulliver House, Madeira Walk, Windsor,
Berkshire, SL4 1EU • 01753 727 400
www.theaward.org

EARTH CENTRE
A charity that promotes sustainable living.
Denaby Main, Doncaster DN12 4EA •
01709 513 933
www.earthcentre.org.uk

EARTHSCAN
Publishers of books on the environment
and sustainable development.
120 Pentonville Road, London, N1 9JN
www.earthscan.co.uk

EARTHWISE BABY
Informative online baby store.
Lollipop Childrens' Products Ltd,
Freepost SWB 40983, Bosigran,
Pendeen, Penzance, Cornwall, TR20 8ZZ
• 01736 799 152
www.earthwisebaby.com

EBAY
Online auction for second-hand goods.
www.ebay.co.uk

EBONY SOLUTIONS
Sells fuel made from cooking oil.
www.ebony-solutions.co.uk

ECO-BABES
Providers of real cloth nappies and
organic baby goods for environmentally
conscious parents.
17B Paradise Road, Downham Market,
Norfolk, PE38 9HS • 01366 387 851
www.eco-babes.co.uk

ECO SALVAGE
Removes abandoned cars and derelict
equipment.
www.rayzume.com/ecosalvage

ECO SCHOOLS
Aims to get everyone in a school
community involved in improving the

school environment.
www.eco-schools.org.uk

ECO SOLUTIONS LTD.
Environmentally friendly DIY products.
Summerleaze House, Church Road,
Winscombe, North Somerset BS25 1BH,
United Kingdom.• 01934 844 484
www.ecosolutions.co.uk/

THE ECOLOGIST
The world's longest running
environmental magazine.
The Ecologist, Unit 18 Chelsea Wharf,
15 Lots Road, London SW10 0QJ
www.theecologist.org

ECOLOGY BUILDING SOCIETY
A building society dedicated to improving
the environment by promoting sustainable
housing and communities.
18 Station Road, Crosshills, Keighley,
BD2 7 EH • 08456 745 566
www.ecology.co.uk

ECOS ORGANIC PAINTS
Makers of odourless, solvent-free gloss
and emulsion paints.
Unit 34 Heysham Business Park,
Middleton Road, Heysham, Lancs, LA3
3PP • 0152 485 8978
www.ecospaints.com

ECOTEC
Products aimed at improving car fuel
consumption.
Priestley House , 28-34 Albert Street,
Birmingham B4 7UD • 01844 212 939
www.ecotekplc.com

ECOVER UK LTD
Manufactures environmentally friendly
detergents and cleaning products.
165 Main Street, Greenham Park,
Berkshire, RG9 6HN • 01635 574 553
www.ecover.com

ECOZONE
A range of eco-friendly products for use in
and around the home.
www.ecozone.co.uk

EDEN PROJECT
An permanent outdoor exhibition with
over 100,000 plants from all over the
world, that highlights our relationship

with plants.
Bodelva, St Austell, Cornwall PL24 2SG
01726 811 911
www.edenproject.co.uk

EDIRECTORY
Wide range of goods that can be bought
using secure online shopping
www.edirectory.co.uk/

ELECTRIC CAR ASSOCIATION
Blue Lias House, Station Road, Hatch
Beauchamp TA3 6SQ.
www.avt.uk.com

ELLIE POO PAPER COMPANY
Makes paper from the dung of the Sri
Lankan elephant.
1 Heritage Courtyard, Saddler Street,
Wells, BA5 2RR • 01749 670 570
www.elliepoopaper.com

EMAGAZINE
A magazine on environmental issues.
www.emagazine.com

EMPTY HOMES AGENCY, THE
Highlighting the problems of empty
property in England, and bringing them
back into use.
020 7828 6288
www.emptyhomes.com

ENERGY EFFICIENCY
Range of products and services for
business and public sector organisations
to help reduce energy consumption.
0800 585 794
www.actionenergy.org.uk

ENERGY+
Energy efficient refrigerators and freezers.
5 South Parks Road, Oxford, OX1 3UB
01865 281 211
www.energy-plus.org

ENERGY SAVING TRUST
Promoting sustainable and efficient uses
of energy.
www.est.org.uk

ENERGY STAR
Provides information on energy saving
and the energy saving star rating.
www.energystar.gov

ENGLISH NATURE
Responsible for conservation of wildlife and geology in England.
Northminster House, Peterborough PE1 1UA • 01733 455 101
www.english-nature.org.uk

ENMAX
Canadian energy company providing useful energy tips for home and business.
www.enmax.com

ENVIRONMENT AGENCY
Information on energy rating schemes.
0800 80 70 60
www.environment.agency.gov.uk/savewater

ENVIRONMENTAL DISCOVERY HOLIDAYS
Environmental holidays for young people aged 6-16 during the summer in Dorset.
YPTENC, 8 Leapale Road, Guildford, Surrey, GU1 4JX • 01483 539 600
www.yptenc.org.uk

ENVIRONMENTAL INVESTIGATION AGENCY (EIA)
An international organisation committed to investigating and exposing environmental crime.
62/63 Upper Street, London, N1 0NY 020 7354 7960
www.eia-international.org

ENVIRONMENTAL MOBILE CONTROL
Provides recycling solutions for surplus mobile phone equipment.
Unit 3 Glensyl Way, Hawkins Lane Industrial Estate, Burton on Trent, Staffordshire, DE14 1LX.• 01283 516 259
www.emc-recycle.com

ENVIRONMENTAL TRANSPORT ASSOCIATION, (ETA)
Motoring organisation campaigning for a sustainable transport system.
68 High Street, Weybridge, KT13 8RS 01932 828 882
www.eta.co.uk

EOSTA
Distributes organic and biodynamic fruit and vegetables from around the world.
www.eosta.com

ERASMUS SCHEME
Opportunities for undergraduates to learn new languages, experience new cultures, and gain new perspectives.
www.erasmus.ac.uk

ESSEX COUNTY COUNCIL
An excellent recycling/waste products and services page with an A-Z directory of recycling tips.
www.essexcc.gov.uk

ETHICAL CONSUMER
Alternative consumer organisation researching the environmental and social records of the companies behind the brand names.
Unit 21, 41 Old Birley Street, Manchester, M15 5RF • 0161 226 2929
www.ethicalconsumer.org

ETHICAL INVESTMENT RESEARCH SERVICE (EIRIS)
Provides research into corporate behaviour for ethical investors.
The Ethical Investment Research Service, 80-84 Bondway, London, SW8 1SF • 020 7840 5700
www.eiris.org

ETHICAL JUNCTION
Information on ethical organisations and ethically made products.
124 Northmoor Road, Manchester M12 5RS. • 0161 224 0749
www.ethical-junction.com

ETHICAL MATTERS
Information on ethical living and ethically made products.
Unit A2, 2nd Floor, Linton House, 39-51 Highgate Road, London, NW5 1RS 020 7419 7258
www.ethicalmatters.co.uk

ETHICAL TRADING INITIATIVE
An alliance of companies, NGOs, and trade union organisations working together to promote ethical trade.
www.ethicaltrade.org

ETHICAL WARES
Ethical mail order company run by vegans who trade without exploiting animals, humans or the wider environment.
ww.ethicalwares.co.uk

ETHICAL WILLS
Promoting the use of ethical wills.
www.ethicalwill.com

EUROPA
Website of the European Union.
www.europa.eu.int

EXODUS TRAVELS
Walking, adventure, biking, wildlife and cultural holidays worldwide.
Grange Mills, Weir Road, London SW12 0NE • 020 8675 5550
www.exodus.co.uk

EXPERIENCE CORPS
Encourages volunteering in local communities.
020 7981 2500
www.experiencecorps.co.uk

EXPLORE WORLDWIDE
Adventure holidays around the world.
01252 760 000
www.exploreworldwide.com

FACSIMILE PREFERENCE SERVICE
Opt out of receiving unsolicited sales and marketing faxes at home.
DMA House, 70 Margaret Street, London, W1W 8SS • 020 7291 3330
www.fpsonline.org.uk

FAIRTRADE FOUNDATION
Promotes fair trade and campaigns to encourage the growth of global fair trade.
www.fairtrade.org

FARM
Campaigning for a viable future for independent and family farms.
PO Box 26094,London SW10 0XZ
020 7352 7928
www.farm.org.uk

FARM AROUND
Box scheme delivering seasonal organic food to your door.
Offices B140-143, New Covent Garden, Nine Elms Lane, London SW8 5PA
020 7627 8066
www.farmaround.co.uk

FEDERATION OF CITY FARMS AND COMMUNITY GARDENS
Sustainable and community-led projects

working with people, animals and plants.
The Green House, Hereford Street, Bristol, BS3 4NA • 01179 231 800
www.farmgarden.org.uk

FEMCARE PLUS
Healthier, safer and environmentally-friendly feminine hygiene products.
68-307 E. Palm Canyon Dr., #101, Cathedral City, CA 92234
www.femininehygiene.com

FESTIVAL EYE
Listings of camps, festivals and other outdoor events in the UK.
BCM 2002, London, WC1 N3XX
0870 737 1011
www.festivaleye.com

FIELD STUDIES COUNCIL
An educational charity committed to teaching environmental issues.
Montford Bridge, Preston Montford, Shrewsbury, Shropshire, England SY4 1HW • 01743 852 100
www.field-studies-council.org

FOOD DOCTOR
Independent professional advice on nutrition and health.
76 - 78 Holland Park Avenue, London W11 3RB • 020 7792 6700
www.thefooddoctor.com

FOOD FOR THOUGHT
Vegetarian London restaurant.
31 Neal Street, Covent Garden, London WC2H 9PR
020 7836 0239 or 020 7836 9072

FOOD STANDARDS AGENCY
Valuable information on food labelling, organic food, food safety and GM crops.
Aviation House, 125 Kingsway, London WC2B 6NH • 020 7276 8000
www.foodstandards.gov.uk

FOREST STEWARDSHIP COUNCIL
An international NGO dedicated to promoting responsible management of the world's forests.
Unit D, Station Buildings, Llanidloes, Powys, SY18 6EB • 01686 413 916
www.fsc-uk.info

FOUR SEASONS PROJECT
School-based projects and environmental
education resources.
www.4seasons.org.uk

FREE WHEELERS
Campaigns to reduce pollution by
reducing car usage.
www.freewheelers.com

FRESH FOOD COMPANY
Organic fruit, vegetables, meat, fish, wine
and bread and organic recipes.
The Orchard, 50 Wormholt Road, London,
W12 0LS. • 020 8749 8778
www.freshfood.co.uk

FRESH WATER FILTER CO.
Water filters for the home.
895 High Road, Chadwell Heath, Essex
RN6 4HL • 020 8597 3223
www.freshwaterfilter.com

FRIENDS OF CONSERVATION
Funds international community
conservation projects and works with the
travel industry to promote sustainable
tourism.
16-18 Denbigh Street, London SW1V
2ER. • 020 7592 0110
www.foc-uk.com

FRIENDS OF THE EARTH
A national environmental pressure group
with local groups who campaign on
environmental issues.
26-28 Underwood Street, London N1 7JQ
0207 490 1555
www.foe.co.uk

FRIENDS OF THE EARTH – SCOTLAND
www.foe-scotland.org.uk

FRIENDS PROVIDENT
Ethical financial products and services.
Pixham End, Dorking, Surrey RH4 1QA
08706 083 678
www.friendsprovident.co.uk

THE FUNERAL COMPANY LIMITED
Provides green funerals and other
alternative interments for all
denominations.
19 Stratford Road, Milton Keynes MK12
5LJ • 01908 225 222
www.thefuneralcompanyltd.com

FUTURE FORESTS
Plants trees to help neutralise carbon
dioxide emissions.
4 Great James Street, London WC1N 3DB
• 0870 241 1932
www.futureforests.com

FUTURE HEATING LTD
All types of heating installation, including
solar.
37 Highworth Road, New Southgate,
London N11 2SN • 020 8351 9360
www.future-heating.co.uk

GALEFORCE
A company supplying wind turbines.
Renewables House, 230 Portglenone
Road, Randalstown, County Antrim,
Northern Ireland BT41 3RP
02879 65 9 775
www.galeforce.nireland.co.uk

GET ETHICAL-ONLINE
Shopping portal that promotes ethical
shopping and supports social enterprises
in the UK.
www.getethical.com

**GLASS MANUFACTURERS
CONFEDERATION**
Promotes glass as the leading choice for
containers.
British Glass, Northumberland Road,
Sheffield S10 2UA • 01142 686 201
www.britglass.co.uk

GLOBAL WITNESS
Campaigns to end the links between
natural resource exploitation and conflict
and corruption.
PO Box 6042, London N19 5WP
020 7272 6731
www.globalwitness.org/about_us/

GOSSYPIUM
An ethical eco-cotton store that
manufactures fairly traded clothing.
2-3 St Andrew's Place, Southover Road,
Lewes, East Sussex BN7 1UP
01273 897 509
www.gossypium.co.uk

GREEN BATTERIES
Promotes the use of rechargeable
batteries.
www.greenbatteries.com/

GREEN BOARD GAMES
Ethical games for all ages.
Unit 112a, Cressex Business Park,
Coronation Road, High Wycombe, Bucks
HP12 3RP • 01494 538 999
www.greenboardgames.com

GREEN BOOKS
Environmentally inspired books on a
range of subjects.
Foxhole, Dartington, Totnes TQ9 6EB
01803 897 509
www.greenbooks.co.uk

GREEN BUILDING STORE
Safe, sustainable building products.
11 Huddersfield Road, Meltham,
Holmsirth, HD9 4NJ.• 01484 541 717
www.greenbuildingstore.co.uk

GREEN CHOICES
A guide to greener living.
PO Box 31617, London SW2 4FF
www.greenchoices.org

GREEN CHRONICLE
Information on growing, buying, eating
and living organically.
www.greenchronicle.com

GREEN CONE LTD
Compost bins for food and garden waste.
11 Grisedale Court, Chilwell, Nottingham
NG9 5NN • 0115 943 6888
www.greencone.com

GREEN CUISINE LIMITED
Healthy organic cooking, with recipes and
courses on cooking, food and health.
Penrhos Court, Kington, Herefordshire
HR5 3LH • 01544 230 720
www.greencuisine.org

GREEN ENERGY
Encourages sustainable and green sources
of energy.
The National Energy Foundation,
Davy Avenue, Knowlhill,
Milton Keynes MK5 8NG.
www.greenenergy.org.uk

GREEN FIBRES
Organic clothing and home products
made from organic cotton, linen, hemp,
wool and silk, with a wedding list service.
99 High St, Totnes, Devon, England
01803 868 001
www.greenfibres.com

GREEN FUTURES
A magazine on environmental solutions
and sustainable futures published by
Forum for the Future.
www.greenfutures.org.uk

GREEN GLOBE ACCREDITATIONS
World wide certification scheme for
sustainable travel and tourism for
consumers, companies and communities.
GPO Box 371, Canberra, ACT, 2612,
Australia
www.greenglobe21.com

GREENGUIDE
Database of organic, eco-friendly and
ethical businesses and organisations.
Green Guide Publishing Ltd, PO Box
17568, London N1 2WQ • 020 8815 4730
www.greenguideonline.com

GREENMATTERS
Site designed to help busy people live a
greener life.
www.greenmatters.com

GREEN METROPOLIS
Online bookstore for buying and selling
second hand books, with contributions to
the Woodland Trust from every sale.
www.greenmetropolis.com

GREEN SHOP
Sustainable and low-impact products for
the home.
Cheltenham Road, Bisley,
Gloucestershire GL6 7BX • 01452 770629
www.greenshop.co.uk

GREEN STATIONERY COMPANY
Environmentally friendly stationery
products.
Studio 1, 114 Walcot Street, Bath, BA1
5BG • 01225 480 556
www.greenstat.co.uk

GREENPEACE
Campaigns to expose global
environmental problems and their causes.
Canonbury Villas, London, N1 2PN
020 7188 1068
www.greenpeace.org.uk
see also: Greenpeace's campaign against

toxins.
www.greenpeace.org.uk/Products/Toxin

GREEN PRICES
Compares products and prices of green
energy suppliers in Europe.
www.greenprices.com/eu/index.asp

GREENWAYS
An offshoot of the Countryside Agency
that works for quieter lanes.
John Dower House, Crescent Place,
Cheltenham, Gloucestershire GL50 3RA
01242 521381.
www.greenways.gov.uk

GREEN WORKS
Redundant office equipment for schools,
charities, community groups and start-up
businesses.
Second Floor, Tower Building, 11 York
Road, London SE1 7NX
020 7981 0450
www.green-work.co.uk/

GROUNDWORK
Environmental regeneration charity
working for sustainable development in
some of the UK's poorest communities.
65 Villa Road, Handsworth, Birmingham
B19 1BH • 0121 507 6500
www.groundwork.org.uk

GUIDE TO AROMATHERAPY
The UK's Aromatherapy practitioners and
suppliers, with a link to the worldwide
listings.
www.fragrant.demon.co.uk/ukaromas.ht
ml

GUSTOGUIDE
Online organic food and restaurant guide
for the UK.
145 Junction Rd, Tufnell Park N19 5PX
0705 065 4228
www.gustoguide.co.uk

HAPPY HIPPIE
Provides tips, information and resources
on a wide range of ecological products.
PO BOX 7482, San Diego, CA 92107
www.happyhippie.com

HAWK AND OWL TRUST
Working to conserve birds of prey, and
their habitats, from human pressures.
c/o The Zoological Society of London,
Regents Park, London, NW1 4RY
01626 334 4864
www.hawkandowl.org

HEALTHY HOUSE
Products for a healthy environment, at
home and in the office.
The Old Co-Op, Lower Street, Ruscombe,
Stroud, Gloucestershire GL6 6BU
01453 752 216
www.healthy-house.co.uk

HEMP SHOP
Farms, processes and distributes hemp
products across the country.
22 Gardner Street, North Laine, Brighton
BN1 1UP • 0704 131 3233
www.thehempshop.net

HEMP UNION
Provides hemp products for consumers
and industry. Also provides hemp recipes.
24 Anlaby Road, Hull, East Yorks HU1
2PA • 01482 225 328
www.hemp-union.karoo.net

**HENRY DOUBLEDAY RESEARCH
ASSOCIATION (HDRA)**
Dedicated to researching and promoting
organic gardening, farming and food.
HDRA, Ryton Organic Gardens, Coventry,
Warwickshire CV8 3LG • 02476 303 517
www.hdra.org.uk/

HIGH & WILD
Responsible Adventure travel specialists.
1 Heritage Courtyard, Sadler Street,
Wells BA5 2RR • 01749 671 777
www.highandwild.co.uk

HIKING WEBSITE
Helps make the most of hiking
experiences, with gear, trails and more.
www.hikingwebsite.com

HIPP ORGANIC
Producers of organic baby food.
165 Main Street, New Greenham Park,
Newbury, Berkshire, RG19 6HN
0845 050 1351
www.hipp.co.uk

HIPPO THE WATER SAVER
Water saving device for toilet cisterns.
01989 766 667 (order line)
www.hippo-the-watersaver.co.uk

HOMECHECK
Guide to flooding, subsidence, crime and more in your neighbourhood.
www.homecheck.co.uk

HONESTY COSMETICS
Wide range of skin and hair products, suitable for vegetarians and vegans.
Lumford Mill, Bakewell, Derbyshire, DE45 1GS • 01629 814 888
www.honestycosmetics.co.uk

HORSE DIRECTORY
Services, products and information on horses and horse riding.
www.horse-directory.co.uk

HOSTELS.COM
Huge selection of hostels worldwide.
www.hostels.com

H2OUSE
Information and advice on how to use water efficiently.
www.h2ouse.org

IMPROVEMENT AND DEVELOPMENT AGENCY (IDEA)
An agency promoting the involvement of local authorities in Local Agenda 21.
Layden House, 76-78 Turnmill Street, London EC1M 5LG • 020 7296 6599
www.idea.gov.uk or www.scream.co.uk/la21

INSTITUTE OF SOCIAL AND ETHNIC ACCOUNTABILITY
Enhancing the performance of companies' sustainable development records.
Unit A, 137 Shepherdess Walk, London N1 7RQ • 020 7549 0400
www.accountability.org.uk

INTERMEDIATE TECHNOLOGY DEVELOPMENT GROUP (ITDG)
Advocates sustainable use of technology to reduce poverty in developing countries.
The Schumacher Centre, Bourton-on-Dunsmore, Rugby, UK, CV23 9BR
01926 634 506
www.itdg.org

INTERNATIONAL DARK SKY ASSOCIATION
Campaigns to protect the night-time environment and ensure stars are visible.
3225 N. First Avenue, Tuscon, Arizona, 85719 USA
www.darksky.org

INTERNATIONAL RIGHT TO KNOW
A public information resource on US multinationals and their actions.
See also: Friends of the Earth
www.irtk.org

I-TO-I
Promotes voluntary travel with community projects overseas.
Woodside House, 261 Low Lane, Leeds LS18 5NY
www.i-to-i.com

IVILLAGE
The website for women.
www.ivillage.co.uk

IWANTONEOFTHOSE.COM
Suppliers of the solar torch.
www.iwantoneofthose.com

JUNIPER GREEN
Provides organic dry gin, distilled using natural ingredients such as organic juniper, coriander, angelica and savory.
Meadow View House, Tannery Lane, Bramley, Surrey, GU5 0AB
01483 894 650
www.junipergreen.org

JUST GIVING
Processes charity donations online.
www.justgiving.com

KIDS ON THE MOVE
Campaigns to increase child mobility, by promoting initiatives developed by schools, transport operators and local authorities.
Publication copies are available from env_pubs@cec.eu.int
www.europa.eu.int/comm/environment/youth/air/kids_on_the_move_en.html

KINGFISHER NATURAL TOOTHPASTE
Producing natural toothpaste with no added preservatives or colourings.

White Lodge Estate, Hall Road, Norwich,
NR4 6DG • 01603 630 484
www.kingfishertoothpaste.com

LA LECHE LEAGUE
Help and advice for breastfeeding mothers.
PO Box 29, West Bridgford, Nottingham,
NG2 7NP • 020 7242 1278
www.lalecheleague.org.uk

LANDLIFE
An environmental charity that works to
bring people and nature closer together.
0151 737 1819
www.landlife.org.uk

LETS GO GARDENING
Information about gardening in the UK.
www.letsgogardening.co.uk

LIFTSHARE COMMUNITY SCHEME
Car Sharing Scheme.
www.liftshare.org

LIGHT SWITCH
A partnership to promote the use of
energy efficient lighting in the non-
domestic sector.
www.lightswitch.co.uk

LINGUAPHONE UK
A global language learning company.
www.linguaphone.co.uk

LION & LAMB PROJECT
Campaigns to stop the marketing of
violence to children.
4300 Montgomery Avenue- Suite 104,
Bethesda, Maryland, 20814, U.S.A.
www.lionlamb.org

LITTLE RED HEN NURSERIES
Sells and delivers organic plants grown in
peat-free compost.
91 Denholme Road, Oxenhope,
Keighley,W. Yorkshire BD22 9SJ
www.redhens.co.uk

LOCAL EXCHANGE TRADING SYSTEM
Local community-based networks
allowing people to exchange goods and
services with each other without the need
for money.
12 Southcote Road, London, N19 5BJ •
020 7607 7852
www.letslinkuk.org

LONDON CYCLING CAMPAIGN
Campaigns to make London a world-class
cycling city. • 020 7928 7220
www.lcc.org.uk

LOW IMPACT LIVING INITIATIVE
Promotes harmonious ways of living with
the environment.
Redfield, Winslow, Bucks, MK18 3LZ •
01296 714 184
www.lowimpact.org/about.htm

LP GAS ASSOCIATION
Commercial propane and butane gas.
Pavilion 6, Headlands Business Park,
Salisbury Road, Ringwood, Hampshire,
NH24 3PE • 01425 461 612
www.lpga.co.uk

MAILING PREFERENCE SERVICE
A register you can put your name on to
stop unsolicited junk mail.
DMA House, 70 Margaret Street,
LondonW1W 8SS • 0207 291 3310
www.admar.co.uk/mps.htm

MAKE A DIFFERENCE ADVENTURES
Small group tours to Africa and South
America, each of which supports a local
community project.
24 Ringwood Road, Farnborough,
Hampshire GU14 8BG • 0845 122 1304
www.mad-adventures.com

MAKING COSMETICS
How to make cosmetics at home from
natural and manufactured raw materials.
PO Box 251, 8905, Arni, AG, Switzerland
• +41 56 640 1507
www.makingcosmetics.com

MAN IN SEAT 61
Journey advice from a man who has
travelled the world by rail and sea and
worked within the railway sector.
www.seat61.com

MANY MOONS
Menstruation products produced using
either organic or reusable products.
pacificcoast.net/~manymoons

MARSHMALLOW
Advice and tips on making your own
beauty products.
www.marshmallow.co.uk

MAST ACTION UK
Fights the insensitive siting of mobile phone and TETRA masts, and offers advice on how to effectively object.
MAUK Head Office, PO Box 312, Hertfordshire, EN7 5ZE • 08704 322 377
www.mastaction.org

MCSPOTLIGHT
Anything you need to know about McDonald's or McLibel contained within 21,000 files.
www.mcspotlight.org

MEADOW SWEET
Range of natural cosmetics, toiletries and essential oils. Suitable for vegetarians and vegans.
Unit 1, Uplands Court Yard, Stowupland Road, Stowmarket, Suffolk IP14 5AN
01449 676 940
www.meadowsweet.co.uk

MEDIA FAMILY
Helps families and educators maximise the benefits and minimise the harm of mass media on children through research, education and advocacy.
606 24th Avenue South, Suite 606,Minneapolis, MN 55454
+11 888 672 5437 or 011 612 672 5437
www.mediafamily.org

MEDICINES & HEALTHCARE REGULATORY AUTHORITY (MHRA)
Information about the work of the Medicines sector of the MHRA. Includes a detailed section on DIY homeopathy.
Market Towers, 1 Nine Elms Lane, London SW8 5NQ • 020 7273 0000
www.mca.gov.uk

MERCY CORPS
Alleviating suffering, and poverty by helping people build secure communities.
www.mercycorps.com

MILLENNIUM VOLUNTEERS PROGRAMME
An initiative for people aged 16-24, offering the chance to build on skills, and use time constructively.
Colville House Resource Centre, School Road, Oulton Broad, Lowestoft, NR33 9NB • 01502 530632
www.millenniumvolunteers.co.uk

MOUNTAIN BIKING UK
Info on mountain biking in the UK.
Beaufort Court, 30 Monmer St, Bath BA1 2BW • 01225 442 244
www.mbuk.com

MUMSNET
A website on parenting run by parents for parents.
www.mumsnet.com

NAPPY LADY
Offers practical advice on how to swap from disposable to cloth nappies.
16 Hill Brow, Bearsted, Maidstone, Kent, ME14 4AW • 0845 456 2441
www.thenappylady.co.uk

NATIONAL ASSOCIATION OF FARMER'S MARKETS
A source of information on farmers' markets, and a list of markets in the UK.
South Vaults, Green Park Station, Green Park Road, Bath, BA1 1JB
01225 787 914
www.farmersmarkets.net

NATIONAL ASSOCIATION OF NAPPY SERVICES
Voluntary organisation that promotes the use of cotton nappies and increases public awareness of the environmental and health problems associated with disposable nappies.
0121 693 4949
www.changeanappy.co.uk

NATIONAL ASSOCIATION OF PAPER MERCHANTS, (NAPM)
The trade association representing the interests of UK paper merchants.
Hamilton Court, Gogmore Lane, Chertsey, Surrey, KT16 9AP
08707 500 249
www.napm.org.uk

NATIONAL CANINE DEFENCE LEAGUE
Dog-welfare related issues.
17 Wakley Street, London EC1V 7RQ • 020 7837 0006
www.ncdl.org.uk

NATIONAL CENTRE FOR BUSINESS AND SUSTAINABILITY
A consultancy set up to help organisations improve their environmental and social

sustainability.
Giant's Basin, Potato Wharf, Castlefield, Manchester M3 4NB • 0161 819 1102
www.thencbs.co.uk

NATIONAL CHILDBIRTH TRUST (NCT)
Runs a range of antenatal classes, helplines, and educational and social events, to give confidence to new parents.
Alexandra House, Oldham Terrace, Acton, London, W3 6NH • 020 8992 2616
www.nctpregnancyandbabycare.com

NATIONAL ENERGY FOUNDATION
A UK charity that provides free advice on energy efficiency and renewable energy.
The National Centre, Davy Avenue, Knowlhill, Milton Keynes, MK5 8NG
01908 665 555
www.natenergy.org.uk

NATIONAL FOX WELFARE SOCIETY
Charity committed to preserving fox populations in the UK.
135 Higham Road, Rushden, Northants, NN10 6DS • 01933 411 996
www.nfws.org.uk

NATIONAL HEDGE LAYING SOCIETY (NHLS)
To encourage the art of hedge laying and keep the local styles in existence.
'Way Post' Vines Cross, East Sussex BN21 9EG • 01959 565 678
www.hedgelaying.org.uk

NATIONAL INSTITUTE OF MEDICAL HERBALISTS
A professional association of practitioners of herbal medicine.
56 Longbrook Street, Exeter, EX4 6AH
01392 426022
www.nimh.org.uk

NATIONAL PLAYING FIELDS ASSOCIATION
Committed to protecting and improving playing fields.
Head Office, Stanley House, St Chad's Place, London WC1X 9HH • 0207 833 5360
www.npfa.co.uk

NATIONAL RECYCLING FORUM
A guide to products available in the UK that contain recycled materials.
c/o Wastewatch, 96 Tooley Street, London, SE1 2TH • 020 7089 2100
www.recycledproducts.org.uk

NATIONAL SOCIETY OF ALLOTMENT AND LEISURE GARDENS
Maintaining the British heritage by establishing co-operation between agriculturalists and the organisation of smallholdings and allotments.
O'Dell House, Hunters Road, Corby, Northants NN17 5JE • 01536 266 576
www.nsalg.demon.co.uk

NATURAL CARPETS 4 U
Offers a range of natural carpets.
29/31 High Street, Thrapston, Northants, NN14 4JJ • 01832 735 225
www.naturalcarpets4u.com

NATURAL COLLECTION
Online catalogue with a range of eclectic, unusual, useful and interesting products chosen to contribute to a better world.
0870 331 3335
www.naturalcollection.com

NATURAL DEATH CENTRE
Helping people to arrange inexpensive and environmentally friendly funerals.
6 Blackstock Mews, Blackstock Road, London, N4 2BT • 020 7359 8391
www.naturaldeath.co.uk

NATURAL ECO TRADING
Environmentally friendly household cleaning products.
Natural Eco Trading Ltd, PO Box 115, Tunbridge Wells, Kent, TN4 8WJ
01892 616871
www.greenbrands.co.uk

NATURAL FRIENDS
Introduction agency for ethically-minded and environmentally-sensitive people.
15 Benyon Gardens, Culford, Bury St Edmunds, Suffolk, IP28 6EA
01284 728 315
www.natural-friends.com

NATURAL HISTORY MUSEUM, (NHM)
Museum whose collections promote an enjoyment and responsible use of the natural world.
Cromwell Road, London SW7 5BD
020 7942 5011
www.nhm.ac.uk

CONTACTS

NATURAL RESOURCES DEFENSE COUNCIL
An environmental action organisation.
40 West 20th Street New York, NY 10011
• +1 212 727-2700
www.nrdc.org

NATURE SAVE – POLICIES LIMITED
Provides ethical insurance policies.
Freepost SWB30837, Totnes, TQ9 5ZZ •
01803 864 390
www.naturesave.co.uk/home.html

NEW ECONOMICS FOUNDATION
Promotes solutions to social,
environmental and economic problems.
3 Jonathan Street, London, SE11 5NH •
020 7820 6300
www.neweconomics.org

NHBS MAIL ORDER BOOKSTORE
A bookstore specialising in natural
history, the environment, science and
sustainable development.
2-3 Willis Road, Totnes, Devon TQ9 5XN
01803 865 913
www.nhbs.com

NHS ORGAN DONOR NET
Provides information on organ transplants
and how to become an organ donor.
UK Transplant, Fox Dean Road, Stoke
Gifford, Bristol, BS34 8RR
0845 300 6727
www.uktransplant.org.uk

NO SWEAT
The UK campaign against sweatshops.
PO Box 36707, London SW9 8YA
07904 431 959
www.nosweat.org.uk

NORWICH AND PETERBOROUGH BUILDING SOCIETY
A building society in the UK with strong
environmental policies.
Principal Office, Peterborough
Business Park, Lynch Wood,
Peterborough, PE2 6WZ • 0845 300 6727
www.norwichandpeterborough.co.uk

NOT TOO PRETTY
Information on cosmetics and associated
products that contain dangerous
phthalates.
www.nottoopretty.org

OFFICE OF ENERGY EFFICIENCY AND RENEWABLE ENERGY
Aims to bring a future of clean, affordable
and abundant energy.
www.energysmartschools.gov/energysm
artschool/index.html

OFFICES OF WATER SERVICES
England and Wales's sewage and water
industry's regulator.
Centre City Tower, 7 Hill Street,
Birmingham, B5 4UA • 0121 625 1373
www.ofwat.gov.uk

OIL BANK
Find the location of your nearest oil bank
to recycle old oil and filters.
c/o The Environment Agency, Rivers
House, Waterside Drive, Aztec West,
Aldonsbury, Bristol, BS12 4UD
0800 663 366
www.oilbankline.org.uk

OLLIE RECYCLES
A website for children to learn the 3Rs –
reduce, reuse and recycle.
www.ollierecycles.com/uk

ONE HUNDRED AND ONE CANDLES
An extensive range of candles and
accessories.
358 Green Lanes, London, N13 5TJ
020 7247 1038
www.101candles.com

ONE TREE HILL ALLOTMENT SOCIETY, (OTHAS)
Essential information for
cultivating/gardening in the UK.
www.othas.org.uk

ONEWORLD INTERNATIONAL
Dedicated to harnessing the democratic
potential of the internet to promote
human rights and sustainable
development.
17th Floor, 89 Albert Embankment,
London SE1 7TP • 020 7735 2100
www.oneworld.net

ONLINE UK CHARITY ORGANISATIONS AND SHOPS
Provides information on a selection of UK
charities.
www.avoidtherush.co.uk/shopping/2005/
charities.htm

ORGANICA J

A company offering a collection of organic, GM-free products, from clothing to healthcare.

Boghead Croft, Finzean, Banchory, Kincardineshire AB31 6LY
01330 850 257
www.organicaj.co.uk

ORGANIC CONSUMERS' ASSOCIATION

A non-profit organisation campaigning for food safety, organic agriculture, fair trade and environmental sustainability.

6101 Cliff Estate Road, Little Marais, MN 55614, USA • +1 218 226 4164
www.organicconsumers.org

ORGANIC DELIVERY COMPANY

An organic food delivery service especially for Londoners.

70 Rivington Street, London, EC2A 3AY
020 7739 8181
www.organicdelivery.co.uk

ORGANIC DIRECTORY

A comprehensive guide for the organic movement, listing organic retailers, box schemes, farm shops, restaurants and much more.
www.theorganicdirectory.co.uk

ORGANIC FOOD, UK

Anything and everything you want to know about organic food.
www.organicfood.co.uk

ORGANIC HOLIDAYS

Information about holiday accommodation on organic farms and smallholdings.

Organic Holidays, Tranfield House, Tranfield Gardens, Guiseley, Leeds LS20 8PZ • 01943 870791
www.organic-holidays.com

ORGANIC SHOP

Delivers a selection of organic food and wine from Britain and around the world.

Freepost, Alderley Edge, Cheshire SK9 7YG • 0845 674 4000
www.theorganicshop.co.uk

OVER THE GARDEN GATE

A community site dedicated to wildlife in the garden and surrounding countryside.
www.overthegardengate.co.uk

OXFAM

A relief and campaign organisation committed to finding lasting solutions to poverty and suffering around the world.

Oxfam House, 274 Banbury Road, Oxford, OX2 7DZ • 0870 333 2700
www.oxfam.org.uk

OZONE FRIENDS LTD

Collects and reuses your discarded white goods.

Units 6-8, Buzzard Creek Industrial Estate, River Road, Barking IG11 0EL
020 8591 6333
www.ozonefriends.co.uk

PARROT FISH COMPANY

Provides educational resources about issues around the world.

The Parrot Fish Company, 51 North Street, Maldon, Essex CM9 5HJ
01621 858 940
www.parrotfish.co.uk

PATAGONIA

Outdoor clothing and equipment manufacturer that places an emphasis on environmentally friendly manufacturing and support.
www.patagonia.com

PEOPLE & PLANET

UK Student Action on world poverty, human rights and the environment.

People & Planet, 51 Union Street, Oxford OX4 1JP • 01865 245678
www.peopleandplanet.org

PESTICIDE ACTION NETWORK UK

An independent, non-profit organisation that aims to reduce our dependence on toxic chemicals and pesticides.

Eurolink Centre Unit 16, 49 Effra Road, London, SW2 1BZ • 020 7274 8895
www.pan-uk.org

PHENOLOGY NETWORK

Gives a detailed insight into nature's calendar, and information on how to become involved in phenological activities.

The Woodland Trust, Autumn Park, Dysart Road, Grantham, Lincs NG31 6LL
01476 581 111
www.phenology.org.uk

PHONE CO-OP
A telecommunications provider that takes an ethical and environmentally responsible approach to business.
5 The Millhouse, Elmsfield Business Centre, Worcester Road, Chipping Norton, Oxon OX7 5XL • 0845 458 9000
www.phonecoop.org.uk

PLANTLIFE
A national membership charity dedicated to conserving plant life in its natural habitat.
21 Elizabeth Street, London SW1W 9RP
020 7808 0100
www.plantlife.org.uk

POLYMER REPROCESSORS LIMITED
Developing recycling techniques in the plastics industry.
Reeds Lane, Moreton, Wirral CH46 1DW
0151 606 0456
www.polymer-reprocessors.co.uk

POWABYKE
A company offering electric bikes as an eco-friendly alternative to cars.
Powabyke Ltd, 3 Wood Street, Bath BA1 2JQ • 01225 443737
www.powabyke.com

POWERPLUS
A company specialising in fuel saving and emission reduction technology.
42 St Leonards Road, Eastbourne, East Sussex BN21 3UU • 01323 417 700
www.powerplus.be

PRELOVED
A website allowing you to buy and sell second-hand items.
www.preloved.co.uk

PUMPKIN CARVING
For information on celebrating halloween and growing pumpkins.
www.pumpkin-carving.com

PURE H2O
A water purification company that provides water systems for residential and commercial uses.
Unit 5, Egham Business Village, Crabtree Road, Egham, Surrey TW20 8RB
01784 221 188
www.pureh2o.co.uk

PURE ORGANICS LIMITED
Producers of organic food.
Stockport Farm, Stockport Road, Amesbury, Wiltshire SP4 7LN
01980 626263
www.organics.org

PUREWINE COMPANY
Provides over 175 different organic, vegetarian and vegan wines.
Ocean house, 51 Alcantara Crescent, Ocean Village Southampton SO14 3HR
02380 238 214
www.purewine.co.uk

QUADRIS ENVIRONMENTAL INVESTMENTS
A company that runs socially responsible investment funds.
Regent House, 19-20 The Broadway, WOKING, Surrey GU21 5AP
01483 756 800
www.quadris.co.uk

RAINFOREST ACTION NETWORK
Works to protect tropical rainforests and the human rights of those living in and around them.
Dolphin House, 4 Hunter Square, Edinburgh EH1 1QW • 0131 622 7188
www.ran.org

RAMBLERS' ASSOCIATION
An organisation working for walkers across England, Scotland and Wales.
2nd Floor Camelford House, 87-90 Albert Embankment, London SE1 7TW
020 7339 8500
www.ramblers.org.uk

REAL NAPPY ASSOCIATION
For information and advice on all nappy-related issues, for individuals, health professionals, the media and local authorities.
PO Box 3704, London SE26 4RX
01983 401 959
www.realnappy.com

RECLAIM THE STREETS
For information on street-reclaiming action around the world.
PO Box 9656, London N4 4JY
www.reclaimthestreets.net

RECOUP
www.recoup.org

RE-CYCLE
Collects and donates second hand bicycles to communities in developing countries.
60 High Street, West Mersea, Essex CO5 8JE • 01206 382 207
www.re-cycle.org

RECYCLE MORE
Provides information on recycling in the UK, in homes, businesses and schools.
c/o Valpak Ltd, Vantage House, Stratford Business Park, Banbury Road, Stratford-upon-Avon, CV36 7GW • 0845 068 2572
www.recycle-more.co.uk

RECYCLED PAPER SUPPLIES
Provides stationery products, including recycled paper, card and envelopes.
Gate Farm, Fen End, Kenilworth CV8 1NW • 01676 533 832
www.recycled-paper.co.uk or
www.rps.gn.apc.org

RECYCLING HELPLINE
Find out your about your local council's recycling department.
0800 435 576

RECYCLING OF USED PLASTICS
Promotes plastic recycling in the UK.
9 Metro Centre, Welbeck Way, Woodston, Peterborough, PE2 7WH
01733 390 021
www.recoup.org

RED LETTER DAYS
A choice of over 300 experiences you can give as exciting and unforgettable gifts.
0870 444 4004
www.redletterdays.co.uk

REED DESIGN
For information about making and flying your own kites.
0207 738 8373
www.reeddesign.co.uk

REEL FURNITURE
Eco-friendly wooden furniture for home, garden and conservatory.
37 St. Stephens Square Norwich NR1 3SS England • 01603 629396
www.reelfurniture.co.uk/

REFORM FURNITURE
Furniture made from 100% recycled materials.
35 High Street, Higham Ferrers, Northampton, NN 10 8DD
01933 391480
www.re-formfurniture.co.uk

REG-UK
A company that recycles old, non-roadworthy tyres into sources of material for a new generation of environmentally and economically sound products.
191 High Street, Yiewsley, West Drayton, Middlesex, UB7 7XW
01895 444 714
www.reguk.com

REMARKABLE
Everyday items produced from recycled or sustainable sources.
56 Glentham Road, London SW13 9JJ
020 8741 1234
www.remarkable.co.uk

RESCUE PET
An Internet database with details of animal shelters and individual pets in need of a new home.
www.rescuepet.net

RESPONSIBLETRAVEL.COM
Promotes eco-tourism holidays in over 110 countries, designed to benefit tourists, hosts and the environment.
www.responsibletravel.com

RETHINK RUBBISH
Provides information on how to solve the growing problem of household rubbish.
www.rethinkrubbish.com

RETIRED GREYHOUND TRUST
An organisation set up to find homes for greyhounds retired from racing in the UK.
149a Central Road, Worcester Park, Surrey, KT4 8DT • 0870 444 0673
www.retiredgreyhounds.co.uk or
www.adopt-a-greyhound.org

REUZE
A site about where, what and how to recycle in the UK.
www.reuze.co.uk/home.shtml

ROYAL SOCIETY FOR THE PREVENTION OF CRUELTY TO ANIMALS (RSPCA)
A charity working to rescue and re-home animals suffering from distress or cruelty.
Wilberforce Way, Southwater, Horsham, West Sussex RH13 9RS • 0870 333 5999
www.rspca.org.uk

ROYAL SOCIETY FOR THE PROTECTION OF BIRDS, THE, (RSPB)
A charity working for a healthy environment rich in birds and wildlife.
The Lodge, Sandy, Bedfordshire SG19 2DL • 01767 680 551
www.rspb.org.uk

SAFEWASH
Supplies the T-wave laundry disc, an environmentally friendly and money-saving alternative to detergents.
The Safewash Company, 1426 John St, Baltimore, MD 21217, USA
011 410 383 2063 [standardise]
www.safewash.com

SALVO
Suppliers of vintage or antique building materials.
www.salvo.co.uk

SAMARITAN'S PURSE INTERNATIONAL
Runs operation Christmas Child – sending your gift filled shoe boxes to needy children around the world.
Victoria House, Victoria Road, Buckhurst Hill, Essex, 1G9 5EX • 020 8559 2044
www.samaritanspurse.org

SAVAWATT
Promotes the sensible use of electricity, and the elimination of unnecessary and costly waste.
SAVA Building, Waterloo Industrial Estate, Bidford on Avon, Warwickshire B50 4JH • 01789 490 340
www.savawatt.com

SAVE ENERGY
Saving energy in your home.
www.saveenergy.co.uk

SAVE OR DELETE
Campaigns to protect the world's forests from total destruction (see Greenpeace).
www.saveordelete.com

SAVE THE CHILDREN
A UK children's charity working to create a better future for children.
17 Grove Lane, London, SE5 8RD
020 7703 5400
www.savethechildren.org.uk

SAWDAYS SPECIAL PLACES TO STAY
Publishes books with intriguing alternatives to corporate and five star accommodation in the UK, France, Spain, Portugal, Italy, Morocco and India.
The Home Farm Stables, Barrow Court Lane, Barrow Gurney, Bristol BS48 3RW
01275 464 891
www.sawdays.co.uk

SCENTSATIONS POT-POURRI AND GIFTS
Suppliers of biodegradable confetti.
46 The Paddocks, Old Catton, Norwich, Norfolk NR6 7HD England
01603 410205
www.scentsations.uk.com

SCHOOL ENERGY
Kenly House, 25 Bridgeman Terrace, Wigan, WN1 1TD • 01942 332 273
www.schoolenergy.org.uk

SCHOOL GOVERNMENT PUBLISHING CO.
Information about field study and environmental education centres for schools.
www.schoolgovernment.co.uk

SCOOT ELECTRIC
An online shop selling electric scooters.
08707 877 408
www.scootelectric.co.uk

SCOPE
Campaigns to achieve equality for people with cerebral palsy
Library and Information Unit, 6 Market Road, London, N7 9PW
0808 800 3333
www.scope.org.uk

SCOTTISH WILDLIFE TRUST
Protecting Scotland's Wildlife.
Cramond House, Kirk Cramond, Cramond Glebe Road, Edinburgh EH4 6NS • 0131 312 7765
www.swt.org.uk/

SCRIB
Steel Can Recycling Information Bureau.
Everything you need know about can
recycling.
Port Talbot, South Wales, SA13 2NG
01639 872626
www.scrib.org

SEEDS OF CHANGE
Offers organic seeds & food.
www.seedsofchange.com

SHOP AND OFFICE FURNISHINGS
Lists outlets for reusable commercial
furnishings.
www.recycle.mcmail.com

SILVER CHILLI
A company offering fair trade silver
jewellery manufactured by Mexican
craftsmen.
www.silverchilli.com

SIMPLY ORGANIC
Organic soups, sauces, ready meals and
baby food.
196 The Broadway, London SW9 1SN
01609 718 049
www.simplyorganic.co.uk

SIMPLY ORGANIC FOOD CO. LTD
A farm shop, dairy, fish market and health
food shop that delivers organic groceries
and essentials.
Horsley Road, Kingsthorpe Hollow,
Northampton, NN2 6LJ • 01604 791 911
www.simplyorganic.net

SIMPLY SOAPS
Producers of herbal soups that use organic
ingredients suitable for vegetarians and
vegans.
Brilling, Rackheath Path, Norwich NR13
6LP • 01603 720 869
www.simplysoaps.com

SLOW FOOD MOVEMENT
An international movement helping
people rediscover the importance of
careful food production and preparation,
and thus banish the degrading effects of
fast food.
Mendicita Istruita 14, 12042 Bra CN, Italy
0800 817 1232
www.slowfood.com

SMALL WORLD OF TOYS AND HOBBIES
Offers a selection of wooden toys,
dolls' houses and miniatures finished
with non-toxic paint.
01984 64 11 22
www.smallworldtoys.co.uk

SMART WOOD
Provides information about recycled
wood products and runs a wood
certification scheme.
European contact: C/ Maestra Maria Del
Rosario, No. 18, 1F 28320, Madrid, Spain
+34 91 692 2783
www.smartwood.org

SMILE.CO.UK
Online banking.
The Co-operative Bank plc, PO Box 101,
1 Balloon Street, Manchester M60 4EP
www.smile.co.uk

SOAPBASE
Provides information about making soap
and natural toiletries in the UK.
The Mill House, Black Rock Mills,
Waingate, Huddersfield HD7 5NS
01484 304 658
www.soapbase.co.uk

SOAP KITCHEN
Provides a selection of hand-made natural
toiletries and soaps.
11a South Street, Great Torrington,
Devon, EX38 8AA • 01805 622 944
www.thesoapkitchen.co.uk

SOCIETY OF HOMEOPATHS
Registers professional homeopaths
in the UK and provides practice
information and advice.
4a Artizan Road, Northampton NN1 4HU
01604 621400
www.homeopathy.soh.org

**SOCIETY OF INDEPENDENT
BREWERS, (SIBA)**
Provides information about Britain's
micro-brewers.
The Siba Office, PO Box 101, Thirsk
YO7 4WA
www.siba.co.uk

SOIL ASSOCIATION
A campaigning and certification
organisation for organic food and

farming.
**Bristol House, Victoria Street, Bristol
BS1 6BY • 0117 929 0661**
www.soilassociation.org

SOLA LIGHTING LTD
Provides of energy-efficient daylight
solutions for new or existing homes
and businesses.
**Sola House, 17 High Street, Olney,
Buckinghamshire, MK46 4EB
0845 458 0101**
www.solalighting.com

SOLAR ENERGY ALLIANCE
Information and advice on solar
powered energy.
**8A, Battery Green Road, Lowestoft,
Suffolk, England NR32 1DE
01502 515 532**
www.gosolar.u-net.com

SOS (SAVE OUR SEEDS)
An EU-wide campaign to keep
conventional and organic seeds free of
genetically modified plants.
www.saveourseeds.org

SPIRIT OF NATURE LTD
Offers a range of natural and
environmentally friendly products,
including organic clothing, natural skin
care, and eco-household products.
**Units 1-2, Clipstone Brook Industrial
Park, Cherrycourt Way, Leighton
Buzzard, Bedfordshire, LU7 4GP
01525 381 343**
www.spiritofnature.co.uk

SPRINTS
A scheme enabling you to swap empty
print cartridges and old mobile phones for
new school equipment.
0845 130 2050

STUDY STAY
Committed to providing free and
impartial information about UK study to
prospective international students.
**Wickham House, 10 Cleveland Way,
London E1 4TR • 0207 790 8555**
www.studystay.com/htm/courses/exchan
ge_programs.htm

SURFERS AGAINST SEWAGE, (SAS)
A campaign for clean, safe recreational

waters in the UK, free from sewage
effluents, toxic chemicals and nuclear
waste.
**Wheal Kitty Workshops, St Agnes,
Cornwall, TR5 0RD • 01872 553 001**
www.sas.org.uk

SUSTAIN: THE ALLIANCE FOR BETTER
FOOD AND FARMING
An alliance that promotes food and
farming policies and practices to benefit
people, animals, and the environment.
**94 White Lion Street, London N1 9PF
020 7837 1228**
www.sustainweb.org

SUSTAINABLE COTTON PROJECT
Builds bridges between farmers,
manufacturers and consumers to initiate
markets for organic cotton.
www.sustainablecotton.org

SUSTRANS (SAFE ROUTES TO SCHOOLS
INFORMATION TEAM)
A sustainable transport charity that
campaigns for a reduction in motor traffic
and its adverse effects.
**35 King Street, Bristol, BS1 4DZ
0117 926 8893**
www.sustrans.org.uk

SWADDLES
An online organic food home delivery
service.
**Swaddles Green Farm,
Chard TA20 3ZB • 0845 456 1768**
www.swaddles.co.uk

SWAP (STRATEGIC WASTE
MANAGEMENT SERVICES)
An environmental consultant that deals
with sustainable management.
**74 Kirkgate, Leeds, LS2 7DJ
0113 243 8777**
www.swap-web.co.uk

SWEAT SHOP WATCH
A coalition of groups committed to
eliminating the exploitation that occurs in
sweatshops.
**1250 So. Los Angeles St, Suite 214,
Los Angeles, CA 90015, USA
+1 213 745 5945**
www.sweatshopwatch.org

TALKING BALLOONS

A website that specialises in screen-print biodegradable balloons for parties and celebrations.
Matlock Road, Kelstedge, Ashover, Chesterfield, Derbyshire, S45 0DX
01246 590402
www.talking-balloons.co.uk

TEACHING ENGLISH AS A FOREIGN LANGUAGE, (TEFL)

For information on working as a foreign language teacher.
72 Pentyla Baglan Road, Port Talbot SA12 8AD • 020 7691 7074
www.tefl.com

TEARFUND

Works for the elimnation of global poverty – including campaigns on injustice, unfair trade and landmines.
100 Church Road, Teddington, TW11 8QE
0845 355 8355
www.tearfund.org

TELEPHONE PREFERENCE SERVICE

A service set up by the Direct Marketing Association Ltd to allow consumers to opt out of receiving unsolicited sales and marketing calls.
DMA House, 70 Margaret Street, London, W1W 8SS • 020 7291 3320
www.tpsonline.org.uk

TLIO (THE LAND IS OURS)

A group campaigning for ordinary people to access the land and be involved in any decision-making processes that affect it.
The Land is Ours,16B Cherwell St, Oxford OX4 1BG • 07961 460 171
www.tlio.org.uk

TIMEBANK

A national organisation campaigning to raise awareness of the importance of giving time and volunteering.
The Mezzanine, Elizabeth House, 39 York Road, London, SE1 7NQ
020 7401 5420
www.timebank.org.uk

TOMS OF MAINE

Creates natural toothpaste and other products using ingredients from nature.
Tom's of Maine UK, Ltd. PO Box 1873,
Salisbury, UK, SP4 6WZ
020 7985 2944
www.tomsofmaine.com

TOOLS FOR SELF RELIANCE

Works with local organisations in Africa to provide tools and training.
TFSR, Netley Marsh, Southampton SO40 7GY • 02380 869697
www.tfsr.org/about.htm

TOTNES GENETIX GROUP

Campaigns against genetically modified farming and promotes locally grown food that maximises nutritional value and minimises environmental damage.
PO Box 77, Totnes, TQ9 5ZJ
0803 840 098
www.togg.org.uk

TOURISM CONCERN

A membership organisation campaigning for ethical and fair traded tourism.
Stapleton House, 277-281 Holloway Road, London, N7 8HN • 020 7753 3330
www.tourismconcern.org.uk

TRAFFIC INTERNATIONAL

Works to ensure that trade in wild plants and animals is not a threat to nature conservation.
Traffic International, 219a Huntingdon Road, Cambridge, CB3 0DL
01223 277 427
www.traffic.org

TRAIDCRAFT PLC

A Fair Trade organisation that campaigns to help poor communities work their own way out of poverty.
Kingsway, Gateshead, Tyne and Wear NE11 0NE • 0191 491 0591
www.traidcraft.co.uk

TRAVELLING NATURALIST, THE

Provides guided wildlife holidays with a special emphasis on birds.
PO Box 3141, Dorchester DTI 2XD
01305 267 994
www.naturalist.co.uk

TREES FOR LONDON

Works to improve London's urban communities through tree-planting schemes.

CONTACTS

Prince Consort Lodge, Kennington Park,
Kennington Park Place, London, SE11
4AS • 020 7587 1320
www.treesforlondon.org.uk

TRIBES
Organises holidays run on fair trade
principles.
01728 685971
www.tribes.co.uk

TRIODOS BANK
A European ethical bank, financing
initiatives that deliver social,
environmental and cultural benefits.
Brunel House, 11 The Promenade,
Clifton, Bristol, BS8 3NN • 01179 739 339
www.triodos.co.uk

TYRE DISPOSAL
Campaigns to raise awareness on tyre
disposal and recycling tires.
www.tyredisposal.co.uk/

U REFILL TONER LTD
Provides DIY toner refill kits.
305 Telsen Centre, Thomas Street,
Aston, Birmingham B6 4TN,
0121 693 2644
www.refilltoner.com

UK ATTRACTIONS
A wealth of information on attractions
across the UK.
www.uk-tourist-attractions.co.uk

UK COMPUTER RECYCLING
An environmentally-friendly computer
disposal service throughout Great Britain.
www.uk-cr.org.uk
enquires@uk-cr.org.uk

UK PHENOLOGY NETWORK
Initiative by the Woodland Trust with the
Centre for Ecology & Hydrology to
monitor and evaluate changes in nature.
01476 581 111
www.phenology.org.uk

UK RECYCLED PRODUCTS GUIDE
See Wastewatch.
www.recycledproducts.org.uk/index.htm

**UNITED NATIONS ENVIRONMENT
PROGRAMME (UNEP)**
UNEP DTIE , Tourism Programme, 39-43,
Quai André Citroën, 75739 Paris Cedex
15, FRANCE • +33 1 44 37 14 41
www.uneptie.org/tourism

UNICEF
The United Nations programme to
promote health, education, equality and
protection for every child.
Africa House, 64-78 Kingsway
WC2B 6NB • 020 7405 5592
www.unicef.org

UNIT-E
Supplies renewable energy products to
homes and businesses.
Freepost (SCE9229), Chippenham,
Wiltshire SN15 1UZ • 0845 456 1640
www.unit-e.co.uk

URL BARON
For a selection of email cards.
www.urlbaron.com

USWITCH
A company that helps customers take
advantage of the lowest prices on gas,
electricity, home phones and digital TVs
from a range of suppliers.
PO Box 33208, London, SW1E 5WL
0845 601 2856
www.uswitch.com

VAUDE
Stocks VauDe outdoor gear – tents,
sleeping bags, rucksacks and clothing.
CDA Ltd., Unit 6C, Greensfield Park,
Alnwick, Northumberland NE66 2DE
01665 510660
www.vaude.co.uk

VEGAN SOCIETY
A society for vegans with information on
ethical, compassionate lifestyles that
benefit humans, animals and the
environment.
Donald Watson House, 7 Battle Road,St
Leonards-on-Sea, East Sussex. TN37
7AA • 01424 427 393
www.vegansociety.com

VEGETARIAN SOCIETY

Working towards a future where vegetarianism is accepted as normal.
Parkdale, Dunham Road, Altrincham, Cheshire WA14 4QG • 0161 925 2000
www.vegsoc.org

VISION AIDS OVERSEAS

A charity dedicated to improving the vision of poorly sighted people in developing countries. Recycles spectacles and optical instruments.
12 The Bell Centre, Newton Road, Manor Royal, Crawley, West Sussex RH10 2FZ
01293 535016
www.vao.org.uk

VOLUNTEER DEVELOPMENT ENGLAND

A UK charity providing support and advice to local volunteer agencies.
New Oxford House, 16 Waterloo Street, Birmingham, B2 5UG • 0121 633 4555
www.vde.org.uk

VOLUNTEER DEVELOPMENT NORTHERN IRELAND

A Northern Ireland charity providing support and advice to local volunteer agencies. Volunteer Development Agency, 4th Floor, 58 Howard Street, Belfast BT1 6PG • 02890 236 100
www.volunteering-ni.org

VOLUNTEER DEVELOPMENT SCOTLAND

A Scottish charity providing support and advice to local volunteer agencies.
Volunteer Development Scotland, Stirling Enterprise Park, Stirling FK7 7RP • 01786 479593
www.vds.org.uk

VOLUNTEER DEVELOPMENT WALES

A Welsh charity providing support and advice to local volunteer agencies.
Baltic House, Mount Stuart Square, Cardiff Bay, Cardiff, CF10 5FH
0870 607 1666
www.wcva.org.uk

VOLUNTEERING IRELAND

An Irish Charity providing support and advice to local volunteer agencies.
Coleraine House, Coleraine Street, Dublin 7, Republic of Ireland
00 353 1 872 2622
www.volunteeringireland.com

WAGS

The Wavendon and Allotment and Garden Society promotes Allotments and Vegetable Gardening in Milton Keynes and the Surrounding Area.
www.btinternet.com/~cbownes/wags/

WASTEAWARE

For information on household waste and recycling.
www.wasteaware.org.uk

WASTECONNECT

An online database for searching local recycling points in the UK.
www.wasteconnect.co.uk or www.wastepoint.co.uk
01743 343 403

WASTE WATCH WASTELINE

An organisation that promotes and encourages waste reduction, reuse and recycling.
96 Tooley Street, London, SE1 2TH
020 7089 2100
www.wastewatch.org.uk / www.wasteonline.org.uk

WATER AID

A charity working in Africa and Asia to improve water infrastructure, and provide sanitation, and hygiene education.
Prince Consort House, 27-29 Albert Embankment, London SE1 7UB
020 7793 4500
www.wateraid.co.uk

WATER MATTERS

A charity working to provide safe water, sanitation and hygiene to the world's poorest people.
Prince Consort House, 27-29 Albert Embankment, London SE1 7UB
020 7793 4500
www.watermatters.org.uk

WEDDING FAVOURS

A company offering biodegradable confetti.
PO Box 91, Batley, West Yorkshire, WF17 7XL • 01924 503 237
www.wedding-favours.com

WHALE AND DOLPHIN CONSERVATION SOCIETY (WDCS)

Working for the protection of whales,

dolphins & their environment worldwide.
**Brookfield House, 38 St Paul Street,
Chippenham, Wiltshire SN15 1LY
0870 870 0027**
www.wdcs.org

WHITEDOT
An organisation that campaigns to reduce
the amount of TV we watch.
PO Box 2116, Hove, East Sussex BN3 3LR
www.whitedot.org

WIGGLY WIGGLERS
Supplies wormeries, gardening accessories,
and wildlife products for your garden.
**Lower Blakemere, Herefordshire
HR2 9PX • 01981 500 391**
www.wigglywigglers.co.uk

WILDFOWL AND WETLANDS TRUST
An organisation to research and protect
wildfowl and their habitats.
**WWT, Slimbridge, Glos, GL2 7BT
01453 891 900**
www.wwt.org.uk

THE WILDLIFE TRUSTS
A wealth of information about wildlife
and our environment.
**The Kiln, Waterside, Mather Road,
Newark, Nottinghamshire NG24 1WT
0870 036 7711**
www.wildlifetrusts.org.uk

WILDWINGS
Runs wildlife eco-tours.
**577-579 Fish Ponds Road, Bristol
BS16 3AF • 01179 658 333**
www.wildwings.co.uk

WILLING WORKERS ON ORGANIC FARMS (WWOOF)
Provides information about volunteering
on organic farms around the world.
PO Box 2675, Lewes BN7 1RB
www.wwoof.org

WOMAD
World of Music, Arts and Dance
www.womad.org

WOMEN'S ENVIRONMENTAL NETWORK
Campaigns on issues which link women,
environment and health.

**PO Box 30626, London, E1 1TZ
020 7481 9004**
www.wen.org.uk

WOODCRAFT FOLK
Provides a programme of games, drama,
craftwork and education for young
people.
**13 Ritherdon Road, London, SW17 8BQ
020 8672 6031**
www.woodcraft.org.uk

WOODLAND TRUST
Working for the protection of Britain's
native woodland heritage.
**Autumn Park, Grantham, Lincolnshire,
NG31 6LL • 01476 581 135**
www.woodland-trust.org.uk

WORLD DEVELOPMENT MOVEMENT
Working to tackle the underlying causes
of poverty, and change the policies that
keep people poor.
**25 Beehive Place, London, SW9 7QR
020 7737 6215**
www.wdm.org.uk

WWF-UK
An international conservation
organisation working to protect species
and their natural habitats.
**Panda House, Weyside Park, Godalming,
Surrey, GU7 1XR • 01483 426 444**
www.wwf.org.uk

YOUNG PEOPLES TRUST FOR THE ENVIRONMENT (YPENTC)
Encourages young people's understanding
of the environment.
**YPTENC, 8 Leapale Road, Guildford,
Surrey, GU1 4JX • 01483 539600**
www.yptenc.org.uk

ZEROWASTE
A trust encouraging us to work towards
zero waste production.
www.zerowaste.co.nz